CREATING TRAINING MIRACLES

CREATING TRAINING MIRACLES

ALASTAIR RYLATT & KEVIN LOHAN

Pfeiffer
An Imprint of Jossey-Bass Inc., Publishers

Copyright © 1997 by Pfeiffer, An Imprint of Jossey-Bass Inc., Publishers

® The words Mind Map are a registered trademark of Tony Buzan

ISBN: 0–7879–0992–0

Library of Congress Cataloging-in-Publication Data

Rylatt, Alastair
    Creating training miracles / by Alastair Rylatt & Kevin Lohan
        p. cm.
    Includes bibliographical references and index.
    ISBN 0-7879-0992-0
    1. Employees—Training of. I. Lohan, Kevin. II. Title
HF5549.5.T7R95   1997
    658.3'1245—dc21   96-50924

Printed in the United States of America

Published by

An Imprint of Jossey-Bass Inc., Publishers
350 Sansome Street, 5th Floor
San Francisco, California 94104–1342
(415) 433–1740; Fax (415) 433–0499
Pfeiffer (800) 274–4434; Fax (800) 569–0443

Visit our website at: http://www.pfeiffer.com

Printing 10 9 8 7 6 5 4 3 2 1

This book is printed on acid-free, recycled stock that meets or exceeds
the minimum GPO and EPA requirements for recycled paper.

Dedicated
to the learner and
trainer in all of us.

CONTENTS

PREFACE

Making the Big Difference

Creating Training Miracles has been written with the conviction that effective training develops new skills, transforms potential, and increases the capacity of people to meet the challenges that confront them in today's rapidly changing world. Our philosophical position is that seeing a person becoming more empowered as a result of learning is miraculous.

Creating training miracles requires total commitment to excellence and a genuine belief that all people have the capacity to learn and train. In a world where values, beliefs, and self-esteem are constantly being challenged, the business of learning takes on added responsibility. Learning provides the gateway of opportunity that helps individuals to cope with the ambiguity, stress, and transition that these challenges often create.

We see *Creating Training Miracles* as an opportunity to share guidelines and techniques that we believe improve the quality of discovery and learning in a variety of settings, including formal education, workplace learning, and in the community at large.

Discovering the Recipe for Miracles

The wonder and mystery of miracles have been explored since the dawn of civilization. Whether it is worshiping the attraction and power of fire, to the genius of building and flying a hot-air balloon, people have sought to explain how and why the extraordinary and unexpected happen. Likewise, creating miracles in discovery, innovation, and learning has also captured the imagination of many trainers. For example, how is it that some people can stimulate curiosity, excitement, and change while others struggle to do so? Like most people, we have had mentors, coaches, and trainers who have had a profound effect on our lives: from a high school teacher who introduced poetry by studying the words and music of pop/rock songs by artists such as Elton John, Peter Allen, and Bette Midler, to a driving instructor who taught how to change gears in thirty minutes. These people, for some reason, knew the recipe.

It is our view that the recipe for converting ordinary learning to outstanding learning begins in people's ability to believe in miracles and to have the right spirit, high-quality and relevant techniques, awareness of change and learning styles, a resilient character, and excellent training structure. When this occurs, there is an increased likelihood that miracles will occur.

In saying this, we do accept that there are literally hundreds of ingredients that, together, shape the quality of exchanges between a trainer and a learner. After examining and reflecting on many of these ingredients, the following mindsets are seen as a starting point to discovering the recipe for creating training miracles.

Mindsets for Training Miracles

Mindset 1 — Trainers and learners need to discover and contribute in partnership.

Mindset 2 — Training is much more than just a series of courses and activities. It is a daily, never-ending, lifelong process.

Mindset 3 — Training miracles are generated from unconditional support based on trust, integrity, tolerance, generosity, and mutual respect.

Mindset 4 — When miracles are not occurring, something needs fixing or resolving.

Mindset 5 — True miracles strengthen both the resolve and the capabilities of the learner and the trainer.

Mindset 6 — Miracles smash and reform thoughts, fears, and beliefs into a higher level of understanding and consciousness.

Mindset 7 — The trainer and the learner must be prepared to both give and receive if miracles are to occur. Part and parcel of this mindset is an acceptance that every person is a multi-intelligent, unique, and precious individual who has an unlimited capacity to learn and train.

Mindset 8 — A wonderful trainer believes in the capacity and intention of the learner as well as accepting that he or she, as a trainer, will have a message to convey. If the trainer looks after the learner, the learning will look after itself.

Mindset   9— Miracles enable people to learn from the past, acknowledge the present, and release the future.

Mindset 10— Trainers must be prepared to honor, support, and embrace change and learning themselves before expecting others to do the same.

The Ultimate Challenge

Given the importance of training to the world at large, it is imperative that training providers, professional bodies, and associations play an active role in promoting and lobbying the benefits of high-quality learning. To do this successfully, training providers must seek synergetic learning partnerships that display a strong and cohesive image to decision makers from whom resources and support are needed to create training miracles. Ultimately, it is the quality of exchange and discovery between people that will determine whether they will be able to achieve their dreams and aspirations.

Taking the License to Be Different

We recognize that the title *Creating Training Miracles* may appear dangerously over the top or even disturbing to some people. However, we hold the view that training miracles can and do occur.

Creating Training Miracles has been designed to provide a treasure-trove of techniques and strategies on a number of training and learning skills. Having said that, there can be no doubt that the domain of advancing training and learning is far more extensive than the material we have covered. It is our hope that *Creating Training Miracles* will act as a springboard to further publications in the years ahead.

This book has been written primarily for the workplace trainer who performs such functions as researching, designing, presenting, and facilitating. We have used the terms facilitator and trainer interchangeably. As a consequence, many of the examples and materials have been slanted to the world of workplace learning rather than a purely teaching or educational environment. However, we do see enormous potential for people other than workplace trainers to apply many of the principles of *Creating Training Miracles*. These people include teachers, line managers, and any person responsible for the training and coaching of others.

Getting Your Full Money's Worth

The book is intended to be a quick and practical reference guide to a wide number of training skills. Recognizing that many people will read only what interests them, each chapter begins with a brief outline of the chapter, after which storytelling is used in conjunction with practical tips, models, and frameworks to enhance understanding. There is also a summary at the end of each chapter that gives a broad overview of what is contained within. Finally, there is a bibliography at the end of each chapter for those who wish to pursue the topic further. In all cases, the material that is shared is based on our real-life observations and experiences in creating training miracles. In some cases, we have supported the chapter material with practical resources found in appendixes at the end of this book.

Exploring the Ingredients

Like a chef designing and presenting a new menu for which each meal will contain different combinations of herbs, spices, and food groups, the process of creating training miracles requires a similar combination of creativity and a desire to try the new and different.

Creating Training Miracles supplies the ingredients that help achieve extraordinary results. Within the first eleven chapters of the book, many such ingredients that can create this combination are discussed. Beginning with an overview of future and emerging trends in training, the remaining chapters provide suggestions on important advanced training skills. Topic areas include gaining involvement and support for training in the workplace, competency-based training, self-directed learning, neurolinguistic programming, accelerative learning, role plays, case studies, outdoor learning, and facilitation of learning and group dynamics. *Creating Training Miracles* ends with a final chapter entitled "Reaching for the Stars," which provides an overview of what it takes to be an outstanding trainer.

Alastair Rylatt
Director
Excel Human Resource Development
Newtown NSW Australia

Kevin Lohan
Director
Endeavour Training and Development
Wamberal NSW Australia

ACKNOWLEDGMENTS

Completing a project of this magnitude can only be done with the encouragement and support of many people. First, we would like to thank the Australian Institute of Management (NSW), University of Technology (Sydney), Australian Institute of Training and Development, Australian Human Resources Institute, the American Society for Training and Development, and the International Alliance for Learning for their ongoing interest in our professional and personal growth.

Second, we would also like to thank the hundreds of clients and thousands of learners whom we have worked with over the past ten years. Without your gratitude and cooperation, this publication would never have been created.

Third, we would like to thank the following people for their constructive feedback on *Creating Training Miracles:* Tony Jollye, Manager, Australian Institute of Management; Sandra Cormack, Professional Development Manager, Australian Human Resources Institute; Glenn Capelli from the True Learning Centre; Kaylie Smith from Prentice Hall Australia; Merran Dawson, Manager, Staff Development and Training, at the University of Technology; Ann Rolfe-Flett from Synergetic Management; and Betty Sheppard from Betty Sheppard and Associates.

We would also like to thank a large number of mentors and friends who have had a significant impact on our careers at vital stages. To name but a few: Steve Camarsh, Peter Mulhall, Marlys Hanson, Ann Herrmann-Nehdi, Linda McDonald, Michael Morgan, Luke Shields, Paul Stevens, David Taylor, and the Dodd family. We would also like to thank Tony Buzan for kindly granting us permission to use the term "Mind Map"® in our book.

Finally, we would both like to acknowledge the love we have received from our families and close friends over the past four decades. Without them, none of this would have been possible.

We thank you all.

Alastair Rylatt
Director
Excel Human Resource Development
Newtown NSW Australia

Kevin Lohan
Director
Endeavour Training and Development
Wamberal NSW Australia

EMERGING TRENDS IN TRAINING

This chapter provides a thumbnail sketch of the major global trends in training. It will help trainers gain a better understanding of what is currently happening and what will occur in the future in order that they may learn how to better plan their careers.

Gems Mined from These Pages

- Trainers will benchmark their skills against international best practices.

- Responsibility for lifelong learning and performance will involve everyone.

- Team learning will be a major catalyst for managing change.

- In the future, the focus will be on enhancing adaptability.

- High technology will allow the delivery of learning across time and place.

"The most exciting breakthrough in the next century will not occur because of technology, but because of an expanding concept of what it means to be human."

JOHN NAISBITT

Sometime in the Future

The business of helping travelers to fly into remote and exotic locations to rub shoulders with, and learn from, people of cultures that have survived for thousands of years continues to be a profitable business for the global economy. Ongoing advances in international jet travel continue to build the available marketplace for short and flexible tour options to unprecedented levels. In short, the future of travel looks very rosy for travel organizations provided they remain up-to-date, informed, and competitive in a vibrant and dynamic marketplace. The statistics of travel business failure within the rapidly growing and highly lucrative marketplace of Asia Pacific are startling. Of the new businesses established each year, only 5 percent survive the first twelve months of operation.

One organization that has survived the turbulence and growth of the past decade is Small World Travel. To find out how this organization continues to power forward into lucrative market segments you only need to see how it trains its people.

Kirin Sharma, the marketing manager, and the other senior management staff from Small World Travel are reviewing the final draft of the training plan for next year, covering 1,200 staff members in sixteen countries including Cambodia, Fiji, Papua New Guinea, and New Zealand.

The biggest challenge to Kirin, as for many other managers and team leaders in the company, is how to maintain the competency of such a diverse and dispersed workforce. Kirin, for example, oversees twenty-two field staff members who are responsible for forty-six holiday destinations. Kirin's office is located in Melbourne, Australia, but over 50 percent of Kirin's time is spent visiting the tour operators. Kirin's primary responsibility as marketing manager is to be a coach and mentor who focuses on people management, team coordination, and strategic thinking. To keep up-to-date on training and business trends, Kirin actively networks among other professionals and shares best practices with them. This includes meeting people from both within and outside the travel industry, including managers, sales representatives, learning specialists, and internal training providers from a full spectrum of industries and countries.

Yesterday, while meeting with a new head-office instructional designer, Kirin clearly recalled the words of the managing director at last year's annual meeting. She said, "It is fascinating how the delivery of training has changed dramatically in the past decade. In the past, our training was piecemeal, to say the least. People learned everything by accident and often from our customers. Word of mouth was the only way they learned about the various holiday destinations they managed. Local and head-office training was uncoordinated and ineffective. The only regular training was at a semiannual regional conference, and that only involved a few senior- and middle-level staff. This is especially bizarre given that in those days the full-time workforce was 30 percent larger than it is today. In the past, company information was communicated solely by facsimile and phone. Unfortunately, due to the geographical spread of the workforce and high staff turnover, change rarely happened. As a result, there was a history of the head office wanting to control everything, which led to high frustration levels, less innovation, and poor performance."

Kirin also told the new employee how the general manager, in a less diplomatic fashion, had echoed the managing director's comments to the attendees at a regional management meeting last January. "If the business is to remain viable, field staff must be more actively involved in all aspects of workplace learning. We have recognized that the field staff can no longer wait for the head office to give directions, or for a training provider to come and run a token seminar every six months. Local field staff must now manage the just-in-time learning for each of the three hundred full-time and nine hundred part-time staff members operating within the region. Get it clear, training is no longer a voluntary activity; it is the cornerstone of our business survival."

In this regard, Kirin said, "It is imperative that we follow those new directions by ensuring that all instructional design and training delivery is competency-based, accelerative, culturally sensitive, cost-effective, and relevant to the business." I am confident that together we can achieve that objective. For example, Vida Martinez from Manila recently asked for a distance-learning package on negotiation skills for the tour operators. As a result, a number of learning books, audiotapes, and seminars were produced in English and Filipino in conjunction with a consultancy firm based in Singapore. To meet this high standard of excellence, a pool of committed internal and external learning consultants provides a regular fee-for-service training business for staff."

Kirin then began to brief the new employee on the progress of the current review of this year's training plan. Kirin said the process had begun last week when all twenty-two field managers were asked to provide input on a number of training issues. This was done by using a computer conferencing capacity within their electronic-mail system. The three areas the conference addressed were general feedback and results on past training initiatives, future learning needs, and budgeting forecasts.

This consultation process, which coincidentally crossed seven time zones, was completed within forty-eight hours, after which Kirin organized a telecommunication conference involving a steering committee of six field staff. Their role was to review the field submissions and develop an overall strategy.

The two-hour steering committee meeting had been held the previous evening at 10 p.m. Melbourne time. There, Kirin facilitated the telecommunication conference using a networked computer system in which every person had the video image of every other person on their screen simultaneously. The background reading had been faxed to them the day before using the same computers they were now talking through.

Everyone was able to fully participate, even though Nada Ismail had to rely on a laptop system that incorporated an integrated telecommunications system and a hand-held video camera on location 120 miles west of Shanghai. Nada simply connected the camera to the laptop, and the built-in telephone and modem in the laptop dispatched Nada's words and image over the worldwide digital communications network.

Six highly exciting recommendations came out of the meeting.

1. Continue to push toward competency-based training, continuous learning, and culturally sensitive training in all regions.
2. Increase the number of existing languages that the staff members need to learn, focusing particularly on Mandarin, English,

French, and Vietnamese. The delivery methods should include more workbooks, face-to-face training, as well as interactive multimedia.

3. Undertake a best-practice study to explore the distance/open learning options for training tour operators in the areas of business management and customer service. Taiva Williams from Fiji offered to lead a team to investigate this area.

4. Continue to use the new electronic-mail messaging service to communicate the latest trends and industry information.

5. Increase the number of face-to-face training programs for tour operators in team learning and coaching skills.

6. Allocate a bigger proportion of funding to the learning resource centers within each of the regions.

The mood of the meeting was exuberant. People were excited by the future initiatives, but most importantly they drew comfort from the fact that they were able to discuss tough issues face-to-face, in real time.

Kirin always liked to close such meetings with a ritual during which people shared their thoughts and feelings on the outcomes discussed. So, for fifteen minutes the seven participants shared a personal perspective on the results achieved at the meeting.

After this ritual had been completed, it was obvious to everyone that the meeting and recent moves toward decentralization had been very beneficial. Some of the claimed successes included increased business performance, greater innovation, improved skills, and dramatically heightened morale.

Vida, from Manila, summed up the mood of the meeting by saying, "It is obvious to me that we are on the 'right track.' Our experimentation with new trends in training seems to be doing much more than just improving performance. It seems to be adding extra vitality and confidence to everyone in the business."

After a moment's pause, Nada yelled through on the mobile phone in China, "Yes, you're right Vida; it's a miracle."

Predicting an Uncertain Future

What is going to happen to the field of training in the next twenty years? Will the predictions of increased sophistication in computer and communications technology eventuate? Will formal training be replaced by a "virtual reality" or will there still be a place for a traditional relationship between the learner and the trainer?

These questions and many more can arise when people explore their hopes, dreams, and fears of the time ahead. Many people would argue that the circumstances described in the story "Sometime in the Future" are already happening in their workplaces.

People already operate within a highly competitive marketplace reliant on exemplary skills development. During the past five years there has been a rapid increase in smaller and more transient workplaces that are exploring and perfecting the art of best-practice training products and services and high technology. Mirroring these innovations is the increase in empowered work teams, total quality management, and just-in-time learning. As a consequence, the nature and importance of training has been elevated to an essential part of business strategy.

Conversely, there are a multitude of organizations who are lagging behind in the development of practices and policies that promote outstanding learning. In this regard, the messages of just-in-time learning and multi-point delivery of training seem more like a dream than a reality. In many cases, decision making by key individuals is based on "fire fighting" rather than "fire prevention." We are training people simply to catch up with what they do not know instead of preparing them for the future by developing their capacity to cope with the pressures of ambiguity and skills associated with resilience and creativity.

Predicting future trends in training is subject to many difficulties and uncertainties, particularly since each person, team, workplace, and industry is uniquely affected by different societal, economic, political, and environmental factors. However, to create training miracles, it is imperative that both the learner and the trainer have some sense of the certain and uncertain dimensions of their respective futures.

How to Paint a Picture of the Future

An excellent way of getting a picture of the future is to undertake a "research project" to predict it. There are a large number of activities that could supply a wealth of information on future possibilities and emerging trends. Possible activities include the following:

- Contact six industry opinion leaders and ask them to share their views of the future. Explore issues such as what knowledge, skills, and attitudes will be most important within the next five years. Be sure that the leaders represent different backgrounds and positions. For example, senior executive, front-line staff, university expert, industry adviser, author, and training consultant. Extend your knowledge pool by asking these people to recommend other contacts or reference sources.
- Undertake an information search and knowledge exchange through national and international CD-ROM, on-line, or Internet database services. Be careful to narrow the output data options by inserting key words such as "training; future (area of application), (industry)." When displayed, the data can then be examined by date of publication, which can further assist the retrieval of more recent information.
- Join a professional association of trainers and establish a research project regarding the future.
- Choose some relaxing music, find a quiet place, and spend thirty minutes visualizing the future at your workplace. Describe the products and services being used in five and ten years' time.
- Visit a best-practice organization in training. Form a partnership of cooperation and exchange information.
- Attend a training conference where skills, ideas, and products for the future can be discussed and observed.
- Write an article on the future for an industry journal or workplace newsletter and ask for responses on your view.
- Visit your local library and glance though the daily newspapers from the last six months for press releases and editorials focusing on training or learning trends.
- Spend time in a management and education bookshop looking at the new and different products.
- Study existing business and strategic planning documents at your workplace. Ask to be involved in data-gathering and consultation processes.
- Make notes of the training implications of leading-edge futuristic magazines, television programs, videos, or radio programs.

- Draw a time line illustrating how training has evolved over the past thirty years in your industry. Extend your time line through the next twenty years.
- Collect and classify your thoughts and observations of the future, using the worksheet in Exercise 1.1.

EXERCISE 1.1. GAZING INTO YOUR CRYSTAL BALL

From the data you have collected, group your observations under the following headings.

1. *What is the likelihood that this prediction will occur?*
    (1) Will happen.
    (2) 75 percent certain it will happen.
    (3) 50 percent certain it will happen.
    (4) 25 percent certain it will happen.
    (5) Won't happen.
2. *What is the impact of these observations?*
    (1) On yourself?
    (2) On your workplace?
    (3) On your internal and external customers?
    (4) On your industry?

Trends for the Future: A Personal Perspective

To explain our view of existing emerging trends in training, we have conducted some of the activities described earlier and have arrived at eight trends that we believe are having a profound impact on worldwide training and learning strategies and methods.

In describing these trends, we found two major driving forces that weave their way across all the issues identified. The first is the desire for performance solutions and the second is the desire to find practical strategies that inspire human potential and contribution. From our observations, we have found that the workplaces and individuals who have been best able to consistently achieve best-practice training outcomes are those that have been able to form a strong connection between these two, often opposing, forces. It is our view that the miracle of learning can only be realized when the task of providing people with greater meaning, enjoyment, and choice in their lives is seen as equally important as the effort to improve effectiveness and efficiency.

1. Globalization

During the past decade, organizations and governments have become more global in their perspectives. There is no place, individual, team, or industry that is escaping this trend. Advances in communication technology, distance education, and travel have meant that industries have increasingly recognized that they are in fact only "small fishes in a big sea" and that they need to form strategic alliances and partnerships to survive in today's global economy.

In every industry and country the message is the same. To remain viable, the workplace must produce better quality products and services. The last decade has, for the most part, jolted any complacency that may have existed in the past. More people now realize that it is imperative that workplaces maintain a level of competency comparable to that of worldwide skills and best practices to maintain viability, performance, and capability. To do this, training providers have needed to become more strategic in their operations by being more actively involved in the every-day and long-term leadership of the business. As a consequence, people with training, facilitation, and change-management skills are now applying their talents to diverse business issues such as helping to shape and articulate the vision for change, reengineering workplace structures and systems, exploring best practices, improving quality and customer service, coaching others to become self-directed and resourceful learners, and finally, to being resources and mentors.

Gone are the days when businesses could accept formal training courses as the only outcome of the training profession. Ultimately, the performance and potential of an organization on a global and regional plain is heavily contingent on training professionals being prepared to expand their marketability and skill base while helping others to do the same.

As well as the need to be marketable and credible, it is increasingly being recognized that training is a major growth industry in the world's economy. The market opportunity for training products and services is enormous. Advances in the quality of systems and curriculum design, technology, or specialist skills are very marketable commodities. As a result, there is a rapid growth of organizations that are expanding their core business to include training products and services. An example of a new market could be a hotel chain conducting customer-service training to the staff of retail stores.

Underlying this trend of expanded market opportunity is an increasing awareness that the products and services must be tailored to the unique needs of the client. For example, if an organization were to approach a client of a different ethnic culture, it would be essential that all dealings were sensitive to the people's beliefs, customs, and expectations. This also includes adapting to needs that are affected by regional, socioeconomic, and political issues. To address these needs, organizations need to seek out people who are sensitive to these regional variables.

Currently, countries such as Germany, Japan, the United States of America, and Australia are in a cycle of innovation and reinventing. As a consequence, in these first-world areas, people are demanding training that supplies a strategic and leading-edge advantage over their competitors. Examples include the use of interactive multimedia, accelerative learning, and performance-enhancement technology.

In the second world, for example in parts of the old Eastern European bloc, decision makers are seeking training that helps people to cope with the rapid decentralization of once centralized economies. Here, training on topics such as strategic thinking, team development, and project management are currently very popular.

In the third world, including countries and regions such as Cambodia, Central America, and Brazil, people are seeking more training expertise that helps convert outdated technology to modern alternatives. Recent examples include telecommunications and computer-assisted manufacturing.

Finally, the area of greatest humanitarian need is to help the fourth world deal with survival, starvation, and self-sufficiency.

2. Decentralization of the Learning Function

Closely associated with the trend toward globalization is the dismantling of bureaucratic structures that inhibit the capacity of organizations and industries to deal with change.

During the past twenty years, the revolution in restructuring and reengineering has led to much smaller, more dynamic, and flatter organizations. Allied with this trend is the increased growth of part-time, temporary, and subcontract staff. As a consequence, training is no longer conducted just for full-time staff. The audience is now a much wider pool of people including suppliers, customers, subcontract staff, telecommuters, and benchmark partners.

As indicated in "Sometime in the Future," the days in which it was acceptable to wait for a training professional to run a course as a solution to a performance problem are diminishing. Today's successful organization sponsors and celebrates learning everywhere, from the general manager's boardroom to the work cafeteria.

To achieve this, employees will be increasingly expected to demonstrate an ongoing commitment to workplace learning and skill enhancement. People will be required to take full responsibility not only for learning for themselves but also for their teams.

Everyone will be encouraged to use learning as an agent for positive change. In this regard, line managers and team leaders will be coached on how to ask questions, guide team learning, and manage on-the-job learning. To ensure that this happens, organizations will use management systems to reward people who excel in achieving learning milestones that contribute to business and individual performance enhancement. To secure this learning relationship, employment contracts and "enterprise agreements" will specify the responsibilities of the organization, manager, and individual in the training and development process.

The impact of this trend will mean a shift in the power and accountability of training away from centralized functions to decentralized work locations. Trainers who hold centralized positions within organizations will become learning consultants who will help, guide, and support local workplaces to improve innovation and performance on a regular basis. This role will afford them a greater opportunity to cement a stronger working relationship between learning and strategic business planning activities.

To cope with this added responsibility, it will be necessary for individuals and teams to learn how to do the following:

- Select best-practice training;
- Screen consultants, products, and service providers;
- Budget and forecast learning needs;
- Coach others;
- Achieve bottom-line results with training;
- Use learning tools and resources to the team's advantage;
- Manage high technology sensibly and effectively;
- Facilitate team learning and multiskilling within both dispersed and fixed location teams;
- Undertake on-the-job training;

- Support the use and application of self-directed learning; and
- Measure workplace learning outputs.

Chapter 2 offers more information on how to decentralize learning.

3. Self-directed Learning Teams

In the last decades of the Twentieth Century, the workplace has seen a quantum leap in the use of teams. This trend is expected to continue. Whether it is in a formal training room, on the job, during a telecommunication conference, or as an agent of change, the team process will continue to swell in both application and incidence.

As highlighted in the story "Sometime in the Future," people will be required to operate in teams even though they may not actually live or work near one another. Telecommuting will be used more and more, and the nature of teams will change as a result.

More and more organizations will conduct their work functions from a large number of small and frequently moving conglomerates. People will be required to interface and learn within teams dispersed across the full spectrum of time, place, function, and salary level. As a consequence, teams will become ad hoc, temporary, and more diverse.

Quite simply, dispersed and single-location team processes will become integral to all organizational activity. The training industry will have a vital role in coaching people in the skills of team learning and project management so that the benefits of innovation, personal growth, and performance can be reaped.

An ongoing hurdle for trainers and team leaders will be how to convince individuals who crave independence and autonomy that teamwork is an important way to manage complexity and achieve results.

As a consequence, training and workplace-learning teams will need to take every opportunity to build people's confidence and skill in the team process. Behaviors such as coaching, mentoring, team evaluation, and valuing diversity will need to be demonstrated and improved at every opportunity. These efforts will also need to be supported with human resource and business systems that celebrate and support teamwork.

In this regard, the centralized trainer, in his or her role as an on-the-job learning consultant, will need to spend greater time dealing with the quality-assurance roles associated with teams. The trainer might accomplish this, for example, by offering expertise or tools to help team performance.

4. Performance Improvement and Support

As in recent times, the future will require people to improve business performance, employee fulfillment, and customer satisfaction. A major driving force for performance improvement will be that people will be expected to implement or improve on internal and external benchmarks and/or best practices. In many cases this process of achieving "the best" will be linked to salary and incentive programs.

In the future, there will be a need for performance-enhancement tools that improve employee output. In addition to investing in capital such as better equipment and facilities, organizations will need to supply people with learning resources that will dramatically enhance their capacity to perform and learn. Examples include modems, personal computers that have interactive multimedia learning equipment, touch-sensitive screens and input devices totally different from today's keyboard, voice-activated technology, adaptive technology to help people with physical disabilities, on-line help desks, workbooks, resource centers, client-friendly computer software, competency standards, and expert systems. All of these must be backed up by people who are skilled in helping learners to get the most from these technologies.

People will be required to demonstrate how such performance-enhancement tools and training have contributed to positive change. For example, in "Sometime in the Future," Kirin and the field staff team will need to show how the upgrading of language training in Mandarin, English, French, and Vietnamese has impacted on the competency of the learners or the capabilities of their workplaces.

As a result, people will be investing much more time to measure the competencies of learners before, during, and after training. Also, they will be measuring business performance improvement by such indicators as testimonials, new ideas, new markets, less wastage, and customer feedback.

In addition, learning will be used to improve individual and business performance. The methods that will increasingly be used are as follows:

- Reflecting on critical incidents to resolve business challenges;
- Experimenting with existing methods and procedures;

- Holding regular learning sessions with experts and mentors;
- Seizing the opportunity to learn from mistakes and successes;
- Asking people to share their learning and experience with others;
- Sharing stories of how new or past learning has affected the bottom line; and
- Exploring the most critical discovery out of a specific situation or experience.

5. Highly Flexible and Competency-based Training

The development, revision, and assessment of competencies will be commonplace in organizational, industrial, and national restructuring and skill formation processes in the future. As Chapter 3 discusses, instructional design, delivery, and assessment of learning will need to be increasingly based on competency outputs. This will result in learning in the future being more flexible, relevant, and receptive to people's needs and prior experience. People will be able to learn in a multiplicity of ways rather than solely through traditional training methods such as lectures.

Organizations will increasingly link training initiatives to industry and international standards as well as customizing the material to meet their own unique constraints and challenges. Related to this trend toward competency-based learning, there will be a continued expectation by governments and industries that all training providers meet agreed accreditation requirements.

Competency-based learning will increase in its sophistication as people incorporate improved understanding of mental diversity, accelerative learning, and self-directed learning. To meet this aim of better application of competencies, training providers will need to experiment with and encourage a wider range of learning methods, techniques, and strategies than they have done in the past. Notably, people will need to explore how they learn and how this builds confidence and resilience. Allied with this trend is the increased weighting in the area of assessment methodology and measurement. This will involve the use of methodologies outside traditional ones (such as written tests), including on-the-job observation, peer assessment, and learning contracts.

To reap the full benefits of competency-based training, organizations, individuals, industries, and governments will allocate more resources to areas such as functional and basic literacy and vocational education that will help enhance the portability of skills and the receptivity of learners.

6. Lifelong Learning

As the future approaches, the best training will need to convince people that learning can be enjoyable and insightful and can add important meaning and personal power to their lives. Unless this emotional attachment is made, the potential for learning as an agent for change will often not be realized.

Rather than seeing learning as just a training course, leading organizations and trainers will be able to make the connection between learning and the areas of greater hope, improved self-esteem, and expanded self-determination.

The better training and workplace initiatives will be seen as focusing on much more than pure competency development and skills acquisition; they should also facilitate lifelong personal growth and renewal.

Training and workplace learning should support behaviors that encourage lifelong learning. These behaviors include the following:

- Learning from experience;
- Stamping out behaviors and systems that stifle learning;
- Applying what you learn from others;
- Experimenting with ideas, concepts, and actions;
- Locating and developing mentors and protégés;
- Reframing beliefs and thoughts that are inhibiting learning;
- Celebrating and sharing with others new insights and competencies that you discover;
- Identifying strengths and areas for personal growth; and
- Learning to become both trainer and learner at the same time.

7. Investment in Adaptability Skills

Without doubt, the pace and intensity of change requires exemplary skills and tremendous resolve. Historically, training and workplace learning programs have developed people's flexibility, portability, and transferability. Included in this push toward flexibility has been the development and enhancement of various technical, human, and conceptual skills that have helped people to adapt. Typical examples include computer keyboarding (technical skills), communicating face-to-face (human skills), and strategic thinking (conceptual skills).

In the future, instructional design, delivery, and assessment will need to highlight the importance of adaptability to a much greater level than has been done in the past. As a consequence, learning initiatives will need to be extended to incorporate adaptability as a fourth category of skill on top of the traditional areas of technical, human, and conceptual, thereby providing greater potential and visibility for portability, transferability, and flexibility of skills.

Some of the key competencies of adaptability follow:

- Staying calm and assured while coping with the overpowering and complex;
- Using accelerative learning and networking to gain information quickly and efficiently;
- Creating and communicating vision, inner purpose, and values when dealing with ambiguous change and ethical dilemmas;
- Seeking opportunities to enhance adaptability in all aspects of one's life;
- Demonstrating resilience and pliability when responding to pressure and uncertainty;
- Dealing with ambiguity in both structured thinking and unstructured thinking;
- Investing in lifestyle changes that support emotional and physical health and well-being;
- Loving change and embracing risk rather than defending against it;
- Inspiring trust and trustworthiness in others; and
- Setting realistic, challenging, fulfilling, and self-nurturing life goals.

8. Multi-point High Technology Delivery

Ultimately, the success of the training profession in the decade ahead will be determined by its capacity to access a wider population. Training, therefore, will need to move from traditional up-front delivery to one where people can learn if and when they desire. As highlighted in the story "Sometime in the Future," high technology now makes it possible to link people with databases, information, and advanced instructional design more than was ever possible before. As the level of interactivity, cost availability, and quality improves, so will the potential to access even more people across any time zone and distance.

The multi-point delivery for high technology can be explored by examining Table 1.1. Here, current technology is grouped under time and place. Thus, if you are training people who are in the same place as you at the same time as you are there, you can use technology such as electronic whiteboards, a personal computer screen, and other electronically supported meeting tools. The level of sophistication of the technology increases as we move away from the same place and away from the same time. Likewise, the options available to learners become more sophisticated. Therefore, if you are training people who are in a different place at a different time, you will use technology such as electronic mail and on-line help desks and computer-assisted video production. In recent times the increases in the sophistication of telecommunications, authoring software, and instructional technology has meant that learners can access the Internet to keep up to date while also enhancing skills. For many the classroom and library have

TABLE 1.1. MULTI-POINT DELIVERY OF HIGH TECHNOLOGY

		Same	**Different**
PLACE	**Different**	*Distance learning* ● audio, graphic, and video conferencing ● interactive viewer-response systems ● Internet-based training (World Wide Web and User Groups) ● intranet (internal network) training ● pay, broadcast, and interactive television ● radio ● screen sharing ● telephone	*Messaging* ● computer conferencing ● computer-assisted video production ● electronic mail ● electronic tutorial ● interactive CD-ROM tutorials ● on-line help desks, expert systems, databases ● shared files and calendars
	Same	*Face-to-face meeting* ● electronic whiteboards ● electronically supported meeting ● laptop connected presentations ● multimedia ● PC screen	*Learning centers* ● CD-ROM databases, expert systems ● CD-ROM interactive multimedia ● library, audio, and videos ● virtual reality
		Same	**Different**
		TIME	

Source: Adapted from Ehlen, D. "The coming revolution in training technology," *Training and Development in Australia,* July 1994, vol. 21, no. 3, pp. 11–14. Reproduced with permission.

shifted from those places we knew in the past to ones we can access from the comfort of our home, office, or some remote location by simply keying in or touching a computer screen. This new point of delivery has not only changed the nature of knowledge acquisition and distance learning forever, but has opened up a whole new marketplace for training providers.

This model shows how the advances in technologies such as telecommunication and computer software are changing the face of training. In stating this, it is important to add that, firstly, no technology is intrinsically superior to any other. What is paramount is that the technology meets both business and learner requirements and is backed up by suitable support. That means adequate time, funding, and people to support the systems are available. Otherwise the technology will become a white or, "silicon" elephant. Secondly, as advances and sophistication of technology and communication increase, so will the potential for flexibility and versatility between distance-learning, messaging, face-to-face, and learning-centers technologies. For example, you could participate in a highly interactive role play, involving 3D image, sight, sound, and touch, which is being driven by a computer in a totally different time and place.

Summary

It can confidently be said, as we enter a new millennium, that the business of improving learning competencies and skills will remain one of the world's fastest growing industries and priorities.

With this exciting and rapid growth, there will be many more opportunities to create training miracles, particularly as people learn to blend advances in high technology with the improved understanding of human behavior.

Predicting the future still remains a challenging task; however, the success of learning necessitates constant exploration of uncertainty as a norm rather than as an exception.

Bibliography

Calvert, G., Mobley, S., & Marshall, L. (1994, June) Grasping the learning organization. *Training and Development, 48*(6), 38–43.

Caudron, S. (1996, May). Wake up to new learning technologies. *Training and Development, 50*(5), 30–35.

Ehlen, D. (1994, July). The coming revolution in training technology. *Training and Development in Australia, 21*(3), 11–14.

Galagan, P.A., & Carnevale, E.S. (1994, May). The future of workplace learning and performance. *Training and Development* (supplement), *48*(5), S36–47.

Marquardt, M., & Reynolds, A. (1994). *The global learning organization*. Burr Ridge, IL: Irwin.

McLagan, P. (1996, January). Creating the future of HRD. *Training and Development, 50*(1), 60–65.

Morris Baskett, H.K. (1994, March). Advice to the learnlorn. *Training and Development, 48*(3), 61–63.

National Centre for Vocational Education Research Ltd. (1994, June/July/August). *Australian Training Review Special Feature on Flexible Delivery; Paraprofessional Training; Adult Apprenticeship*, no. 11.

Pickett, L. (1994, July). The challenge of the global paradox (interviews with John Naisbitt). *Training and Development in Australia, 21*(3), 15–17.

Rhinesmith, S. (1993). *A manager's guide to globalization*. Alexandria, VA: American Society for Training and Development/Burr Ridge, IL: Irwin.

Rhinesmith, S. (1994, May). Trends that will influence workplace learning and performance in the next five years. *Training and Development* (supplement), *48*(5), 29–33.

Robinson, D.G., & Robinson, J.C. (1995). *Performance consulting: Moving beyond training*. San Francisco, CA: Berrett-Koehler.

Rylatt, A. (1994). *Learning unlimited: Practical strategies and techniques for transforming learning in the workplace*. Sydney: Business & Professional Publishing.

Thach, E.C., & Murphy, K.L. (1995, December). Training via distance learning. *Training and Development, 49*(12), 44–46.

Tkal, L. (1993). *Technology survey report: Educational technologies 1994*. Sydney: Open Training and Education Network, New South Wales Department of School Education, TAFE, Redfern.

Watkins, K., & Marsick, V. (1993). *Sculpturing the learning organization*. San Francisco, CA: Jossey-Bass.

Wulf, K. (1996, May). Training via the Internet: Where are we? *Training and Development, 50*(5), 36–42.

GETTING TRAINING RESULTS IN THE WORKPLACE

This chapter provides an overview of the key considerations for gaining support and momentum for training in the workplace.

Gems Mined from These Pages

- Promote quality dialogue to gain commitment.

- Do not struggle with change; see it as an opportunity.

- Establish learning partnerships that support the training effort.

- Link training accountability to strategic and operational planning.

- Focus on delivering and providing resources for just-in-time learning.

"The question is not whether organizations have learning resources. The key question is 'How effectively are the resources being used?'"

MALCOLM
KNOWLES

Let's Call in the Training Department

It was two months ago when Eric Freemann, the senior manager of the Information Services Division, first left a message on the answering machine for Toni and Robin from the training department. Eric screamed, "Will one of you call me regarding this damn employee attitude survey?" After this outburst the message abruptly ended.

Concerned by the aggressive and somewhat rude attitude, Toni and Robin made some quick inquiries of their manager (Human Resources Department) before calling Eric back.

Their manager informed them that, as with the feedback from the other seven divisions of Pacific Trust Bank, the survey results of the thirty full-time staff and ten subcontractors from the Information Services Division were not favorable. However, these results were not within the norm; they were far worse than any from other parts of the company and showed the morale of the staff in the division to be at rock bottom. The general manager was so disturbed with these findings that she sent a directive to Eric to fix the problem as quickly as possible.

When Eric received this directive, he must have immediately picked up the phone and left his message on the answering machine. The manager of Human Resources said the hostile and abrasive message was not surprising given the directive of the general manager and the track record of the Information Services Division in not wanting to complete surveys in the first place. Robin and Toni were then advised to call Eric back but to tread carefully.

When they did contact Eric, it appeared that he had calmed down considerably. This time, in a more relaxed tone, Eric advised Toni and Robin that a divisional steering committee, consisting of a senior project leader, a systems analyst, and a maintenance subcontractor, had been established to look into the matter. Toni and Robin were asked to attend the first meeting the following morning at 9 a.m.

The first meeting of the steering committee lasted about three hours. Toni and Robin spent most of the time answering questions about the validity and credibility of the employee survey or, in other words, to what extent the results could be believed.

The view of the senior project leader seemed to sum up the initial tone of the meeting. The project leader said, "The staff are never happy. They are just using this survey to complain and let off steam." However, after some rigorous questioning and information sharing most of the steering committee's concerns were resolved. The final thirty minutes of the meeting addressed what to do next. It was decided that Toni and Robin should conduct on-site discussions during the following week to determine appropriate strategies for action.

To do this, Robin and Toni suggested a combination of one-on-one discussions and small-group meetings. When the senior team leaders and Eric heard this recommendation, they requested that they all be seen individually as well as having the permission to attend group discussions with the staff.

The on-site day went according to plan, with both Toni and Robin gathering some very useful facts and opinions regarding the current situation. The day began with a very short meeting with Eric. He claimed that the survey results reflected how under-resourced the workplace was at the moment. He stated that the division was "being swamped by too many demands." However, the words that stuck most in Toni and Robin's minds were those depicting the senior manager's views on the future. He said, "The way forward is more of the same. We must keep a firm hold and control over what is happening at the moment. We cannot afford to rock the boat or take any unnecessary risks. Let's try to fix this little problem by cheering the staff up a little."

After this insightful meeting with Eric, Toni and Robin held discussions with the three other members of the steering committee. Each of them expressed the view that things were not as bad as the survey results indicated. They all felt that the major problem was that staff members wanted more authority and responsibility but that they were not quite ready for it yet. When quizzed on what this meant, the senior project leader stated, "In the past, several staff meetings were held but nobody ever spoke up. Staff meetings are a waste of time, particularly when we have so much work to do."

For the rest of the day, Toni and Robin listened to the remainder of the staff. They noticed that on the couple of occasions when senior management attended, the dialogue quickly became hesitant and uneasy. As a consequence, both Robin and Toni concentrated on meeting and talking to staff members informally, away from the senior management for the remainder of the day.

Generally, the staff feedback from the on-site discussions was very interesting. It showed that the low morale was reflective of five factors: first, an ever-increasing workload with less staff; second, a lack of consultation by senior management on project allocation and decisions; third, a management style that was too autocratic and task oriented; fourth, senior management was not prepared to implement required change; and finally, there was genuine concern about job security. This fifth issue was seen as most relevant to full-time staff. The point was backed up by several stories of full-time employees being sacked or moved after complaining about preferential treatment to subcontractors. The grievance centered around the feeling that all too often the interesting work was being given to the subcontract employees and, as a result, full-time employees were left with the boring and mundane work. Because of this they felt undervalued.

When the on-site discussions were over, Toni and Robin scheduled a meeting with the steering committee to explain the findings. On hearing of the meeting, Eric also requested to attend. At the meeting, Toni and Robin carefully shared their observations without disclosing their origins. They summarized their findings into four major themes of trust, cohesiveness, communication, and staff recognition.

When their short verbal report had been delivered, the senior project leader asked, "Given that this gossip is all true, what can be done about it?"

After some brief discussions, the steering committee agreed to accept Robin's suggestion that the division start with a one-day team-development training program. It was recommended that it be scheduled over two consecutive days so that all staff members could attend. Eric was keen on this idea as he felt this was a high-impact way of improving morale without disrupting the office routine. Toni explained that for the program to be a success, Eric should attend both days. "Most importantly," Toni said, "for the program to be a success everyone who attends must be treated equally. In this regard, ground rules will be set to ensure that everyone will be given an equal say. Job status or work title will not be allowed to stifle sharing and teamwork."

The group discussed what could be done, and Eric wanted some assurances from Robin and Toni that the day would not be a waste of time. On hearing this request, Robin cautiously replied, "The number one outcome of both days will be the drafting of a measurable, relevant, and challenging action plan." Toni then added, "We can run a wonderful training program and have a lot of fun but unless you and your staff are prepared to act on the outcomes of the day, nothing will happen—in fact, things could get worse, particularly if expectations for change are not met."

After hearing this reply, the senior manager gave a nervous smile and said, "Well you have my commitment to support change and to attend both days." With these final words, everyone shook hands and Toni and Robin left to develop a training package.

Given the major themes that came from the staff interviews, the two trainers recommended a number of powerful indoor and outdoor activities plus a rigorous action planning and re-view segment. This proposal was submitted to the steering com-mittee and was accepted unconditionally.

The two one-day programs were scheduled and went ac-cording to plan. All of the activities went very well with plenty of debate and learning resulting. Both days finished on a high with respective teams sitting down and agreeing on the way ahead. Key areas for action included increasing the level of del-egation, making appropriate staff level adjustments, promoting senior-management consultation on change, and introducing self-managing teams—all of which linked to the themes identi-fied from the on-site day.

In the week following the training programs, Toni and Robin held another series of telephone and on-site discussions with staff members. This research indicated a universal feeling from all staff that the whole experience had been both useful and enjoyable. When they heard this feedback, the steering committee said they were happy with the results so far and were now looking forward to managing the process themselves in the months ahead. Toni and Robin offered their assistance if the steering committee felt it was necessary.

Last week, Nguyen Tan, a full-time computer systems operator from the Information Services Division, called Robin. He said in a frantic voice, "Since the team-development program was completed a month ago nothing has changed. In fact, things have become worse. Three staff members have resigned due to frustration, and the divisional senior management have stonewalled any of the ideas coming out of the two training days. It was suggested by a couple of staff members that a recall day should be held but even this idea was squashed. The general feeling among the staff is that the training course went too well for the managers' liking."

Alarmed by the feedback, Toni called Eric to schedule an appointment. After two days of trying to arrange a time, Toni and Robin physically turned up at Eric's office. The surprised senior manager said that everything was under control and that things were progressing as planned. Robin asked if they could talk for a few minutes about what had been done since the program. Eric said, "Not at the moment. Can't you see I am very busy?"

Frustrated by the lack of action, Toni and Robin spoke to their manager. The next day, the manager of Human Resources raised the matter with the general manager. The day after, the general manager called to say that Information Services would be contacting Human Resources to set dates for two recall sessions. The general manager also asked that Toni, Robin, and the manager of Human Resources see her after the two recalls were completed. The manager of Human Resources did not say what had happened, but it was obvious that the general manager had directed Eric to hold recall meetings sooner rather than later.

As predicted, the head of the steering committee called the next day to arrange for Toni and Robin to facilitate two half-day recall meetings. The goal of the recall was to review the progress since the team-development training. The following week, two emotionally charged recall meetings were held. After a long and very heated debate, the staff agreed to proceed with the idea of setting up three task forces to look at the agreed-on issues of work allocation, change management, and self-managing teams.

The recommendations of the task forces were to be submitted to the steering committee in one month.

At the end of what was a very long and tiring day, Toni and Robin then visited the general manager to give some feedback. When they arrived, the manager of Human Resources was also present as planned.

Both of the trainers sat down and Robin said, "It was obvious that the senior staff members of the Information Services Division were clearly embarrassed and threatened by our direct action on this matter. We are not very popular with the manager there at the moment, even though the rest of the staff feel we are marvelous."

After these opening words, the general manager calmly replied, "First of all, I would like to personally thank you for your decisive and courageous action. Clearly, the situation has been a stressful one for everybody concerned. Obviously, to resolve this matter actions other than just training may be required. I will be taking a very close interest in this matter in the months ahead. Above all else, we should remember that nothing can stand in the way of the company's improving its capacity to perform and introduce change. I understand that the actions you have taken in recent weeks have been very stretching. But let me say this: the company needs people like you if we are going to confront the future with confidence. In my opinion, what you have done over the last two months is a miracle, and I thank you."

Securing a Lasting Impression

The experiences of Robin and Toni in the story "Let's Call in the Training Department" are all-too-common training occurrences in organizations. For too long, training departments have lacked resources and have been used as a quick-fix solution to workplace difficulties. As a consequence, the training department in many organizations has a history of being treated as a scapegoat for somebody else's problems.

Clearly, training can be a wonderful asset; however, it should never be seen as a panacea for all ills. For training miracles to be achieved, many other factors need to coalesce. As we have found on many occasions, even the best training may not be enough. For training to succeed, there needs to be a clear understanding of the critical success factors that make a difference in the capacity of workplaces to get meaningful results from their training investments.

As in the case of "Let's Call in the Training Department," it was not until the general manager intervened that there was a commitment of sufficient muscle for the training effort to make a real contribution. As was also indicated by the general manager, it is quite likely that a number of non-training solutions will need to be adapted. These options could include job redesign, performance management, and staff relocation.

"Let's Call in the Training Department" also highlights a number of other questions. For example, how does the company increase the accountability of people to training and development? What is the optimum role of trainers in bringing about change? Should trainers be located in centralized functions or would it be better to decentralize the function? How do organizations convince people that training is much more than courses, that it is about a lifelong commitment to workplace learning, continuous improvement, and discovery?

To explore these issues, we will now address eight factors that are paramount in bringing about workplace training miracles. As displayed in Figure 2.1, these factors are highly interdependent. This means that people must constantly consider and apply all of the crit-

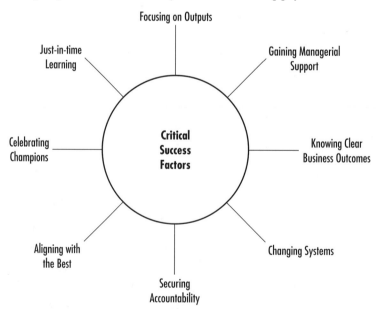

FIGURE 2.1. GETTING TRAINING RESULTS

ical success factors to achieve a lasting impression in both formal and on-the-job training initiatives.

Focusing on Outputs

Trainers need to develop the capacity to engage in conversations that focus on the outcomes of training. A common mistake is for people to spend too much time discussing the inputs of the training process (i.e., course design) rather than investing the necessary time and effort to determine what will be required to bring about a desired change. For example, in "Let's Call in the Training Department," there could have been more time spent examining the intended outcomes of the project. All parties involved should have more clearly identified what was expected as a result of the process, before coming up with the apparently short-term solution of conducting two team-development programs.

Asking people to describe their expectations is a powerful way of surfacing values or demands that could potentially stifle or help a training process. In addition to clarifying intentions, shifting the discussion to outputs increases the likelihood of parties reaching agreement on individual accountabilities, resources, and leadership before the training process starts. For example, in "Let's Call in the Training Department," Toni and Robin could have discussed earlier with the steering committee the importance of holding recall sessions.

For some trainers, asking questions that are designed to secure commitment is a nerve-racking experience, particularly when the trainer is seen as holding a less senior position. It is essential that trainers see their role as much more than just that of a presenter, instructional designer, or administrator. Today's trainers must see themselves as learning consultants and change agents who are vitally interested in getting above-average results for the client by asking quality questions and promoting expansive inquiry. Creating training miracles starts by promoting healthy and creative exploration of multiple options. Only then can the best strategy be engaged.

Powerful Questions for On-site Consultations

Questions that can help focus clients on outputs include the following.

- In twelve months' time, if the training were perfectly successful, what would be happening? If I were to visit you then, what would I see, hear, or feel that would be different frwere om now?

- Which milestones will you need to complete for a perfect outcome to occur?
- What are the key competencies that need to be addressed for your goal to be achieved?
- What resources will you need? What resources will you supply?
- Which non-training issues will need to be resolved before a successful outcome is achieved?
- How do you see your role (client) and our role (trainer) in making this training a success?
- How will you measure success?

Alternatively, if a client already has a training solution in mind, the trainer may need to have the person spell out his or her needs more specifically. For example, in "Let's Call in the Training Department," Robin and Toni could have asked the steering committee, "If you agree with Robin's suggestion to conduct a team-development program, what needs do you see this will best meet?" followed by, "Which needs will be neglected if we use this approach?"

Gaining Managerial Support

Having managerial support is central to securing results. The degree of endorsement will vary from one organization to another and from one project to another. However, it is important to get management's endorsement as that will raise the priority of training.

When asking for support, it is important to clearly state what you desire. It is imperative to ask for visible and relevant contributions to the training process. Five popular strategies used by decision makers to demonstrate their commitment follow:

1. Help articulate the desired performance and competency levels that need developing.
2. Attend the training as an observer, presenter, or participant.
3. Ensure that key people and stakeholders participate.
4. Follow up on workplace and/or learner application of the training.
5. Assign mentors, coaches, and back-up resources for the learning being undertaken.

There will be times when nonmanagerial support may be required initially, particularly if "grass-root" support is being sought from employees, customers, suppliers, and trade unions. In some cases, having senior-management support up front may create an image that training is being "done to" people rather than being "done for" them. What is most important is that people feel that they own the process rather than that they are just participating in it. Seeking and obtaining people's permission is an integral part of the support process.

Knowing Clear Business Outcomes

Irrespective of whether a trainer is employed in the private sector, in the government arena, or by a community-based organization, all training should lead to improvements in people and business performance.

Leading organizations recognize that managing change and business complexity requires highly skilled and motivated people. The importance of understanding this equation cannot be underestimated. People are an organization's most expensive and flexible resource, and training must play a vital role in stimulating the capability and potential of this resource. With this in mind, it is essential that trainers take the lead in embracing change as an exciting opportunity rather than treating it as a draining and difficult roadblock to learning. When the commitment is made to let go of the struggle, all of a sudden, change can become a friend to learning rather than an enemy.

Closely associated with the acceptance of the inevitability of change and the opportunities associated with it is the need for trainers to learn the skill of linking training to business needs. Today's world provides trainers with enormous ammunition and evidence to justify their case. As the pace of change increases, so will the opportunity to claim that learning is the best and most effective way of helping people cope with the added pressures and ambiguities of modern life. In fact, the demand for high-quality and best-practice learning is the only remaining constant within the equation of turbulent and dynamic change.

With this great opportunity to sell the merits of learning comes a new and different responsibility, that of ensuring that the training initiatives are well considered, well researched and competency based. Gone are the days when training dollars were given away without justification. Today's decision makers are increasingly asking trainers to provide evidence of success before resources are allocated or reinvested. As a consequence, people must constantly review and assess whether the desired results have been achieved. Finding the most important business reasons for training takes time and effort. Some of the best ways of extracting evidence come from business and operational plans, industry and government reports, field discussions with staff and key customers, competitive information detailing the relative performance of one's operations, best-practice case studies, and results from previous studies of training needs.

Important Business Outcomes

As a consequence of this research, trainers can present business outcomes that can be used to gain support for training, including the following:

- Cost competitiveness—keeping costs down, keeping numbers of staff down, and eliminating unnecessary work, that is, managing more with less;
- Improved change-management skills;
- Improved delegation—increased staff empowerment and involvement, greater trust, and improved risk management;
- Enhanced competitiveness—improving customer satisfaction and producing industry best practices and superior products and services;
- Organizational effectiveness—building workforce flexibility, efficiency, and teamwork;
- Innovative training—breaking new ground in both products and services;
- Better total quality;
- Global and regional competitiveness—improving market performance within the different domains;
- Achievement of identified business targets;
- Compliance with government and industry standards; and
- Political and environmental expectations being met by the organization.

In addition to these general business reasons, each workplace will have its own unique needs for training. For example, in recent weeks, some of our clients have implemented the following learning initiatives:

- Help employees to draft both professional and personal goals.
- Prepare government employees for an impending restructure.
- Train lawyers for a transition to "self-managing teams."

In addition to identifying the business outcomes for training, it is imperative that appropriate and ongoing evaluation be undertaken. This helps to ensure that the desired competencies are gained and that the anticipated business and individual benefits are reaped from the training.

Measuring business benefits can be achieved by quantifying new frontiers or milestones achieved, exploring critical incidents, and assessing testimonials regarding the training. One way to measure these data accurately is by using the control group technique, which compares the results between two sets of people, one of which has undertaken training while the other has not.

Creating Systems that Sing the Praises of Learning

If training is to have a long and established impact on the capabilities of people within a workplace, all of the associated human resource, business, and total quality systems must sing the praises of high-quality learning, innovation, and continuous improvement.

Training cannot be expected to bring about miracles if there are hurtful, unfair, or inferior practices occurring within the workplace. As implied in the story "Let's Call in the Training Department," training cannot be expected to bring about change when there are people who do not toe the training line. Organizations can no longer afford to have decision makers who are only interested in pursuing self-indulgent agendas. It is sad but true that there are people in organizations today who are not genuinely interested in the development of other people. Key decision makers must ensure that the necessary changes are made to place learning first on the agenda.

Ultimately the capacity of an organization to align its systems to support learning will be contingent on the level of sharing and networking that occurs both inside and outside the workplace. The better informed that people are, the better the chance for change.

As a consequence, trainers must ensure they are totally in tune with, and well-informed about, business trends and challenges. While doing this, attempts must be made to form learning partnerships that encourage the spirited exchange of ideas, the sharing of resources, and the provision of emotional support.

A common area of difficulty in the application of learning is when trainers are not represented, consulted, or involved in human resource or business decision-making processes. As a consequence, the training effort becomes fragmented, piecemeal, and ineffective. Training and human resource systems must therefore be aligned and coordinated to ensure that the importance and spirit of high-quality learning is reinforced. To do this, representatives of the various arms of the human resource effort need to regularly demonstrate that all human resource systems, policies, and activities support high-quality learning.

Showing Clear Linkage Between Training and Human Resource Systems

Common examples of the outcomes of human resource systems that can help training are as follows: ·

- Recruitment practices that attract and hire staff who have a track record of learning;
- Reward structures that acknowledge staff who demonstrate excellence in applying training and learning;
- Performance-management systems that require people to demonstrate how they foster workplace learning;
- Career paths that encourage and provide resources for individuals to achieve their learning goals in line with business priorities;
- Team and job structures that develop the capacity, empowerment, and discovery of employees;
- Staffing practices that reflect the importance of work/life flexibility, value mental diversity, and demonstrate openness and fairness; and
- Enterprise agreements that link productivity and learning.

Securing Accountability

As highlighted in Chapter 1, leading organizations who demonstrate best-practice learning no longer view training and workplace learning as a voluntary activity. They now see it as a mandatory and strategic part of business activity. Ultimately, if training is to get results from everyone within the organization, we must accept that learning is everyone's responsibility, not just the training provider's.

Securing appropriate levels of accountability for training takes time and effort. There are at least six key strategies that need to be acted on if a workplace wishes to secure accountability. However, to do this correctly people must learn to listen and develop empathy with each situation as it arises. Particularly important is personalizing the benefits for training; supplying information and evidence on how, why, and what change may be happening; encouraging people to recall past and successful changes; and providing people with a reasonable time to adjust.

Key Strategies

1. Strategic and Operational Planning

Organizations need to state in their strategic and operational plans that training and workplace learning is an essential part of business activity. One high-leverage way of doing this is to write an organizational value statement that explains in clear and simple language that senior management is 100-percent committed to skill enhancement and continuous improvement.

Implicit in this commitment are two important considerations. First, there must be an expectation that all employees are required to support and promote employee growth in line with business requirements and, second, people who excel in promoting workplace learning need to be rewarded and acknowledged. Conversely, where appropriate, the organization should be prepared to place sanctions on people who deliberately avoid or frustrate workplace learning and training.

2. Funding

Have people bid for and manage their own funding for workplace learning. This transition, combined with the accountability to the business planning process, will provide a greater chance for learning to become a normal and natural part of every employee's daily routine, rather than just a ritual called a training course.

This shift toward line-accountability funding will create a different relationship with internal and centralized training providers. Instead of a training function bearing all of the financial risk of training, the line manager or team leader in the workplace will now need to ensure that the training investment has been worthwhile.

3. Coaching Sessions

There needs to be regular team and one-on-one coaching sessions between employees and their managers regarding career development and workplace learning needs. To reap the benefits of these activities, it is essential that people are coached on how to conduct high-quality and informative dialogue with employees. However, for this to happen, significant resistance may need to be overcome before both the individual and the organization benefit, particularly given that for some the change from being a boss to being a coach will be a very radical and undesired one.

The key to enhancing people's skill and capability through learning is to view on-the-job discovery as the real classroom. As a consequence, structured on-the-job learning and projects need to be carefully allocated to ensure the appropriate level of challenge, recognition, and support. The more balance and diversity a person receives in on-the-job learning, the greater the potential for growth. In regard to formal training, the manager or team leader of people participating should ensure that maximum opportunity is afforded to apply and practice core competencies on the job.

4. Workplace Team Involvement

Workplace teams should be actively involved in all facets of training design, delivery, and assessment. Workplace teams should ensure that training is taken seriously from start to finish. For this to occur, centralized training providers need to help workplace teams take ownership of and custom design their training.

Together with this accountability of workplace teams is the need for people to learn the skill of setting achievable and challenging milestones. Examples of milestones include undertaking clear research of learning requirements, ensuring effective consultation, seeking out best practices, undertaking structured competency-based design, conducting high impact training, and observing good evaluation processes.

5. Resource Provision

Organizations must be prepared to provide employees with the resources to manage their own workplace training requirements. Notable resources include modems that access databases and distance-learning programs; coaching people on how to conduct structured training; providing expertise to design learning materials; providing suitable equipment; establishing informal and formal networks to enable people to exchange and share ideas inside and outside the organization; supplying relevant audio, video, computer, and information resources; recommending mentors; and ensuring that when performance-enhancing tools are made available that adequate time and information is supplied to foster application.

6. Change Agent Development

Finally, special effort must be placed on developing the competency and learning needs of change agents. All too often these people are overlooked or are not supported. As a consequence, it is important that change agents get extraordinary assistance and are valued, recognized, sustained, and developed accordingly.

Aligning with the Best

Creating training miracles requires people to learn from the best. This may be by identifying the most suitable application or by accessing the expertise that can enlighten and stimulate the training effort. Forming high-quality learning partnerships is a vital part of the managing change equation.

As organizations become smaller, more transient, and more global, there is a greater need to locate and align oneself with best practices. The worldwide training profession is full of well-meaning people who are fighting the battles in isolation and, as a result, are "burning out." Given the power of telecommunications and the level of networking at regional, national, and international conferences, fighting such battles on one's own makes less and less sense.

One of the best levers for reform is the fact that ideas can be used in other places and at other times. This is a particularly successful strategy in the case of a decision maker who has tried an idea in the past only to have it fail because of poor implementation, lack of support, or inappropriate timing.

An important extension to this discussion is the realization that organizations are already full of untapped resources and best-practices options. Through better consultation, improved accountability, and more flexible categories of employment, workplaces can dramatically improve the quality, richness, and diversity of their knowledge pool.

As the quality and range of talent and knowledge expand, so does the chance of having higher leverage learning in the workplace. The ways of expanding the pool of knowledge and expertise are limitless. All that is required is an awareness of organizational and career trends plus plenty of creativity. Examples of how knowledge pools can be expanded include using telecommuters to undertake telemarketing and research, hiring disabled employees to undertake instructional design, using retired or displaced past employees for short-term projects, or creating a job-sharing policy for employees.

Celebrating Champions

Maintaining the enthusiasm and energy that sparks outstanding training results takes tremendous resolve, tact, and skill. Most of all it requires sensitivity and versatility to be able to deal with people's emotions, agendas, and desires.

Gaining the support of others is both a full-time and never-ending occupation involving the management of many thousands of communication exchanges each year. Whether it is people meeting face-to-face, on the phone, or in writing, each situation is a "moment of truth" where the need for learning should be sold.

One of the highest priority challenges in gaining commitment is to ensure that organizations identify and celebrate champions. People are more likely to take notice when one of their peers is getting results. Ways of celebrating champions include the following:

- Ensuring that key decision makers understand who the champions are and what makes them so special;
- Publicizing early successes, testimonials, and critical incidents that highlight results;
- Organizing formal and informal meetings between champions and other decision makers;
- Organizing rituals to highlight successes while making sure champions and their staff get all the credit;
- Asking champions to speak out at various internal and external gatherings;
- Holding briefing seminars with senior management;
- Helping champions to organize high-energy kick-off and milestone events;
- Sending information circulars and newsletters that publicize the results to key decision makers; and
- Taking a personal interest in the development of each champion's own career and energy level.

Aiming for Just-in-Time Learning

The guiding philosophy for getting training results is that all training design, delivery, and assessment should either mirror real-life workplace conditions or should be designed to be delivered at the time it is needed. This is important given that, on average, 80 percent of the learning undertaken within organizations occurs on the job.

To successfully achieve just-in-time learning there needs to be a passionate pursuit of continuous learning and skills transfer at the organizational, team, and training activity level. Practical tips for each of these three levels are explained below.

Level 1—Organizational Strategy

Before any just-in-time strategy can occur there needs to be an organization-wide commitment to continuous improvement and learning action. The whole notion that learning should be managed on the job should be supported and resourced.

Key issues for this level include the following:

- Senior decision makers demonstrating and role modeling just-in-time learning;
- Supplying people with self-study packages, learning tools, training, and information resources that support self-management, learning, and change;
- Ensuring that all key people are coached on what is required;
- Connecting people with best practices; and
- Creating a norm where people are encouraged to challenge the status quo and the assumptions of the decision makers.

Level 2—Teams

Teams provide the best leverage to manage just-in-time learning in a flexible and synergetic way. There are many ways in which teams can support just-in-time learning. These methods include the following:

- Discussing learning needs for the workplace in relation to business challenges;
- Developing the strategy for teams to manage their own workplace learning challenges;
- Developing workplace coaches, mentors, and trainers;
- Encouraging peer support and feedback;
- Encouraging cross-functional teams;
- Using high technology to provide multi-point delivery of learning;
- Implementing multiskilling and cross-training processes;
- Experimenting with multiple and fresh approaches to solution finding, continuous improvement, and team learning, for example, self-managing teams and quality circles;

- Organizing forums specifically to exchange and share dialogue and experience;
- Promoting balance and diversity;
- Setting training goals and reviewing outcomes; and
- Celebrating milestones and successes.

Level 3—Training Activities

Just-in-time learning requires excellent instructional design with first-class delivery and evaluation. The following are practical training activity tips that help just-in-time learning:

- Focus on immediate and/or early success in the application of skills.
- Structure learning so that people's past experience is recognized.
- Access the knowledge pool both inside and outside the organization to fast track the learning.
- Communicate realistic expectations and outcomes for actions and results.
- Design, deliver, and assess using a wide range of training activities that reflect real-life problems and challenges.
- Determine projects that give people an opportunity to apply their skills and to discover learning in real life.
- Vary the pace, speed, jargon, and pitch of the training to match the participants' learning styles.
- Build the self-esteem and the self-direction of learners by creating a supportive and nurturing learning environment.
- Take plenty of opportunities to reflect on, share, and celebrate learning.
- Hold recall sessions to reinforce and support workplace application. Well-designed recall sessions can add tremendous momentum to the process of continuous improvement well after the original training has occurred.

Summary

Getting workplace results from learning is one of the greatest challenges confronting organizations. Part of the answer lies in accepting that getting training results is a far more multifaceted process than just developing a wonderful instructional design.

People tasked with the challenge of getting results need to concentrate their efforts on securing greater employee accountability for learning. Key strategies include clarifying roles and responsibilities in learning, flagging key outputs and business contributions, discovering from best practices, celebrating training champions, designing training that delivers just-in-time learning, and removing and changing systems that stifle discovery and innovation.

Bibliography

Australian and New Zealand Training and Development Management Manual. (1992). Sydney: CCH (Update service).

Bellman, G. (1992). *Getting things done when you are not in charge.* San Francisco, CA: Berrett-Koehler.

Chawla, S., & Renesch, J. (1995). *Learning organizations: Developing cultures for tomorrow's workplace.* Portland, OR: Productivity Press.

Field, L. (1990). *Skilling Australia.* Melbourne: Longman Cheshire.

Gill, S.J. (1995, May). Shifting gears for high performance. *Training and Development, 49*(5), 25–31.

Marquardt, M.J. (1996). *Building the learning organization.* New York: McGraw-Hill.

Nilson, C. (1990). *Training for non-trainers.* New York: AMACOM.

Robinson, D.G., & Robinson, J.C. (1989). *Training for impact.* San Francisco, CA: Jossey-Bass.

Rylatt, A. (1994). *Learning unlimited: Practical strategies and techniques for transforming learning in the workplace.* Sydney: Business & Professional Publishing.

Senge, P. (1990). *The fifth discipline.* New York: Doubleday Currency.

Smith, A. (1992). *Training and development in Australia.* Sydney: Butterworths.

Sredi, H.J., & Rothwell, W.J. (1987). *The American society for training and development reference guide to professional training roles and competencies, Volumes 1 and 2.* Amherst, MA: Human Resource Development Press.

Tracey, W. (1992). *Designing training and development systems* (3rd ed.). New York: American Management Association.

COMPETENCY-BASED TRAINING

This chapter explains what competencies are, how they are used in training, what their many benefits and applications are, and how to develop them.

Gems Mined from These Pages

● Competencies are a description of the essential skills, knowledge, and attitudes required for effective performance.

● Typically, competencies include statements of good performance, the conditions and standards under which the performance will be carried out, and how the performance will be assessed.

● Competency-based training is concerned with the demonstration of competencies (outcomes), not with how they were attained (input).

● Competencies provide extensive benefits for individuals, the organization in which they work, the industry to which the organization belongs, and to the national economy.

● Competencies have applications to a range of human resource and organizational development issues as well as to training.

Almaza Gets Off on the Right Foot

Almaza had been a student of bakery all of her life. Now it was her time to rise.

Almaza Shenouda lived above her parents' small suburban bakery where they had supplied the local community with bread, cakes, and pastries for the past nineteen years. The cosmopolitan nature of the community meant that the family provided a broad variety of baked products.

Now that Almaza was finishing school she intended to join the business, but her parents advised her to broaden her horizons by first working in another bakery. That way, they reasoned, she would be able to bring new ideas and improved methods to their business.

It was nearly the end of the school year and Almaza decided to see her school's career adviser. It was there that she learned that she would need to go to a college for four more years to study for a Bakery Certificate. "But I am already a good baker," Almaza correctly informed the adviser. She was dismayed to learn that her current skills made no difference. She had to go through the system just like everyone else.

Almaza was an assertive young woman and had plenty of initiative. She thus decided to search the newspaper want ads for a job. She found a listing for an entry-level baker at a nearby hotel. Almaza prepared one of her famous choux pastry delights and made the trip to the hotel in a bus. There, she insisted on meeting the head chef. When the head chef came out to meet her she revealed her pastry. "I'm very sorry," the chef said. "I cannot hire you for this job unless you have a Bakery Certificate, but I might be able to take you on for a four-year apprenticeship."

Feeling disappointed and frustrated, Almaza returned to her parents and explained the situation. "I can earn more here as a baker than by taking a job as an apprentice," she explained.

Setting the Scene

Almaza's story typifies one of the reasons for the growing interest in competency-based learning. The story shows that it is unlikely that Almaza needed the entire four years of further study to make her a competent baker. Perhaps she needed only to complete a bridging course and some on-the-job practicals. However, the system demanded a four-year course and so that was what she was required to do.

Competencies and competency-based training are being hailed as a more efficient approach to training. In this chapter we will explain the principles of competencies and competency-based training from a general perspective.

We will discuss the following topics:

- What are competencies?
- Using competencies in training
- Benefits of competencies
- Applications of competencies
- How to identify job competencies

What Are Competencies?

Competencies are a description of the essential skills, knowledge, and attitudes required for effective performance in a work situation. Essentially, they detail the outcomes of work and should be stated in terms of worldwide best practices so that the outcomes they describe are the best that they can be.

Competencies explain the major functions or skill groups of a job. They are therefore usually expressed in broad terms. The broad statements are then defined more specifically by the various elements of competency. These describe the specific tasks that comprise competence in the major function or skill group. As well as these task specifications, it is important to add the criteria for successful performance (performance criteria). Finally, there will be a statement of the conditions under which the performance is expected to be performed and a specification of what evidence is required to demonstrate satisfactory competence (evidence guide). Typically, a comprehensive set of competencies will be structured along the following lines.

A number of key roles will describe the broad activities that a person engages in during his or her work. For example, a manager may have roles in the management of financial and human resources and also in some technical field such as engineering. Each role will comprise a number of units of competency that reflect the major functions, activities, or groups of skills required for that role. Each unit of competency, in turn, comprises a number of elements of competency that describe the units in more detail, explaining the output of a person who can perform the competency and a number of performance criteria that specify the desired level or standard of performance for each element of competency.

Each element of competency will also contain a statement of the conditions under which the competency is to be performed and the variables that might affect these conditions. These variables could include equipment to be used, manuals, procedure documents, possible client groups, environmental contexts, and whether or not assistance will be available.

The element of competence will also be accompanied by an evidence guide that shows ways in which an assessor (or the learner) can determine competency. The evidence guide may include a variety of strategies for assessing competency depending on the competency itself. It may, for example, require on-the-job assessment via demonstration of a skill, assessment under simulated conditions, a written or oral test, or the use of role plays.

The competency standards for a complete job will comprise a number of units of competency, each of which has its own set of elements. Figure 3.1 illustrates how the competencies for a job might be displayed and shows the divisions of the unit of competence: elements, performance criteria, conditions, and evidence guide.

Almaza's parents also felt her frustration; however, they had heard of a college that was trying a new system of training. "It's called competency-based training," her mother told her. "I read about it in a trade journal last month." She retrieved the journal from her library and showed it to Almaza.

"Look," said her mother, "Here it is. In this system of training the college will assess your current skills and you only need to attend the training that will be required to give you all the skills of a certified baker. They even list all of the skills."

Almaza looked at the journal's listing of the competencies required of a certified baker. She then pointed out one of the units of competence to her mother and said, "Can you see the way they have described the competencies here? This is one that I can definitely do well."

What Almaza was showing her mother was the unit of competence entitled "Prepare pastry, cakes, and yeast goods." It contained four elements and each element had performance criteria assigned to it.

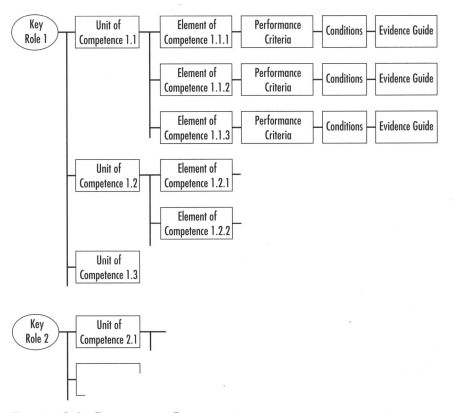

FIGURE 3.1. DESCRIBING COMPETENCIES

Source: Adapted from the National Training Board, *National Competency Standards, Policy and Guidelines* (2nd ed.). National Training Board, Canberra. Reproduced with permission.

If, as her mother said, Almaza was required to only study for the skills she did not already have, then she would be able to complete the course in much less than the four years she was told it would take.

Almaza decided to call the college and see about enrolling in the course they offered. She made an appointment with the admissions officer and went to see her about the course for bakers.

"I understand you have a Baker's Certificate course that is competency-based," said Almaza, trying to sound knowledgeable. "Can you tell me all about it?"

"Certainly," said the admissions officer. "I think we should begin by having a chat about using competencies in training and the principles of competency-based training."

Element	Performance criteria
Prepare, decorate and present pastries	• Sweet and short pastry produced to basic standard recipe. • Puff, filo, and strudel dough pastry-based products correctly identified. • A variety of choux-based products prepared and presented to standard recipe. • A variety of pastry products produced to restaurant dessert trolley standard.
Element	**Performance criteria**
Prepare and produce cakes and yeast goods	• A selection of sponges and cakes prepared and decorated to standard recipe. • A variety of yeast-based products produced and served to industry standard.
Element	**Performance criteria**
Prepare and decorate petits fours	• Petits fours selected to complement given situation. • Petits fours prepared and decorated to industry standard.
Element	**Performance criteria**
Apply portion control and storage procedures	• Portion control applied to minimize wastage. • Storage procedures identified and applied correctly for cakes and pastry products.

FIGURE 3.2. UNIT OF COMPETENCY: PREPARE PASTRY, CAKES, AND YEAST GOODS (TYPICAL STATEMENT OF COMPETENCY FOR ONE UNIT)

Source: National Training Board, *National Competency Standards, Policy and Guidelines* (2nd ed.). National Training Board, Canberra. Reproduced with permission.

Using Competencies in Training

Competency-based training (CBT) is concerned with the attainment and demonstration of specified skills and knowledge and the consistent application of those skills to meet the required enterprise or industry standards in the workplace. It focuses on the demonstration of competence rather than with an individual's achievement relative to that of others, as we often see in traditional education where learners are graded relative to their peers.

The definition also implies that the assessment procedure used to determine a person's competence will be based only on the demonstration of competencies that are specified using clear performance criteria.

"In other words," said the admissions officer, "we don't care whether you come first or last in a class. We only care about whether you can perform the skills required. Furthermore, we assess you by having you actually demonstrate the skills."

CBT is concerned with outcomes of training, that is, the demonstration of competence, however it is attained. It is in contrast to the focus that some more traditional training has on inputs, that is, the delivery style and methodology. This shift in focus from input to output is driven by a number of guiding principles.

Put simply, CBT covers training that is designed to develop specific, performance-based competence, however attained. It is therefore flexible in its process and allows people to acquire competence in any way. As a result, it demands some unique design characteristics, especially when applied to competencies such as those in vocational trades.

"The following nine principles will help you to understand what competency-based training is and how it is used for the Bakery Certificate program," said the admissions officer.

1. Use Meaningful Benchmarks

Competencies should reflect essential business requirements. They should be statements of industry or vocational standards of excellence, based on international best-practice benchmarks rather than minimum standards of performance, which may serve to create mediocrity. In this way we will be assured of developing worldwide competitiveness.

2. Focus on the Acquisition of Learning

One of the key differences between CBT and traditional training is the focus on the acquisition of learning, not the delivery of training. In CBT, we are only concerned with *whether* people acquire the competencies involved and not with *how* they are acquired. Learning processes are focused on helping people learn and not on delivery techniques and strategies. There is also a strong emphasis on the portability of skills learned. They should be transferable across artificial boundaries such as differences in accreditation across different states.

3. Promote Flexibility

As a result of the concern for the acquisition of learning, there is now a greater flexibility in the way people learn. Learning may take place in a variety of settings and there may be many different methods used for it, from instruction to reading to trial and error (and by learning informally in your parents' bakery). This flexibility ensures that the learning people engage in on an informal basis is a valid process. As long as they can demonstrate competence, the way in which the learning was acquired is irrelevant. Therefore, when people engage in projects of a self-directed nature there is a possibility that these will be validated in a process of assessment that verifies the acquisition of competence. In Chapter 4 we will explain how this self-direction can be adapted for workplace learning.

4. Recognize Prior Learning

Competency-based training should recognize that learning may have occurred prior to a person's formal training. The recognition of prior learning allows for flexible entry points to training. It will no longer be necessary for people to always begin "at the beginning" and finish "at the end." A person can enter and exit at many positions throughout the learning program, and indeed can complete the training in any sequence.

"This is where I come in," interrupted Almaza. "You see, I have worked for many years in my parents' bakery and I already know a lot about the job. I don't think I need to go to college for another four years. I only need to learn a few new skills."

"Then CBT is for you," said the admissions officer. "The fifth principle is also relevant here."

5. Allow the Pace to Vary

CBT is not concerned with *how long* it takes you to learn, only *if* you learn. Traditional training requires you to complete the term, regardless of how quickly you learn the competencies. In a CBT environment, flexible learning methods allow you to speed up or slow down your learning to suit your own pace and, in theory, you can learn as fast as you like. It is conceivable that a person might complete a four-year training program in one year.

6. Use Appropriate Assessment Techniques

CBT is concerned with the demonstration of competence. Therefore, it is necessary for people to be assessed to determine whether they are competent in order to award qualifications. Since learning may have occurred in many settings, we must be confident that people claiming competence are indeed competent. Assessment methods used to determine competency must be carefully designed to ensure that they measure the actual attainment of competence. The methods must be reliable. This means that any assessor would reach the same conclusion about a person's competence. They must also be valid, which is to say that the method must actually measure what it says it measures. Asking a person to explain how to bake a loaf of bread, for example, is not a valid way to assess whether they can bake.

The issues to consider for appropriate assessment include the encouragement of self-assessment and progressive assessment. Both of these strategies will keep assessment costs low while encouraging learners to continue as a result of the personal responsibility and continuous feedback that is maintained. The actual methods used will reflect the nature of the competence. For example, role play would be an appropriate method when assessing interpersonal skills.

In other cases, on-the-job observation may be the best way to appropriately assess competence. This is often the situation when the conditions of performance are difficult to simulate.

7. Ensure Ongoing Monitoring and Evaluation

"The way people bake today will differ from the way they bake in twenty years' time," said the admissions officer. "Changes in the chemistry of raw materials, the introduction of baking technology, and the changing demands of consumers will all influence the way a baker goes about his or her daily functions. It is important, therefore, that competencies change to reflect the changes to an occupation. It is also important that people who learn how to bake today are retrained to reflect the changes to their industries. Therefore, for competency-based training to be effective, we need to ensure there is a system in place that monitors the development of competencies over time to reflect changes to requirements. This system should also monitor training providers to ensure they are providing learning processes that deliver the appropriate competence. This means that here at the catering college we need to keep up to date, too, or else we will lose our license to teach baking."

Ultimately, the true benefits of competency-based training are contingent on linkage to national accreditation. Principles 8 and 9 make a vast difference to the success of competencies as a viable framework for training. It is these two principles that ensure, for example, that the effort expended to develop competencies and design flexible training to achieve these outcomes is worth the investment.

8. Maintain National Consistency

Traditionally, occupational training has been performed by many providers including tertiary institutions, commercial institutions, consultants, and training staff employed by individual organizations. Each of these providers has a distinct way of deciding what is to be learned. Often, this leads to inconsistencies in the skills and knowledge among learners who are performing the same function. Competency-based training relies on the demonstration of competencies that are nationally consistent with the requirements of the industry in which they are to be applied. As a result, people who learn the skills in one place will be able to relocate anywhere in the country and remain confident that they will be employable.

"What this means," explained the admissions officer, "is that the competencies we teach have been endorsed by a national accrediting body as appropriate to the baking industry across the country. It doesn't matter where you go to learn to be a baker; you will learn these same competencies."

"I've always been a bit cynical though," said Almaza. "How do I know that you are really going to be able to teach me those things. You might say you will but then be really bad at it or not keep up to date as you say you will."

"That's where the final principle comes in," said the admissions officer.

9. Accredit Learning

A system of accreditation ensures that there is national consistency among providers of training. That is to say, institutions that provide training for bakers, for example, must have their curriculum approved by a central authority before they can promote their course as one which will turn out bakers certified as competent.

To summarize these principles, competency-based training is a process by which the things to be learned are expressed in terms of measurable competencies, and a variety of student-centered rather than teacher-centered learning methods are employed to enable learners to acquire and demonstrate the competencies. Learners can learn the competencies in any setting, at any pace, and in any way they choose as long as they can demonstrate competence. For the process to be effective there needs to be a network of controls that ensures competencies are kept current and that providers are providing the right training.

Typically, the government will provide those controls with the establishment of national authorities. In Australia there is the Australian National Training Authority (ANTA). In New Zealand there is the New Zealand Qualifications Authority (NZQA). In the United Kingdom there are The National Council for Vocational Qualifications (NCVQ), The Scottish Vocational Educational Council (SCOTVEC), and the Training and Development Lead Body (TDLB). Canada has the Canadian Labor Force Development Board (CLFDB) and in the United States there are the Departments of Labor and Education.

Benefits of Competencies

Competencies have a number of benefits to employees, organizations, industry as a whole, and to the national economy if adopted as a national framework.

Benefits for Employees

- Clarifies the relevance of prior learning, the transferability of skills, the value of recognized qualifications, and the potential for career progression.
- Provides an incentive for individuals to seek training through access to national certification based on standards.
- Fosters goal setting as a means of career growth.
- Details a benchmark for what is expected in order to meet a competency within an enterprise or industry.
- Creates a common language for mentoring and skill enhancement.
- Provides evidence of the value that an organization places on learning and growth (based on the currency of the competencies and the use of their benefits).
- Clarifies career change options. To change to a new occupation, a person can compare current competencies to those required in the new occupation. The new competencies required may only be 10 percent different from the ones already possessed.
- Allows for more objective performance assessment and feedback based on clearly defined competency standards.
- Increases portability of skills and marketability of employees.

Benefits for Organizations

- Allows for accurate mapping of required and existing competencies of the workforce.
- Improves recruitment effectiveness by matching competencies required in a job to those offered by applicants.

- Focuses training on skill gaps and specific enterprise skill requirements.
- Facilitates access to cost-effective training based on industry needs and the identification of internal and external providers based on the competencies identified.
- Increases decision makers' confidence that people actually have the skills that were intended to be acquired in training.
- Provides for reliable and consistent assessment of both prior learning and outcomes of training.
- Increases individuals' capacity to transfer their skills to new situations as a result of having developed broad competency rather than having been restricted to a particular set of tasks.
- Supports clear communication of expectations about employee skills and knowledge.
- Facilitates change by identifying competencies required to manage the change.

Benefits for Industries

- Allows for better identification and match of overall skills needed for the industry.
- Facilitates greater access to public-sector training provisions relevant to the industry.
- Provides a basis for common and clear understanding of course outcomes across the industry through competency certification.
- Inspires greater confidence that industry needs are being met as a result of assessment based on standards.
- Provides the basis of a national system for industry-specific qualification.
- Allows greater efficiency in delivery and reduces the duplication of training effort.
- Enhances accountability of education and training providers for outcomes.
- Encourages skill development that is broad and relevant to the future.

Benefits for National Economy

- Enhances skill formation for competition in international markets.
- Encourages new international investment in industries for which a skilled workforce is a major requirement.

- Provides more cost-efficient, relevant, and accountable vocational education and training.
- Allows access by individuals to industry-recognized and relevant competencies that are portable within and across industries.
- Promotes nationally consistent assessment against relevant industry standards.
- Enhances equity and access of individuals by clear expression of requirements by industry and through recognition of prior learning against preset standards.

Applications of Competencies

Competency-based training is only one application of competencies. There are many more strategic uses of competencies that can contribute to the business bottom line. As Figure 3.3 illustrates, training is merely one application.

FIGURE 3.3. APPLICATIONS OF COMPETENCIES

1. Training

As we have already discussed, competency standards can be used to design training programs both on-the-job and in formal settings. The standards are descriptors of the core skills, knowledge, and attitudes that will form the basis of the program. They will guide decisions about content. The standards also help with decisions about which learning and assessment methods to offer to learners.

2. Strategic and Business Planning

Having predetermined competencies can help when planning the strategic direction the organization needs to take. In most strategic planning processes, there is a stage in which the organization needs to examine its strengths and weaknesses, along with its opportunities and threats. The strengths and weaknesses may well relate to the level of competence of the staff, and the organization may then choose to capitalize on these strengths or take a direction that is designed to overcome the weaknesses. In its search for a competitive advantage, the organization may find the ability of its people to be its greatest asset and the perfect opportunity to gain better leverage in the marketplace. On the other hand, the comparative lack of competence may be the greatest threat to the future of an organization.

For example, if the organization is planning to move into new markets in Southeast Asia, it would be necessary to examine the competencies required to succeed. Implementing such a plan may take years of planning and research about the market opportunities. Meanwhile, the organization could do what was necessary to provide its staff with the appropriate competencies for such a move, such as languages, cross-cultural awareness, and even knowledge of differences in packaging preferences in the new markets. When the time comes to act, the people will be ready.

From another perspective, competency standards can help with short-term business plans. Imagine an organization that is about to launch a saturation advertising campaign for a traditional product. Competency questions include "Do the staff members have the necessary competencies to cope with the increased demand?" "Can the productivity be increased?" "Can deliveries be increased?" "Will quality standards be maintained under this new pressure?"

3. Performance Management

Performance-management systems rely on a clear understanding between management and staff of the required standards of performance. Competency standards are, of course, exactly that. With a complete set of competency standards for a particular job it is much easier to have meaningful dialogue about required performance and how current performance compares. The outcome of the discussion should be about plans for improvement—either building on strengths or developing areas that need improvement.

4. Succession Planning

Organizations can assess the most suitable candidates for promotion and transfer by examining their levels of ability compared to the required competencies. A planned and open approach to the identification of competency required in different positions and of what will be done to help people develop those competencies can create motivation for people who see the acquisition of competencies as a stepping stone.

5. Career Development

From an individual's perspective, competency standards serve two key functions. First, the standards can be used to help compare the present level of performance against a desirable benchmark that can then help to determine immediate training and development needs. This knowledge can help a person to realize how he or she might go about developing skills to the required standard for his or her current job. Second, the standards can be used for long-term career planning. If, for example, learners are already competent in their present jobs, they can use the competency standards to determine how they can develop their skills for the future. Having these competencies in place can also help to develop a learning organization and to encourage people to take responsibility for their own development over the short and long term.

6. Human Resource Information Systems

Competencies can also serve as a database of the human resource requirements of the organization. The standards indicate what people are needed. When this database is compared to the already existing competencies in the organization, training and recruitment needs can be determined. The Human Resource Information System stores and processes the data to help make the comparison and ultimately make the necessary decisions about the organization's staff. An important ethical consideration has to do with participation. People must voluntarily participate in the process; otherwise it may be seen as a "big brother" approach. Staff members may feel that the organization is spying on them. Many people are uncomfortable with the notion that their details exist on databases.

7. Recruitment

The existence of clear competencies that specify required levels of performance can also assist people who are trying to fill a job vacancy or to complete a short-term project. Interviewers will be assisted by the competencies since they can now assess the applicants in light of the elements of competence and performance criteria.

8. Job Design

Competencies can help with the job-design process and the formation of such structures as self-managing work teams. A comprehensive list of competencies required for successful performance is an excellent baseline for decisions about who will do what and how many people in each category will be needed. The skills required for effective performance as well as those for working in an autonomous team will be specified. The competency standards, in effect, serve as a statement of duties and include performance criteria and range (conditions under which the performance will be expected to be performed).

9. Enterprise Bargaining

When organizations and their staff members negotiate salaries, work reforms, and the consequent learning needs that are related to them, the definition of competencies will be a useful benchmark. Both management and staff will have a clear idea of what is expected for the fulfillment of job requirements and can use this for discussions about changes to applied skills and appropriate rewards for any increases.

How to Identify Job Competencies

Competency standards are the building blocks that describe the work roles implicit in a job. As such, they describe the broad requirements of what a person might be expected to perform in that job. They are a combination of hard-skill competencies, for example, "prepare drawings," that describe in behavioral terms a skill that is easily observable and soft-skill competencies, for example "relate to the feelings and needs of others and convey interest and respect," that are more intangible and difficult to quantify.

It is important that the competencies that describe a job use both of these domains. Otherwise, there will be a tendency to create robots who can perform observable functions but who fail to apply concepts such as commitment, imagination, perseverance, and innovation.

Developing such a set of competencies involves a combination of techniques that are designed to break a work role down into its component parts. A brief description of some of the major techniques follows.

1. DACUM

DACUM (Develop a Curriculum) technique requires a facilitator and a group of expert job holders who together review an occupational area and identify the general areas of competence. It operates under the assumption (as do many of these techniques) that a group of expert workers is better equipped to define their work than anyone else.

In general, the group attempts to identify between eight and twelve key statements of competence that describe the work function. Although this number is flexible, the intention is to refine the requirements into a workable number and eliminate any duplication by combining similar competencies. When the group has identified the broad competencies, they then work through each of the statements and identify the core skills, knowledge, and attitudes that comprise each of these broad areas.

The facilitator's role is to act as guide and prober through the process. He or she is responsible for checking items such as previous and subsequent steps in working procedures, what assumptions have been made, what is done when things go wrong, and what initiative is required on the part of the worker.

2. Delphi

This process involves recognized experts (who may either be expert workers or experts in the field from academia) making a best guess about the requirements of the work. It typically involves a number of "rounds." Each round may be done in a group or by correspondence. In each round, the facilitator asks the members to present their opinions about the matter at hand. The information is then collated and returned to the members for further comment. This is repeated until the group reaches agreement on the issue.

For example, in round one the members are asked to identify the competencies of say, an electrician. The results are tabulated and returned to the group for round two with instructions that might say "The following list comprises the competencies identified by the whole group. Please delete any that you see as unnecessary and give your justification." The replies are again tabulated and the competencies that were deleted by the majority are now removed. Round three now begins and the list is again returned with instructions such as "This list represents the competencies that are seen as important. Please identify the top ten in priority order and combine or reword any that you believe need to be expressed differently." The responses that are received next may be the competencies you are seeking.

3. Functional Analysis

This is another group process that relies on groups of expert workers and a facilitator. It involves the group in a search of the key function or purpose of a work role in its wider context such as teams or in its particular enterprise.

The facilitator leads the group through an analysis of this key purpose to determine what must be done for that purpose or outcome to be achieved. This is the first stage and will determine the core competencies for the work role. Each of these core competencies is then broken down further by repeating the process. The same question is repeated for each step in the process until the functions are broken down into units and elements. It is important that the results include all the components required for the work role being examined, including technical skills and knowledge and soft skills such as communication and motivation.

Once the group reaches the point at which the units being described for one core competency are clear and concise and cannot be confused, they move on to another of the core competencies developed in the first stage. One way of checking the integrity of the units and elements identified is to ensure that they cannot be confused by another person reading them. That is to say, anyone reading them must reach the same conclusion about what they mean. In an example of the competencies for real estate agents, a unit that says "create listings" may be interpreted many ways, but it is broken down to smaller components, such as "develop and implement strategies to develop a sales network," that are more meaningful.

4. Critical Incident Technique

This technique involves a group of workers (or individuals) who have problems posed to them in the form of critical incidents that they may face on the job. How they respond to this critical incident helps identify the competencies required for effective performance. Successful outcomes are compared to unsuccessful ones to reveal core competencies for mastery of the task.

Another way to use the method is to ask workers to describe exactly what they do when there is a failure of a critical nature. Often this is done in a group context using written critical incidents. The participants respond individually in writing, and then the whole group discusses and clarifies the responses and determines effective and ineffective behavior. For example, you might suggest to a group of forklift drivers that a critical incident consists of a load falling from the forklift. The discussion should then highlight the skills and abilities that would prevent this from happening and also identify what would lead to such an incident.

More than one hundred such incidents may be necessary to define the competencies that make up a whole job role. It is then the facilitator's role to get the group to refine the list to a core of eight to ten competencies.

Almaza enrolled in the CBT Bakery Certificate program. She completed the course in nine months and was awarded the Certificate in record time. She returned to her career adviser at school and showed the Certificate to her, proud of her achievement.

The career adviser was dumbfounded and could merely exclaim, "It's a miracle!"

Summary

In this chapter, competencies were defined as a description of the essential skills, knowledge, and attitudes required for effective performance; their benefits for individuals, organizations, industries, and the national economy were outlined. The application of competencies is not restricted to training, and the framework from this chapter may be used to explore many opportunities to maximize the benefits of competencies.

Competency-based training was discussed and nine principles were provided to assist in the application of this training in an organization. Finally, a number of examples of strategies that can be used to develop competencies were provided, including DACUM, delphi, functional analysis, and critical incident technique.

Bibliography

Blank, W. (1982). *Handbook for developing competency based training programs.* Englewood Cliffs, NJ: Prentice Hall.

Field, L. (1990). *Skilling Australia.* Melbourne: Longman Cheshire.

Fletcher, S. (1991). *Designing competency based training.* London: Kogan Page.

MCI. (1992). *MCI pocket directory: Middle management standards.* London: Author.

National Training Board. (1992). *National competency standards, policy and guidelines* (2nd ed.). Canberra: Author.

National Training Board. (1993). *Highlights: Fourth annual report.* Canberra: Author.

Rutherford, P.D. (1995). *Competency based assessment: A guide to implementation.* Melbourne: Pitman Publishing Asia Pacific.

SELF-DIRECTED LEARNING

This chapter provides an explanation of the practicalities of self-directed learning: what it is and how to apply it to help foster a learning organization.

"Please do not teach me; I wish to learn."

GRAFFITI ON A
FIJIAN SCHOOL
BUILDING

Gems Mined from These Pages

- Self-directed learning is both a method of learning and a character trait.

- In this age of rapid change, we have to stop teaching people and help them learn how to learn.

- People already know how to learn; the challenge is to help them apply this talent in formal settings.

- There is a profound shift in the role of a trainer from being a subject-matter expert to being a resource expert and helping people access resources to learn.

- One way to help people apply self-direction in formal settings is through the use of learning contracts.

Please Do Not Teach Me; I Wish to Learn

Jai Ram studied the soil in which his small garden crop of vegetables grew. It was rich and black and crumbled easily in his hands as he squeezed it. Not so long ago it was barren and full of rocks and stone chips.

When Jai bought his home three years earlier, it had barely a scrap of grass on it. The building process had killed almost everything, and the soil was filled with the refuse of the builders. Jai knew nothing of gardening but was determined to fix it. At first he achieved some success with common sense. He tilled the soil and removed many of the stone chips and rocks by hand. However, a neighbor suggested to Jai that the soil also needed enriching. Jai invited the neighbor to dinner and spent several hours quizzing her about the intricacies of soil enrichment.

He began to visit his local library and there he found many books on native plants. He was soon propagating his own cuttings from the plants he came across in neighbors' gardens all around the community. He joined a local garden club and heard many of the members speak on various garden issues. He even began to experiment with some grafting of fruit trees.

Suddenly, Jai came out of his daydream and brushed the soil from his hands. He would have to hurry if he was to make it to work on time. Today he was attending a training course and he didn't want to be late.

When he arrived at the training course he noticed that things seemed a little different. There was no customary book of training notes on the table in front of him, and the back of the room was filled with books, audiotapes and videotapes. Before long, the trainer arrived and began to speak to the participants about learning in their lives. Jai thought the trainer looked familiar but couldn't quite place him.

The trainer spoke about how many people learn on their own, at their own pace, with resources they choose, and at times that suit them. "In other words," the trainer said, "we make most of the decisions about how and what to learn ourselves." Then the trainer said something that made Jai's ears prick up. "For example, many of us learn gardening in this way."

"Typically though," the trainer continued, "in training, the trainer makes all of those decisions for us. In this course, we are going to let you use that talent for learning. You will be able to make those decisions yourself and I will help you."

Next the trainer said something that really started Jai thinking. He said, "Instead of my teaching you, you are going to learn."

Later, during one of the breaks, Jai approached the trainer. "Where are you from?" he asked.

"I grew up in Fiji," said the trainer. "Why do you ask?"

"Because just now you said something that reminded me of something I experienced as a young boy. One of the other boys in my school had painted on the school building "Please do not teach me; I wish to learn.'"

"That was me," said the trainer excitedly. "I wrote that because I felt that the teachers at school were often creating obstacles for me. Instead of allowing me more freedom to pursue my own learning goals, they insisted that I stay with the class, often despite the fact that I knew the material they were teaching. Now I am carrying that same philosophy into my job. I want to help people to recognize that they are already skilled learners and that if they apply these skills in workplace learning they will have a lot more success. How are you finding the idea so far?"

"How am I finding it?" repeated Jai. "It's a miracle."

Competencies and Self-directed Learning

In the previous chapter we explained that one of the principles of competency-based training is that it is flexible. It allows for multiple entry and exit points in training and allows for the occurrence of informal learning, just like Almaza in her parents' bakery. Another of the principles is the recognition of prior learning so that a person may not have to complete an entire training program—only those parts for which he or she has not yet acquired competence.

Self-directed learning is a means to facilitate both of these processes. It supports informal learning because it encourages a person to seek learning outcomes in whatever way suits his or her circumstances. It is also a means by which a person may acquire "prior learning" that will later be recognized by an assessor when that person is seeking entry to a training program at a midpoint, for example.

In short, self-directed learning is an important process that supports competency-based training. The two are a set like a knife and fork. They can exist separately but things just work better when both are employed together.

What Is Self-directed Learning?

This book was written with the aid of three different computers: an Apple Macintosh, an IBM desktop clone, and an IBM notebook clone. Neither of us has ever completed a computer training course, but we have quite capably learned the intricacies of various applications of these machines. Occasionally, we consulted friends who know about these things. Less frequently, we consulted the manuals that come with the hardware and software. Most of the time, we used the "help screen" function and trial and error.

There are many things we do not know. However, as far as we do know, we have not yet had the need to know these things. If the need arose, we would no doubt undertake to learn them as we have done for so many other things.

By most definitions, what we have engaged in has been a series of self-directed learning projects. Everyone does this. How have you learned to cook? What about car maintenance, gardening, and do-it-yourself projects? Although there are training courses for such things, the vast majority of people learn these things independently of formal guidance.

Self-directed learning describes the process by which learners make decisions about their learning that might, in other circumstances, have been made by a teacher or trainer. Self-directed learning is therefore, in a sense, the opposite of teacher-directed learning. It is the process of learner control or a means by which people can learn.

However, the term self-directed learning also describes a personality trait of a person who engages in the search for learning and discovery. Many self-directed learning practitioners have advocated the need to develop this trait in learners. Self-directed learning thus becomes an end product or an outcome of the process.

Self-directed Learning as a Process

Self-directed learning is most commonly associated with the process by which learners initiate their own learning and diagnose their own needs, define the goal, identify resources, decide on the methods by which they will learn, and evaluate their progress.

It is more likely, however, that taking initiative for (or control over) these things is not a simple event in which you either do or you don't. Instead, the level of learner control exists on a continuum with learner control at one end and trainer control at the other. Learning or teaching methods can then be positioned along this continuum to describe their level of self-directedness (see Figure 4.1).

Self-directed learning as a process must therefore be defined contextually. A degree of trainer control does not preclude self-direction. Both can exist together.

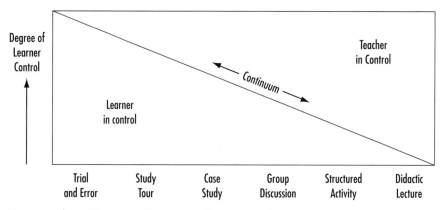

FIGURE 4.1. TRAINER/LEARNER CONTROL CONTINUUM

The benefits obtained from increasing the degree of learner control in learning situations are, of course, the reasons for the growth in the popularity of the method. Later, under the heading "Why Employ Self-directed Learning?", we will explain these benefits. Then, under the heading "How to Implement Self-directed Learning," we will provide some ideas for how to develop increased learner control or self-direction in training.

Self-directed Learning as a Personality Trait

The definition of self-directed learning that is suggested by the way we learn about gardening and cooking, for example, is difficult to apply in a workplace setting. This kind of everyday learning may be argued to be a natural by-product of personal growth or of the motivation that exists in the search for a fulfilling life (gardening) or in the need for basic living skills (cooking).

It may also be a consequence of a person's search for fulfillment of innate motivators. Innate motivators are those activities from which a person has derived pleasure since early childhood. These motivators reveal themselves as patterns and may manifest themselves, for example, in a child who builds with blocks and then continues to build as he or she grows older, perhaps moving on to treehouses. Many of us can recognize these motivators in ourselves. Perhaps you have always enjoyed word puzzles or studying sea life at the beach. In many cases these motivators emerge in adult life as career choices. For example, the child who enjoyed building may become a construction worker. Just as often, however, our career has little connection to our innate motivators and so we seek to satisfy them in our hobbies. As a result, learning about these innate motivators must be self-directed, since our employers rarely sponsor learning that is not directly related to our employment.

It is possible that similar motivation exists in the working life of people, especially if their motivators are a close match with what they do for a living. If it is possible to inspire this level of motivation for learning about workplace issues to equal the desire for learning about personal issues, then we may be able to tap into the power that exists in all of us to gain deep and lasting learning.

We believe that this is possible. In fact, we have attempted to demonstrate it in the example we gave of our learning about the computer. This was a workplace need and there is little doubt about our motivation to learn it. Yet we know many people who have a similar need (although it may not be as immediate) to learn workplace skills such as understanding computers who have not done so. What is it about one person that gives him or her the ability or desire to take on a learning goal that others lack? This is the foundation for the argument that self-directed learning is a personality trait.

Just as we saw that there are differing levels of self-direction or learner control in the process side of self-directed learning, it is equally true that there are varying levels of learner commitment to self-direction.

The essential feature of a self-directed learner's behavior is a willingness to begin and maintain learning on his or her own initiative. Why people do not do so may be attributed to two factors: preference for trainer-directed learning and personal perceptions about learning.

Preference for Trainer Direction

A preference to "be taught" does exist—in fact, we have witnessed it. Following a self-directed program, one of the participants had not completed any of the personal learning goals. When asked about this, she replied, "I'd rather just come to a course."

There could be a number of reasons for this reaction, one of which is the notion of learned helplessness. That is to say that as a result of always having people "do for you," you become conditioned to accept and expect help to the point at which you are unable to help yourself.

A second reason may be the culturally bound notions of what constitutes valid learning. We have come to accept that "getting the piece of paper" is the only valid way to demonstrate learning. We once met a young man (about three years out of school) who had approached us for career counseling. He was desperate to win a particular job but had no formal qualifications to help him stand out above the crowd. When we advised him to gain some skills and experience by participating in professional association committees or taking on some personal projects such as research and writing for a professional journal, he saw this as inappropriate. His firm belief was that the prospective employer would not see this as valid.

This cultural bias against self-direction is, we believe, a significant barrier to implementing it in the workplace. People find it difficult to translate their self-directed abilities from informal personal learning goals to formal workplace learning goals. Helping people to over come the notion that you have to be taught by an expert in order to have learned is a major challenge of self-directed learning in the workplace.

Perceptions About Personal Learning

Learners' perceptions about their learning ability may influence their self-directedness in that they may hold a number of falsehoods to be true. For example, they may say of themselves, "I'm too old to learn this" or "I'm not a creative person." These self-perceptions are often the result of the accumulation of the assessments by others of that learner. It often leads to what can be called "hardening of the categories":

when people say of themselves, "I see myself as a. . . ." One of our favorite examples is a friend who professes to "have a memory like a sieve" and to be "not very good at math." Yet this fellow is a keen gambler and could tell you about any of several dozen racehorses and greyhounds and their trainers and can calculate the payout odds for any runner in any race. Ask him what $25 at 33/1 will pay and he can tell you in a blink.

These false constructs can be unlearned just as they were learned. Then, once free of these barriers to their progress and growth, learners may find the freedom so long denied them to begin the journey of discovery of which they are capable.

Combining Process and Personality Trait

Self-direction, as a process, attempts to move learning away from its episodic nature. In other words, we want to have people accept that learning does not only occur when they enter a training room or during other episodes of formally structured learning. In order to achieve this, we need to develop a person's ability to learn. The concept of self-directed learning, therefore, incorporates an individual's motivation to pursue learning throughout life rather than the ability of an individual to engage in episodes of learning.

To achieve self-direction as an end (personality trait), we first need to develop it as a means (learning process). Trainers who wish to take advantage of the benefits of self-directed learners who take control over the initiative of learning and who are autonomous in their management of the learning process will first need to help people hurdle the unnecessary barriers. These barriers can be removed by the gradual movement from trainer-direction to learner-direction as illustrated in Figure 4.2. The diagram suggests that the degree of trainer control can be reduced as the maturity of the learner increases toward self-directed learning. It also suggests that there is always a degree of control by the learner since he or she can elect to leave even in the most didactic presentation. There is also always a degree of trainer control since it is often the trainer who has the clearer vision of learning needs to match the goals of the organization.

As a manager of learning, a learning facilitator can gain much from an understanding of the skills of leadership. As Figure 4.2 illustrates, you need to adapt your style for varying degrees of control.

This adaptability requires different levels of trainer control for different situations, depending on the level of learner maturity.

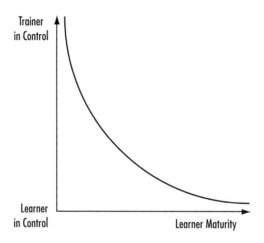

FIGURE 4.2. RELATIONSHIP BETWEEN TRAINER AND LEARNER CONTROL

Learner maturity refers to the skill of the learner to manage his or her own learning. These skills include issues such as setting objectives, identifying resources to help meet the objectives, and assessing personal progress toward the objectives.

Sometimes, trainers who maintain maximum control of the learning process may be described, in leadership terms, as authoritarian learning leaders. They direct learning toward ends that they have identified, using processes they are comfortable with, and measuring outcomes in terms they believe demonstrate success. In other words, they are in control. This style may be appropriate for people with low learner maturity.

Other trainers attempt democratic training/learning styles. Some, for example, meet trainees before the program and conduct pre-course meetings to establish the course agenda. The facilitator commonly reports increased motivation to learn in these situations. However, one is drawn to the possibility of hypocrisy in these circumstances. By giving the participants this opportunity to contribute, is the trainer merely setting up a facade? Does the trainer still decide the real objectives and use processes that he or she is comfortable with? Do the processes vary only slightly from one course to another? In any case, when the learners' maturity at setting meaningful learning objectives is limited, perhaps this style is appropriate in order to maintain quality learning.

A third leadership style—laissez faire—is used in some attempts at self-directed learning. Laissez faire learning facilitation would mean that total control of the learning is given over to the learner. This may lead to directionless learning unless the learner's maturity in self-managed learning is appropriate. Independent learning does not mean independent of learning outcomes. A valid self-directed learning program should still work toward achieving the established outcomes. The learning must be beneficial to the organization that is sponsoring it as well as beneficial to the individual. Yet some self-directed learning programs are without goals, preferring to "give learners their head and see what happens." As Figure 4.2 illustrates, a degree of trainer control must always exist.

Why Employ Self-directed Learning?

Over the years, a number of claims have been made about the benefits of self-directed learning. There are six principal claims:

1. It improves motivation to learn.
2. It improves a person's adaptability to change.
3. It provides improved flexibility in learning.
4. It is aligned with what we understand to be the way adults learn.
5. Results of learning are easier to identify.
6. In the right circumstances, it is the most cost-effective process.

1. Improved Motivation

When you first decided to try your hand at cooking, your motivation to act outweighed your motivation to do nothing. Success was one of the factors that determined the degree to which your motivation to continue would be maintained. For many people, if their first attempt is successful, it creates an increased motivation to continue. This is as true of informal learning like cooking as it is of self-directed learning for formal issues.

We need to show people how they can succeed at self-directed learning, especially with issues that they might have previously regarded as impossible. In other words, we need to remove their invalid constructs or self-perceptions about their learning (as discussed under the earlier heading "Perceptions About Personal Learning"). If we can generate the kind of motivation necessary to continue, to take self-direction further and adopt it as a personality trait, then the motivation to learn as an end in itself will have grown.

2. Improved Adaptability

Learning is, by definition, change. When we learn, we change one set of ideas, behaviors, or known facts for another.

A workforce of self-directed learners can be equated to a workforce of self-directed changers. The personality trait or characteristics of self-direction are complementary to the characteristics needed to adapt to change. If we can generate in people a love for learning that facilitates the desire to actively seek out new learning opportunities, then it is reasonable to expect that these people will be more positive toward change and may even seek it out.

In Chapter 1 we described some of the trends influencing training. These trends reflect the paradigm that the rate of change is accelerating. It is said that only half of what you know now will be useful in five years' time. Learning will therefore take on a new dimension in the workplace. Where once it was necessary to be a master of your job, now it is necessary to be a master of learning so that you can adapt to the changes in your job. Learning will become one of the items on a statement of duties.

3. Improved Flexibility

When a trainer makes all the decisions about what people learn, in what order they learn it, what resources will be used, and with what methods, it is argued that the inflexibility that results will not meet the individual needs of all the learners. Thus, to meet the diverse needs of ten people, we might need up to ten training programs. If each of the programs were of two hours' duration, it would total two hundred hours. Self-direction enables people to pursue their own goals and to meet their own needs. As each person engages in his or her own learning project, it is possible that he or she could learn the material in, say, four hours (for a total of forty hours for all learners). The flexibility of this approach allows people to learn even more in the time available or to pursue other aims that are perhaps not related to learning.

A further way in which self-directed learning improves flexibility is in the way it supports competency-based training. One of the principal issues in competency-based training is the recognition of prior learning and the way this enables a multitude of entry and exit points to and from a training program.

This was highlighted in Almaza's story in Chapter 3, where Almaza worked, learned, and received recognition for a large number of relevant skills prior to seeking formal qualifications at the college. The result is a much more flexible approach for all of the parties involved.

4. Aligned with Adult Learning Principles

As we described in our examples of cooking and gardening, independent learning is a daily occurrence. Self-direction is a fundamental principle that supports the way people learn in their everyday experiences. Furthermore, self-directed learning shares many characteristics with self-actualization, the search for higher levels of growth and potential.

Another way that self-directed learning blends well with contemporary adult learning principles is its link to learning styles. The fact that self-directed learners are, by definition, learning in their own way suggests that they can design a learning project that is consistent with the style of learning they prefer.

5. Easy Identification of Results

It is often argued that we do not know how much people really learn in traditional training courses. The reality of training evaluation still suggests that we rarely go beyond checking learners' reactions to training and that we do not know the level of real learning.

Self-directed learning in a workplace setting requires a clear definition of learning objectives and how they will be assessed. As a consequence, the learners themselves are evaluating their progress as they work on their self-learning projects.

It is not uncommon to discover that learners have not learned a great deal as a result of their projects. However, practitioners will argue that whether learning has occurred or not, at least you know. In traditional training, it is likely that just as many people learn just as little, but we simply do not know who they are since we rarely check.

Knowing who is not learning means that the trainer can intervene and provide help where appropriate so that the learner may be encouraged to get back on track.

6. Cost Effectiveness

The need for a variety of learning resources that can be accessed by self-directed learners creates a high initial set-up cost. As the resources are used, however, the cost may be spread out, and the initial investment becomes further minimized by continued use. The fact that the resources are used independently of a trainer and training room (and thus without the related costs) often results in self-directed learning having a lower per-unit cost over time.

As Figure 4.3 shows, traditional training has a lower set-up (fixed) cost, but the variable costs are higher. For example, imagine you were designing a program for people in branches spread over a large geographical region. Designing a traditional program has a lower fixed cost since the required resources are fewer and their structure of less significance. For a traditional program, however, we typically need to add travel and accommodation to the cost of the trainer's salary, as well as accounting for the training room and other facilities. Therefore, the variable costs rise at a much steeper rate for this type of program

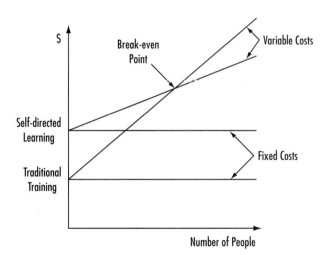

FIGURE 4.3. FIXED/VARIABLE COST COMPARISON

than for a self-directed program in which the learners are able to stay in their local offices to learn. As a consequence, there is a break-even point at which the high set-up costs of self-directed learning begin to pay off and it becomes more cost-effective to use this method than traditional methods.

How to Implement Self-directed Learning

Despite the many benefits of self-directed learning, there is still a need for trainers within an organization to comply with traditional demands for training courses as a way of demonstrating their value to the organization. There is a way to fulfil this obligation while still advancing the cause for self-direction.

Earlier in the chapter, we described the need to turn people away from the notion that learning is a series of episodes that occur in a training room. Nevertheless, if we do not encourage people to engage in some form of episode, then we may never break through the false barriers or constructs that some people have toward the process. To achieve the end result of creating self-directed learners, we need to employ the process of self-directed learning. This was illustrated in Figure 4.2.

Spear and Mocker (1984) suggest that nearly all self-directed learning initiated by people without help is preceded by some change in the learners' environment. However, if we rely on the chance that people will react to change in this way, a lot of learning potential may be lost simply because no opportunities are available to learn. Therefore, it is critical that organizations create circumstances that facilitate the development of the employee, circumstances that provide an opportunity to engage in self-directed learning, particularly in an environment of rapid change.

These opportunities can be created through the design of training programs that start people on the path to self-direction. Doing so will require consideration of the issues involved in the following three areas:

1. Changing your role as a trainer,
2. Developing self-directed learning processes, and
3. Developing self-directed learning skills.

Changing Your Role as a Trainer

Providing self-directed learning opportunities is likely to create a role conflict for many trainers. While many trainers espouse the philosophy that education is linked to giving more responsibility for learning to the learner (that is, promoting self-direction), many workers see the trainer's role as that of running training courses. This suggests an expectation that the number of courses is the key result area for the average trainer rather than a measurable improvement in organization performance. As a consequence, shifting responsibility to the learner is lost in the rush to "train people." So, for many, the old role of expert trainer remains, despite the philosophical paradox.

Conducting self-directed learning programs is, we believe, a new role that reflects a shift in training practice. It will enable a trainer's behavior to be congruent with his or her training philosophy. There will then be a match between what is done by trainers and what they think should be done.

The new role is not just one of a change agent or of an internal consultant (although these roles do have influence), but that of a manager of learning. Just like any manager, trainers have to use the resources at their disposal to achieve their aims. In the context of an organization this also implies that the trainer's aims are congruent with business objectives.

In order to accept the new role, trainers need to adopt what, for many, may be a new set of values about training and learning—values that are associated with an unconditional acceptance of the validity of learners planning and conducting their own learning. This includes accepting that:

- self-directed learning can lead to powerful learning outcomes;
- learners will seek help when they need it;
- learners can make valid choices about the resources they use;
- learners can benefit from coaching and encouragement; and
- learners will expend considerable effort in the quest for self-defined learning needs.

To put it simply, trainers need to realize that significant, meaningful, and well-planned learning occurs all of the time in informal settings without any help from them, and yet this learning can still occur in formal settings. Every time a worker asks a colleague how to do something, the worker is engaging in self-directed learning.

Developing Self-directed Learning Processes

Flexibility is a critical component of managing learning processes that include self-directed learning. Developing self-directed processes relies on it—especially if the organization and the people within it are used to trainer direction as the dominant process.

A gradual adjustment is essential if there is to be long-term acceptance of the process. For some, the suggestion that there should be a mix of trainer direction with learner direction is the antithesis of the ideals that self-direction attempts to create.

However, if a learner chooses to participate in a traditional training course, this does not necessarily mean that he or she is not self-directed. It is often convenient to relinquish the responsibility of deciding on issues such as content and process to the facilitator in order to make the best use of time. A learner who consciously makes such decisions can still be highly self-directed.

The value of instruction is widely supported. It would be folly to abandon all thought of a training environment in which a skilled and knowledgeable instructor efficiently shared some specific skills and knowledge with a group of learners. Just as foolish, however, would be the notion that this is the only way to present learning opportunities to people.

When there are opportunities for self-managed learning as well as formal trainer-directed learning, decisions about participating in one or the other may be taken in the knowledge that a range of other learning options is available. The learners may then allow themselves to make the best of a process they would otherwise be uncomfortable with. Among the things a learner needs for success is a range of educational processes. These processes and their varying levels of facilitator/trainer control are reflected in the power continuum described in Figure 4.1.

The implication of a blend between self-directed and trainer-directed learning is that learning becomes part of the fabric of the organization's values. The strategic needs of the training professional for implementing self-directed learning therefore include the adoption of learning into the culture of the organization—to have learning as a rewarded value and to incorporate learning achievements into the rituals of the organization's life.

If the training department's contribution to development includes a curriculum of learning, then it should incorporate a range of learning processes in that curriculum. Some programs should be in trainer-led format, others in self-taught packages, and others in a format in which a group is facilitated by the trainer.

Imagine an organization that offers a range of learning options and in which learners know that they can take advantage of planning their own learning for some of the issues facing their organization's growth and development. For example, if they choose not to attend a program on time management, they could take advantage of a self-taught package to use in a time and fashion of their own choosing. Only a trainer-led course might be available for the program about new legislation affecting their work, but this is offset by the availability of programs on quality management, supervision, and customer service in self-directed formats.

Lifelong learning is an essential ingredient to success in today's ever-changing world. Professional learning facilitators need to help people realize their true potential as learners and avoid reinforcing the notion that they are merely students for other experts to educate. Offering a mix of trainer-directed and self-directed learning will focus the perception that learning is a joint responsibility and that personal growth is necessary for continuing development in an organization.

Training departments may therefore develop their own self-taught packages that can be used on the job at the time they are needed (just-in-time training). The ideal subject areas are those for which there is an ongoing need or for which the initially high fixed costs (see Figure 4.3) are offset by savings in the variable costs, for example, when there are many learners or when they are spread geographically. Creating self-taught packages generally has a higher fixed cost; however, the variable cost in using them is usually lower, and over time they become a cheaper option.

The development of self-taught packages requires a range of skills that are not normally associated with the skills of trainers. Trainers will now need to become experts in the design of written materials, audiotapes, and video programs. As a place to start, we might learn much from the designers of distance learning programs from educational institutions such as the Monash University in Victoria, Australia; the TAFE Open Training and Education Network in New South Wales, Australia; the New England University in New South Wales, Australia; and the Open Learning Institute in the United Kingdom. The growth in technology such as desktop publishing and computer-assisted video production have made such skills accessible to many people.

Developing Self-directed Learning Skills

The mere existence of self-taught packages does not mean that people will access them. Self-teaching and self-direction may be quite divergent ideas in some contexts. There are many so-called self-taught packages on the market, but very few are presented in an interactive format that maximizes the process of self-direction. The author of these packages often, for example, does little to enable the learner to find the relevant learning points in the program. Audiotapes are a prime example. A learner needs to listen to a great deal of the tape before finding the most relevant parts. A few guidelines for the learner at the start and a content list with accompanying tape counter sequences would go a long way toward helping the learner decide what he or she wants from the resource.

Creating your own programs has several advantages. Among these are the ongoing economics and continuity of established packages. The variable costs of self-taught programs enable substantial savings in the long term, and the existence of such packages allows continuity of learning despite factors such as turnover of training staff. More importantly, if you design your own packages you can increase the level of learner interaction with them and the level of learner control over their use.

Still, we are left with the fact that the level of commitment toward self-direction is variable, and the existence of self-taught packages does not guarantee that people will use them or learn from them.

Clearly then, handing responsibility for learning back to learners should not occur without some level of support. If you intend to pursue a self-directed vision, then as a trainer you need to create suitable structures to assist learners in addressing the following concerns:

1. Where and when to learn;
2. What goals to pursue;
3. Which methods to use in that pursuit;
4. Motivational highs and lows;
5. How to assess success;
6. What to do if they don't understand something;
7 How to access resources; and
8. How they will know when to stop or change course or choose a new goal.

The development of self-direction as an end result requires trainers to help others learn how to learn.

Using Learning Projects to Develop Self-direction

Self-directed learning has long been associated with the use of learning contracts—written statements of what is to be learned that are developed by the learner in consultation with an adviser or mentor. These learning contracts emerge time and again in the relevant literature as a vehicle for helping people become more self-directed in their learning. Most learning-project processes aim to give individuals the skills of setting learning goals, identifying resources, and evaluating outcomes. In effect, learning contracts, or learning projects as we will call them, help people master the concerns that were described earlier.

What Is the Learning Project Method?

A learning project is an agreement made by learners about what they intend to learn, how they plan to go about it, and what resources they intend to employ in their learning. They also specify how they intend to measure success. The agreement may, of course, be made just with themselves; but in the context of an organization, in order to encourage self-direction, it is important to help people learn how to use the process. Thus the agreement is usually made in conjunction with a helper, mentor, or facilitator. The emphasis is on making the learning activities relevant to the learners' jobs and/or personal needs and consistent with the objectives of any training program to which the project may be connected.

A separate project is designed for each learning objective, and each project has all of the components described in terms that are as clear as they can be made. It is important to remember, though, that it is not always possible to specify all issues in the project since the search for learning itself may uncover new and more useful resources or methods that can be used to good effect. It may also alter the original goal as the unfolding discoveries lead the learners down new paths toward the solution they are seeking.

What Are the Advantages of the Project Method?

1. It is an effective way to implement contemporary learning theories about the autonomy of the learner and builds initiative and responsibility for learning.
2. It is consistent with the general principles of autonomy and devolution of control to the individual that are at the heart of much workplace restructuring.

3. It allows learning to be tailored to each learner's needs and therefore is more relevant.
4. It provides an opportunity for the learner to practice techniques learned during a training course when back on the job since this may, in itself, be a part of the project.

What Are the Disadvantages of the Project Method?

1. It is initially a labor-intensive process as many learners clamor for the trainer's time and assistance.
2. It can demotivate passive learners as they discover that they much prefer to be taught and cannot teach themselves.
3. It focuses on an event and may remove the legitimacy of learning that occurs more incidentally.

What Are the Steps in Developing a Learning Project?

1. *Identify what is to be learned.* In this step the learners decide on an aspect of their work that they want to develop further. Competency statements are an excellent resource to help people identify their learning needs since many people "don't know what they don't know" and are unable to decide where to begin. For more information about this, see Chapter 3 on competency-based training.
2. *Rework the broad learning need into a specific task.* Consider all of the learners' present commitments and also their preferred learning styles and specify tasks that will contribute to the development of skills in the area specified. Remember to consider the timing of the tasks in light of their commitments.

   Suitable learning tasks for commuters, for example, may include reading or listening to audiotapes. However, if a person already has too many commitments, then he or she will need to use time-efficient methods—perhaps interviewing experts. The real key is to make the process manageable. One of the most common difficulties in self-direction is that people bite off more than they can chew.
3. *Write a specific learning objective.* It is important to make these specific and, if possible, to write them in behavioral terms (performance, standards, conditions). Some examples follow. Remember, though, that it may be appropriate in the early stages to allow learning objectives to be loose and abstract since the learners may be embarking on a bit of an aimless hunt for ideas and strategies.

When they have nailed these down more clearly, you can encourage them to be more specific about their objectives.

4. *Identify useful resources.* Considering what is manageable and the learning objective that has been established, locate the best resources to help the learner. The resources can be things such as books, audiotapes, videotapes, manuals, journals, and other similar media. However, resources also include experts, the learner's own observations, surveys, self-assessment questionnaires, and experimentation.

5. *Determine what evidence will demonstrate success.* Although projects are for the benefit of the learners, it is also necessary that these clearly specify how the learning or experience will be evidenced. It is then the job of the mentor or adviser (the trainer) to provide feedback and probe learners about what to do next.

Examples of Learning Projects

Example Project No. 1

TOPIC: Time Management

OBJECTIVE: To identify my biggest time-waster and develop a plan to reduce wasted time.

PLAN: On Thursday and Friday, I will keep a daily time log to detail what I do during the day. Then on Monday, I will review the log and identify where my time was wasted by applying a priority grid to the tasks. I will then speak to my supervisor and negotiate a plan with his or her help so that I can cut down on time-wasters.

EVIDENCE:
- Copics of my two time logs.
- My plan to reduce time wasting.
- Two or three paragraphs in my learning journal that I will write two weeks later explaining whether I think I have succeeded.

Example Project No. 2

TOPIC: Team Building

OBJECTIVE: Create a list of at least six ideas I can implement that will help build a cohesive, productive team.

PLAN:
- Go to the library and borrow some books on the subject.

- Read or scan one book per week for the next four weeks.
- Make a list of ideas in my journal.
- Discuss the list with my supervisor and staff, if appropriate.
- Implement ideas.

EVIDENCE: A copy of the list and a short report (in my journal) of the implementation and the discussions.

Example Project No. 3

TOPIC: Leadership
OBJECTIVE: To determine what my staff thinks of me as a leader.
PLAN:
- Give copies of a leadership-style questionnaire to my staff and my supervisor.
- Score them and then compare them to my own assessment.
- Decide on ways to improve my style by analyzing individual questions.

EVIDENCE: Copies of the score sheets and a list of ways to improve.

Example Project No. 4

TOPIC: Delegation
OBJECTIVE: To delegate more effectively.
PLAN:
- Review my work schedule and expose tasks that I have never delegated before.
- Decide on which task for which person.
- Explain to each person why I am delegating the task and how I want it done.

EVIDENCE: A list of tasks outlining who is to do each.
   Note: This project is linked to Example Project No. 3.

Example Project No. 5

TOPIC: General Supervisory Development
OBJECTIVE: To explore new areas of supervision skills.
PLAN:
- Borrow and listen to the videotape set about supervision in the company library.

- Complete the activity booklet accompanying the tapes.
- Borrow the book *Supervision in Australia* by J. Saville (1984) and read it. Take notes in my journal.

EVIDENCE: The activity booklet and my journal.

The Right Mix

Implementing self-directed learning involves many issues unique to the environment in which it is to be used. Prescribing a solution is therefore difficult. Nevertheless, the issues that are seen as important are listed here with some ideas to help with finding your unique solution. You will need to consider the various characteristics of your particular environment and seek to find the right mix of these issues in order to succeed.

1. Trainer Skill and Confidence

The way in which self-directed learning is implemented will be influenced by the trainer's skill and his or her confidence with the change in role we described earlier. That is, a shift from being the authority figure to becoming merely a resource to be used by learners. The skill required includes the ability to become a coach and analyst for learners. They will require help determining what and how to learn but the trainer needs to develop a collaborative relationship in which the learner is allowed increasing levels of control. The trainer also needs to develop a new set of skills that includes how to design high-quality, self-directed learning materials as well as learning to be a resource expert to help learners access the resources they will need for their learning.

2. Resource Opportunities

Learners must have ready access to a wide range of resources on issues relevant to their development. Community, institutional, and company libraries are helpful if they are easily accessible. The development of a library from nothing may take a long time. Perhaps you could encourage the self-directed learners to create the resources for you from what they learn. This might be a simple process in having them write up the results of their learning journeys. Perhaps they can produce an audiotape or a video program ranging from a simple on-camera interview to a documentary.

Learners themselves can also become a resource for future learners. Another excellent resource is access to CD-ROM databases such as "Business Periodicals on Disk" and "A.B.I. Inform," which are available in major libraries. In addition, access to information networks, such as the Internet, via a modem and computer is gaining importance. Some MBA programs have a prerequisite that participants must have access to a modem and computer and that they must learn how to use the Internet.

3. Integrated Self-planned Learning

Foster self-planned learning projects as an integral part of training. Encourage the use of continued learning projects as a part of closure activities in all learning programs. Include sessions about self-directed learning concepts in your training programs. Create a stronger awareness of the significance of the "invisible" learning that occurs as a consequence of self-directed learning, such as learning how to use a library or learning about motivation while researching a project about goal setting.

4. Culture and Commitment

Implementing a self-directed learning program into your training plan will require a match with your organization's culture. Simply put, it will have to be adopted into the value systems of the organization. Learning will have to be seen as a worthy behavior, and success in learning should be built into the reward structure of your organization in a genuine way.

You should employ those who influence the behavior of others in the self-directed learning implementation process. Corporate rituals such as annual dinners and meetings should include elements of the self-directed learning values.

5. The Bottom Line

What is your organization doing? For what reasons does it exist? What are its products, its strengths, and its weaknesses? Who are its competitors? Take these issues into account. It is critical to keep closely to the organization's goals in developing self-directed learning. Marketing self-directed learning in your organization is much more likely to succeed, and the program will have a real (successful) impact, if you focus learning on goals that are congruent with your organization's needs.

6. Cost Comparison

Selling self-directed learning to senior decision makers will be easier if you pay close attention to the fixed/variable cost comparisons illustrated earlier in Figure 4.3. Be sure to get real figures. You would expect your managers to do sufficient analysis prior to big decisions; do so yourself.

7. Evaluation and Assessment

Because self-directed learning happens in so many settings, assessment processes will need to reflect this by evaluating learned competencies. The methods need to be carefully thought out so that the nature of the learning is itself not the issue being measured. We are not concerned about how people learned their skills so much as we are about the skills themselves. In this sense, self-directed learning shares many similarities with the concepts of competency-based training.

8. How Learners Learn

Many people need help to develop their learning skills. They are conditioned to believe that learning means entering a room and emerging when the expert has finished speaking. We need to help remove inappropriate constructs that people possess about the way they learn and the extent of their learning ability. This might be achieved by using the principles suggested in Figure 4.2. That is, initially, when the maturity of the learner is low, provide directive programs that satisfy the need for expert help. Gradually help learners to adopt greater control over the process until they can more successfully manage their own learning projects.

Summary

We are all self-directed. Many people, however, abdicate that skill or effort to a trainer when they engage in what they perceive as "formal" learning or when they perceive that planning their own learning about a particular issue will result in "illegitimate" learning.

The trainer's role is to encourage or assist people to use the self-direction abilities they already possess. It includes helping people to see that self-planned learning is still legitimate learning.

In this chapter we explained the need to develop self-direction as a necessary personality trait for today's changing environment. This will create a new role for trainers who will now need to become more of a resource expert than a subject-matter expert. The new role may uncover conflicts for trainers who have believed themselves to be training technicians skilled at creating an effective training environment. However, we have also explained that total reliance on self-direction is unrealistic and a good mix of trainer-directed and self-directed programs and strategies is desirable.

Implementing self-directed learning will require interventions at the organization level and help for learners who may not be used to the idea of taking charge of their own learning. One method to help learners is by using the learning projects explained earlier in this chapter.

Self-directed learning is consistent with the contemporary movement toward empowerment; if we are to be advocates of that value system then at the very least we need to model it ourselves in the methods we use to help people learn. This is a powerful argument for the implementation of self-directed learning.

Bibliography

Confessore, G., & Confessore, S. (1992). *Guideposts to self-directed learning*. King of Prussia, PA: Organization Design and Development.

Harri-Augstein, S., & Webb, I.M. (1995). *Learning to change: A resource for trainers, managers and learners based on self-organized learning*. London: McGraw-Hill.

Knowles, M. (1975). *Self-directed learning: A guide for learners and teachers*. Englewood Cliffs, NJ: Cambridge Adult Education.

Knowles, M., & Associates. (1984). *Androgogy in action*. San Francisco, CA: Jossey-Bass.

Knowles, M. (1986). *Using learning contracts.* San Francisco, CA: Jossey-Bass.

Saville, J. (1984). *Supervision in Australia.* Sydney: Prentice Hall.

Smith, B. (1989). Adult learning: A monologue. *Training and Development in Australia, 16*(1), 23–27.

Spear, G., & Mocker, D. (1984). The organization circumstance: Environmental determinants in self-directed learning. *Adult Education Quarterly, 35,* 1–10.

Tough, A. (1967). *Learning without a teacher: A study of tasks and assistance during self-teaching projects.* Toronto: Ontario Institute for Studies in Education.

Tough, A. (1971). *The adults learning projects: A fresh approach to theory and practice in adult learning.* Toronto: Ontario Institute for Studies in Education.

STOKING THE FIRE

WARMING UP THE LEARNER WITH ICEBREAKERS AND ENERGIZERS

This chapter highlights some golden rules about getting the best from icebreakers and introduces an explanation of energizers. A model that offers a sound framework is explored.

"You don't get a second chance to make a first impression."
ANONYMOUS

Gems Mined from These Pages

- "Stoke the fire" for a course by adding impact in the first few minutes and establishing a rapport.

- Have a purpose to any activity you might conduct; don't just do it for its own sake.

- Choose activities based on group culture that best fit the program content.

- Activities should allow time for self-introduction to a small subgroup, introduction to the whole group, and introduction to program content.

- Use energizer activities to change the mental or physical state of learners.

Marek Makes a Miracle

Marek Betcher waited just inside the training room for the learners to arrive. This was the first time he had ever coordinated a staff orientation program and he was really looking forward to it. He had arranged for some of the most senior and experienced people in the organization to speak to the group. It would be a good day.

Finally, the first participant arrived. Marek introduced himself and learned her name was Debbie. They shook hands and Marek asked Debbie about her job. They chatted for a minute or so about Debbie's job as a sales representative. "Do you know anyone who will be attending the program today?" Marek asked.

"No, I don't," replied Debbie.

Just at that moment, another person entered. Debbie took a seat as Marek introduced himself to Edward, the new arrival. "Do you know anyone else who will be here today?" Marek asked. Again, the answer was no. Now Marek knew he would need to make some introductions and he did so with Edward and Debbie. "Debbie works in sales for NHT Electrics," Marek explained to Edward, and the two of them began to talk. Marek noticed another two people arrive and went to greet them as he had done for Debbie and Edward.

At last, everyone had arrived and had met Marek and at least one other person to whom they were now talking. Marek stood in front of the group, introduced himself more fully, and explained that he wanted everyone to work on a challenge together. He gave each person an envelope. "Inside the envelope," he said, "are parts of a jigsaw. I would like you to find the other people who have pieces of your puzzle and put it together. You will then discover that it contains a number of questions about the program. I'd like you to try and answer the questions together."

As people mingled to compare pieces, the room erupted into a symphony of voices. However, the conversations soon became quieter as the participants began working together on their respective puzzles and the questions they contained.

Each puzzle had a question about the participants and their backgrounds so that they had to reintroduce themselves to the other people in their new subgroup. The puzzle also contained questions about the organization that were designed as a kind of pretest. Marek hoped that these questions would build some anticipation about the program and about what the speakers would have to say.

After ten minutes or so, Marek began discussing the questions with the group. He learned what the learners knew about the organization and, in some cases, that was quite a bit. He also encouraged each person to answer the question about himself or herself to the whole group this time. He then asked them to discuss, for two or three minutes, their reactions to the exercise.

As they talked, Marek was struck by how easily these strangers talked to one another. He knew that he had successfully broken the ice with this group and had developed a rapport among all of the people, himself included.

Marek had successfully performed an icebreaker miracle.

Breaking the Ice

Imagine the Olympic Games without an opening ceremony. Day one of the games just begins. That's it—no fanfare, no welcome, no excitement, and no anticipation. The athletes arrive, get off the plane, and immediately begin to compete. The television commentary would probably go something like, "Well everyone, thanks for joining us for the 43rd Olympiad. If you've just tuned in, you have missed the first five events."

The Olympic Games would not be the same without that ceremony. It provides a focus for the competitions ahead—a real starting mark that helps to create the mood of excitement and anticipation for both the athletes and the audience. It enables the athletes to be welcomed, to mix with one another, and to hold their heads up proudly as representatives of their countries.

In much the same way, training programs need a similar focus to get things started. We need an opportunity to build some excitement and anticipation about the program. We need to allow the learners an opportunity to meet and greet one another and the trainer.

Icebreakers

Icebreakers are activities that are used to "break the ice." They enable you to establish the kind of climate you would like in the training room. They can, for example, be used to establish a supportive, positive, cooperative climate within the group or may be designed to create a climate of openness and disclosure in order to facilitate interpersonal risk-taking.

Whatever the circumstances or intent, icebreakers should break the ice by helping everyone to get to know one another more quickly, establish and reinforce group relationships, set the tone for the time together, and introduce the subject matter that is to be discussed.

A major purpose of icebreakers is to create rapport. Establishing and maintaining rapport is critical to the success of a program since it will influence the degree to which the learners are willing to follow you. In a program that requires a lot of interaction and trust, or where it is important for people to be open with you, the degree of rapport can make or break the success of the program. An icebreaker that establishes trust and openness is therefore important to such a program and needs to be chosen wisely and conducted thoughtfully.

Rapport can be harmed if participants are asked to participate in unsuitable or unfocused activities. Many participants will not appreciate icebreakers that do not contribute to the learning experience. For example, we once saw a trainer conduct an icebreaker that required the participants to walk around making animal noises, the purpose of which was to find others who made the same noise and thus form a team that would then work together for the rest of the program. The people did not know one another and had come from all over the country for the program, and so the facilitator was taking a risk with this icebreaker—something we fully support. However, when the groups had formed, the facilitator said, "The purpose of that activity was to get you into teams. If you find yourself in a team that you do not want to be in, then you may change." (No other debriefing took place.)

We question the relevance of using an icebreaker to form teams when the learners are told that they may choose a different team anyway. We have nothing against this particular icebreaker; in fact, we have seen it work very well on other occasions. It's just that there was very little real purpose to it on this occasion, and the chance of humiliating the learners was much greater.

This icebreaker might be useful as a means to break down inhibitions. However, we believe that was not its intention on this occasion, so it was unfocused and inappropriate. About the only purpose it would serve would be as a developmental exercise in risk taking for the facilitator. This is something we applaud. However, there are more appropriate times to take this risk.

Energizers

Icebreakers are often confused with energizers. Whereas icebreakers are used to break the ice at the beginning of a program, energizers are used to change the pace of a program as it is progressing. You may wish, for example, to make it more lively, more active, to have more speaking, to have less speaking, or to slow down the pace. Whatever their intended application, one guiding rule should apply for both energizers and icebreakers: there should always be a purpose to them, rather than doing them just for their own sakes.

Marek's orientation program was going well. That is, it was going according to schedule. The company had hired the venue for the event and had thirty-six learners in attendance and a string of presenters. Coordinating the program was difficult because of the many logistic considerations.

Each of the speakers arrived on time and spoke for just long enough. The director of Human Resources spoke on personnel policy, the production manager spoke on Total Quality, the Union delegate spoke on workers' rights and industrial relations issues, the occupational health and safety officer spoke on safety in the workplace, the manager of Corporate Services spoke on the innovation awards policy, and so on.

As Marek observed the procession of speakers, he noticed one common aspect of their presentations. There was very little involvement from anyone but the speaker. Eyelids grew heavy from time to time and there was much yawning as the learners craved oxygen. Furthermore, he noticed that during the breaks the learners were not speaking to one another very much either, despite his earlier success with the icebreaker. The process used by the speakers had not helped rapport at all and everyone was behaving as if they were in a room full of strangers.

With the permission of the general manager, Marek decided to do something about it. Just before coffee break on the first day, he asked everyone to stand at one end of the room, touching the wall.

"OK everyone," he began, "this activity is designed to test your creativity and get you moving around because you've been doing a lot of sitting and listening. What you have to do is walk from this end of the room to this end." As he spoke he walked to the other end. "The only rule is that you cannot get here the same way as anyone else and, since I've just walked here in the normal walking fashion, you can't do that. OK—go!"

Immediately the room exploded with noise as the people began to hop, crawl, run, and walk in all manner of ways to the other end. Marek gently encouraged the stragglers to have a go but didn't insist. Once everyone was at the other end, Marek announced the coffee break.

During the break Marek noticed that the people were talking more than they had all day. The level of discussion was almost at fever pitch. Most of it was about Marek and the activity. But they were talking, and they were also discussing the speakers of the day. Marek listened in.

"No one has spoken much to anyone all day," said one person. "Now look at us. It's a miracle."

Energizers are intended to change the mental or physical state of learners. There are times when the emotional state becomes a barrier to learning. In the example, Marek recognized the sleepy state that some of the learners in the orientation program were falling into and he decided to do something about it.

There is also the possibility that learners may become negative, and an energizer can be used to alter the mood to a positive one. At other times, the level of energy and excitement may be higher than you want. For example, you may want some quiet reflection time to follow on the heels of an intense group activity.

These kinds of changes to the mental state of learners are a key purpose of energizers. However, it is also possible that physical state can present a barrier. For example, when people who are unaccustomed to doing so sit for long periods of time, it is important to provide refresher breaks to enable them to increase their oxygen intake and stimulate their brains.

Energizers can do the following:

- Refresh a group that has been sitting and listening for a long time;
- Revive a group whose energy level is rapidly fading;
- Give fidgeters and kinesthetic learners an opportunity to move around;
- Be an effective transition between topics; and
- Subtly break up cliques and foster whole-group rapport.

Using Icebreakers and Energizers

Icebreakers and energizers, if chosen well, can be an excellent complement to the content of your training session. For example, some are designed to encourage or explore communication and are therefore well-suited to sessions that have a communication theme. However, it is essential to assess the suitability of each activity for your particular group. For this purpose most activities can be divided into three categories:

1. low risk;
2. medium risk; and
3. high risk.

Low-risk activities can be used with groups meeting for the first time or with groups lacking in confidence or self-esteem or with groups that are tense. They are the sorts of activities that do not demand participants to disclose too much of themselves and are therefore "safe" for the trainer as well as the participants. They are generally also culturally acceptable in that they rarely demand unusual behavior. An example of a low-risk activity would be a simple introduction activity such as having pairs introduce themselves to each other.

Medium-risk activities are a little more demanding and are often more successfully used after the group members have begun to know one another, such as in the example that opened the chapter. The people had already met one or two other people, as the trainer introduced them when they arrived. If well selected, medium-risk icebreakers can further enhance group cohesion. An example would be having small groups make a presentation.

High-risk activities usually demand a high degree of disclosure or unusual behavior that seems to go against cultural norms or what people expect to experience at a training event. They are usually more successful in groups that already have an established, stable climate that is open and supportive, such as when the participants all regularly work closely together. They are usually most successful when the facilitator has been given permission by the participants to experiment and try new things. An example would be to ask small groups to create a human sculpture of the organization's culture. Human sculptures require participants to pose, statue-like, in a way that reflects the intended theme. It can also incorporate movement. For example, people may pose close to someone with whom they actively communicate.

If you are not sure where your group is, a guiding principle is to start with activities lower than the risk level you think they may be comfortable with. Remember, your own training ability often has just as much to do with the success of the activity as does the maturity of the group.

A useful process for the introduction of icebreakers is illustrated in Figure 5.1. The model suggests that the icebreaker begins with self, perhaps with personal reflection or by asking individuals to write information down for later discussion. This allows a person to gather his or her thoughts prior to participating. Then participants form subgroups for an activity or discussion. This is intended to help build a sense of esprit de corps and facilitates group development. These small groups may be just two people or as many as four or five, depending on how many people are in the program. Next, the whole group becomes involved, the activity is debriefed, and, finally, it is linked to the content of the program. (Icebreakers should introduce people to the subject matter as well as to each other.)

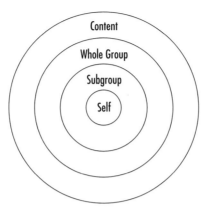

FIGURE 5.1. PROCESS FOR USING ICEBREAKERS

Example of an Icebreaker

If you wanted to use this model for a simple introduction exercise, you would begin with a brief period that allows people to think about a topic that you specify (you could provide guidelines as well, perhaps in the form of a questionnaire for participants to complete about themselves). Next, ask them to pair up and introduce themselves to their partners. The pairs then form quartets and introduce one another. The next step is for one person in the quartet to introduce all of his or her colleagues to the whole group. One of the issues that they talk about in their introductions might be their experiences with the subject matter. This ensures that the icebreaker is related to the content.

An effective icebreaker is one that facilitates lively discussion among the participants about themselves and about the course content. It also begins the process of establishing rapport. However, the real miracle occurs when perfect strangers are "turned on" to the program, creating an air of anticipation and excitement, and when the material discussed in the opening is linked to issues that come up later. The participants' eyes light up and they can sometimes be heard to refer back to their experiences in the icebreaker during other parts of the program.

Energizers

Energizers are about managing the state of the learners and can be illustrated by the graphs in Figure 5.2. It is possible, of course, to create the same effect that energizers create by carefully designing the training processes you use. For example, you can often increase the level of energy during an activity and then bring it down again while debriefing it. The principles illustrated in Figure 5.2 remain the same for energizers or for any training activity that is designed to influence the state of the learners. The vertical axis in each graph represents the level of energy of the group and the horizontal axis represents the duration of the program. You can see, then, that there are a number of approaches to take toward the management of the energy of the group.

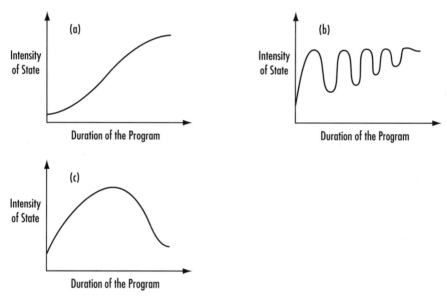

FIGURE 5.2. ALTERING STATE WITH ENERGIZERS

Graph (a) shows how energizers can build the state of the learners gradually to a climax to end the course on a high. This might be important when you want immediate action to be taken after the program and you want to create a sense of emergency and motivation. Graph (b) shows a repeated raising and lowering of the group's energy level. It is being brought to a climax and then relaxed again. This might occur in a program in which there are a number of topics or components, and the trainer wants to create a sense of excitement about each one. Graph (c) illustrates how the group has been brought to a high and then brought down again toward the conclusion of the program. This might be appropriate for a group-development or personal-development program. In such a case, the excitement and energy might come out of personal disclosure and risk taking. The trainer then debriefs the activities so that the emotional and cognitive state of the group is returned to a level consistent with reflection about the program. In other words, the group is not brought to a highly emotional state as a result of disclosure and then left there as the program concludes. This might mean that a wide range of emotional issues are not resolved appropriately.

Guidelines

- Think about the group's expectations, background, and culture when determining the level of risk in the activity and the involvement that will be required.
- Take care to place the icebreaker or energizer at an appropriate time in the program. Take care not to overuse or prematurely use them and make their duration proportionate to the duration of the program.
- Do not insist that participants share confidential or personal information, and always leave a way out for those who do not wish to participate. Also, be sure to keep discussions confidential and to make it clear that this will be the case.
- Icebreakers and energizers can help to develop group cohesion. Make sure you have a clear purpose and that you are using them for that purpose and not just for their own sake. Choose activities that are congruent with your overall goals.
- Ensure that particular individuals do not dominate discussion during the early phase of a program. If necessary, interject tactfully and get back on track.
- Use icebreakers as a means of establishing rapport between yourself and the rest of the group. Your level of participation should demonstrate the degree of risk taking that you value and want from others.
- Clarify your expectations of group behavior during the course by modeling that behavior and reinforcing it during the icebreaker.
- Choose activities that incorporate movement and action to energize the group.
- Select activities that you are comfortable with. If you are not comfortable it will be noticed by the group members and then they themselves may become uncomfortable.

- Choose activities that will work for the size of the group that you will be working with. Some activities lose their intensity with large groups and, likewise, some activities have less impact with small groups.
- Look for and document a range of icebreakers that incorporate different challenges, such as logical or critical thinking, physical or mental exercises, highly structured or spontaneous activity, and highly interactive activity. Keep your list handy for instant use.
- Don't rely on a limited range of activities. Expand your repertoire for your own development and growth.
- Avoid identifying the exercise as an "icebreaker." It may be better to say, "We are going to do an activity."
- Consider the timing of the activity. Different experiences can create the state you need for the beginning of a program, the close of a program, at breaks, at day's end, and during transitions from one subject to another.

Examples of icebreakers and energizers are located in Appendix 1.

Summary

The success of a training program depends on many variables. One of the most crucial moments of any program is the first few minutes. The moment people begin to arrive, they are forming impressions about you, the program, the other learners, and the environment they are in. It is important to make these first impressions positive ones.

"Stoking the fire" is all about creating that effect. It's about providing the fuel for a warm climate. It's about building the energy level in the room and getting things off to a good start so that the rest of the program works well. You can stoke the fire well and come back to it only occasionally, or you can stoke it poorly so that you have to keep returning constantly to add more fuel. So it is with training programs. If you create an appropriate climate with an effective icebreaker, then the group development is off to a good start and rapport is established. Occasional energizers can keep the fires burning and maintain the excitement for the program.

Bibliography

Arch, D. (1993). *Tricks for trainers*. Edina, MN: Resources for Organizations.

Forbess-Greene, S. (1983). *The encyclopedia of icebreakers*. San Francisco, CA: Pfeiffer.

Jones, J., & Bearley, W. (1989). *Energizers for training and conferences*. King of Prussia, PA: Organization Design and Development.

Kirby, A. (1993). *Icebreakers*. London: Gower.

Newstrom, J. (1996). *Games trainers play* (CD-ROM). New York: McGraw-Hill.

Newstrom, J., & Scannell, E. (1980). *Games trainers play*. New York: McGraw-Hill.

Newstrom, J., & Scannell, E. (1991). *Still more games trainers play*. New York: McGraw-Hill.

Scannell, E. (1994). *Even more games trainers play*. New York: McGraw-Hill.

Scannell, E., & Newstrom, J. (1983). *More games trainers play*. New York: McGraw-Hill.

NEUROLINGUISTIC PROGRAMMING

This chapter explains how trainers can improve communication with learners so that they can lead them to greater success.

Gems Mined from These Pages

- Neurolinguistic programming (NLP) describes how the mind and body are conditioned to respond to certain information such as the power of positive thinking.

- NLP is underscored by a number of philosophical principles.

- NLP is not a skill in itself but rather a composite of other skills that together make up the framework that we know as NLP.

- Modalities, or the way we communicate visually, auditorially, and kinesthetically, are one component of these skills.

- NLP is a communication model that can help you to more effectively communicate with learners and others.

"Positive thinking may not give me the skills to take your appendix out if we were stranded on a desert island together and you had severe appendicitis. But wouldn't you prefer that I felt positive about it?"

NORMAN VINCENT PEALE

By George, She's Got It!

Toula Sidaris was feeling very disappointed with her training performance. She had been a trainer now for just over eight months and things weren't going as well as she'd hoped.

Her training technique was as good as she felt she could get it to be. She followed all of the advice she received at her "Train-the-Trainer" program. Her overheads were well designed, her questioning technique was fine, and her group discussions were all focused. Despite doing it right, or at least feeling as though she was, there were still problems with a few learners in some of her programs. She just wasn't able to connect with them. Sometimes she felt that she was making things harder for them rather than easier.

She decided to seek the guidance of her manager, Margaret Davis. Together they decided that Margaret should sit in on one of Toula's programs; then perhaps the two of them might be able to diagnose the problem correctly and establish a plan for improvement. Toula had a safety awareness course coming up that presented a perfect opportunity. The outcome was nothing if not miraculous.

What Is Neurolinguistic Programming?

The concept of neurolinguistic programming (NLP) was first developed by Dr. Richard Bandler and John Grinder in the early 1970s. In essence, they wanted to explore what it was that made the very best communicators so successful. Bandler and Grinder studied these people and attempted to plot their unique abilities. Not surprisingly, the results had quite a lot to do with how messages were filtered, sent, and received, since that is the key tool of communicators. The result was the emergence of what we now know as neurolinguistic programming.

The term "neurolinguistic programming" sounds to some people a bit like the very latest in computer software—a kind of new-age programming language. However, despite the complicated sound of the term, it is quite easy to define if you look at each component separately. "Neuro" relates to the nervous system or the connections between mind and body. "Linguistic" refers to language or information that we process and "programming" is about conditioning and patterns. Neurolinguistic programming describes how we are governed by patterns in the way we process information and how there are patterns to the way in which our mind and body respond to language or information.

Neurolinguistic programming suggests that, although we all have similar experiences, there is no single representation of these similar experiences. Twenty people can witness the same event, for example, and describe it in twenty different ways. Witnesses of a robbery often have quite different descriptions of the robber and the circumstances of the robbery itself. We all adapt the reality of our experiences and create mental representations to fit our perception of the reality.

Just as we individually process what happens around us and create mental models of those events, we also have patterns that shape our behavior. In effect, we pattern our input (experiences), our storage, and our output (behavior). The way each of us does this leads to the notion that there are consistencies in how each of us experience the world and interact with it. Learning how to detect and utilize these processes is the heart of NLP. If you practice some of the ideas in this chapter and accept some of the principles we have described, we believe that you will be able to more successfully communicate with others.

The way we pattern our experiences and behavior creates subconscious rules that help us to handle the complexities of life. They help us to organize and describe our observations as we mentally process them, and they help us to structure our behavior in ways we believe appropriate. These rules are the fundamental framework that defines the programming in NLP. In other words, it is these rules that shape the patterns that govern us. Essentially, these rules fall into three broad categories:

1. Generalizing
2. Deleting
3. Distorting

1. Generalizing

Generalizing helps us to learn from our experiences. When we generalize, we attempt to create a conclusion from our experiences or to explain our experiences in cohesive ways. Doing so means that we can more easily process the information we receive. When we experience an event, we typically try to find ways that that experience matches similar experiences and draw a conclusion based on the context that those earlier experiences provided us with. For example, if one of us began to talk about our car, you would begin to make your own conclusions about the car based on your experiences with cars. Although what we actually say (the reality) may not include any clear descriptions of our car, you will probably begin to create a mental image of it (your pattern). Understanding the way each of us generalizes from our experiences is important to the process of understanding NLP.

EXERCISE 6.1

A man and his son were involved in a car accident. Tragically, the man was killed; the son was rushed to a hospital for emergency treatment. As the boy was being wheeled into the emergency ward, the surgeon rushed over, took one glance at the boy, and cried, "I cannot treat this boy. He is my son."

How is this possible?

(See Appendix 2 for the answer.)

2. Deleting

Every moment of our lives we are being fed countless pieces of information. As you are reading this book, there are distractions that beg your attention. The sounds around you, the images in your peripheral vision, your emotional feelings, and your sense of touch are all sending signals to your brain simultaneously. Trying to actually process all of this information would be very difficult. Our mind filters it so that we can more easily cope with the complex nature of all this input. In other words, we delete some of it so it makes sense.

What many people call "selective hearing" is an example of deletion. As you attempt to comprehend all of the sounds, sights, and feelings around you, you may be deleting what people are saying directly to you. Although their perception is that they spoke clearly and directly to you, it is still possible that your subconscious deleted their words.

EXERCISE 6.2

Read the following figure and determine what you might have deleted.

FIGURE 6.1. DELETION
  (See Appendix 2 for the answer.)

3. Distorting

When we distort, we alter our perception of the information we receive. Distortion enables us to be creative, to daydream, and to imagine the future. When you look at a diagram such as Figure 6.2, what you are really seeing is a two-dimensional image, but you probably distort it as you attempt to look for three dimensions.

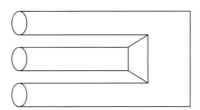

FIGURE 6.2. DISTORTION

We also distort other information to help make sense of it just as we might do with Figure 6.2. An example of this is jargon and other language differences. If I say, "Put a bucket of water in the hole," you assume that I do not mean the bucket as well as the water, thus distorting the words according to your perception of them in order to make sense of them.

We all have these patterns, and for each of us they are unique. Our values and responses to everyday events are other examples of the patterns we create as we learn from our peers and parents during our life experiences. Each of us is conditioned to react differently to different things, and the strength of our conditioning varies from person to person since each of us has different backgrounds. Neurolinguistic programming acknowledges this uniqueness and provides a means by which we can more successfully communicate with others.

Much of what is explained by NLP is really about responding to unique patterns. Because of the way we are programmed, we have developed preferences in the way we communicate. Conditioning (or programming) for a certain language (linguistic) is unique to each person's own neurology.

Potential Users for NLP

Neurolinguistic programming is creating more and more interest in education as well as in many other professions, such as sales and counseling. The lessons to be learned from NLP can significantly influence learning and training effectiveness. Trainers who have had a history of difficult learners may find that by applying the principles of NLP they can create a learning environment that is enthusiastic and energetic and more in tune with learning styles of the group.

Margaret and Toula discussed the way the safety program went. Margaret asked if Toula was aware of neurolinguistic programming and its implications for training. Toula had never heard of it and was sure it wasn't mentioned in her "Train-the-Trainer" course.

"Well," said Margaret, "I think it's about time you did hear about it. You are a very competent trainer and it's now time to take what you learned in your 'Train-the-Trainer' program to a higher level. NLP is something that can help you do that."

"It is not, in itself, a skill in the way we commonly regard skills," Margaret began. "Some people say they 'used' NLP to solve a particular problem or to communicate with another person. However, NLP is more a set of attitudes and communication skills than merely a skill in its own right. To say you 'used' NLP is like saying you 'used' friendliness or you 'used' love."

"Both friendliness and love are combinations of complex attitudes that are conveyed with communication skills. They are not used in the sense we usually give the term. It would be more correct to say that because of your friendliness or because of your love for someone, you were able to get something done. In the same way, we can get things done or achieve more success in training because of our attitudes and communication abilities."

Toula was totally absorbed by what Margaret was explaining and was already trying to figure out how NLP could help her.

"Since NLP is a combination of attitudes and skills, we therefore need to look at NLP from those two perspectives," Margaret continued. "First we have to explore both the attitudinal principles that form the basis of NLP and also some of the skills, or skill patterns, that have been connected to create the NLP framework. These skills and principles together create some exciting learning opportunities for facilitators. These opportunities are generating a growing interest among training professionals and, after observing the safety program, I think they will help you."

NLP Principles

The principles outlined here are the fabric of NLP. They are the canvas on which the skills are painted, the foundations on which the skills are placed to create improvements in learning.

These values and attitudes are an excellent basis for effective communication. Without them the skills are insignificant and perhaps even damaging, for they may simply be seen as a means of trying to manipulate a learner into certain actions and behavior.

In many ways, these principles are as important to educators as the canvas is to the artist; the communication skills that we'll discuss later are like the artist's paint. A palette of paint is worthless without a canvas on which to apply it. The principles are as follows:

1. Representation is not reality.
2. The path to comprehending the patterns of others is to seek rapport, that is to meet them in their world.
3. The measure of communication effectiveness is in the response you get, not in the intent with which it was sent.
4. Individuals have two levels of communication—subconscious and conscious.
5. There are no failures—only outcomes.
6. Present behavior is always the best possible available behavior.
7. Resistance comes about as a result of inflexible communication.

8. The best information about someone is provided by his or her behavior.
9. The intention of all human behavior is positive.
10. The value of people is constant; the value of behavior is open to critique.
11. There is a powerful connection between the way the mind affects the body and the way the body affects the mind.

> Margaret stood up and began to write on the whiteboard in her office. As she wrote, she said to Toula, "Let's look at each of these principles in more detail to explore their meaning and importance to the process of NLP. This is the first one to explore," she said. On the board she had written "Representation is not reality."

1. Representation Is Not Reality

To really understand NLP it is important to accept that what we use to represent something is not the thing itself. A picture of something is not the thing itself, and a word we use to describe a thing is the label for it, not the thing itself. This can sound a little abstract, but what it attempts to explain is that as we create patterns to understand our perception, we create representations of the reality we experience. What then happens is that we begin to assume our representation of something is the reality.

One way of describing this is to go back to the rule of generalizing that we explained earlier. The important thing to consider is that our generalizations are only our representations of reality. We need to accept that the reality itself is different. What we believe to be real is not necessarily real, since other people will have a different representation of the same thing. If our representation was real then everyone else would be wrong.

Another way of explaining this concept is in the notion that we shouldn't judge a book by its cover. The cover is only a representation of the reality. If we see a person dressed shabbily, for example, we may generalize that that person is poor. Our perception or pattern for the representation we perceive from his or her appearance is different from his or her representation of himself or herself. We might discover that the person is actually wealthy and chooses to live that lifestyle to escape the materialistic ways of the world.

Trainers can benefit from this principle by learning to suspend judgment and to objectively observe behavior. Remain in a neutral state and you will see beyond your own subconscious programming; you will see things the way they really are or at least see them the way others may see them. Many NLP practitioners describe this by saying, "The map is not the territory." In other words, the way we perceive the world is not the way it is. We need to perceive things the way others perceive them or at least be open to the possibility of alternative perspectives.

There are several ways in which trainers do not recognize this. For example, when learners see a particular task as difficult, and the trainer knows it is easy, this can become very frustrating for the learner and trainer. The trainer does not see it from the learner's point of view. This frustration can lead to conflict that may damage the important relationship between trainer and learner. Effective trainers realize that the way they perceive the task is not the same as the way the learner does. No matter how easy it seems to you, if a learner says it is difficult, then it is difficult.

Another example of this principle in action is when a trainer explains something and the learner resists it by saying, "That's fine in theory, but we're different." In such circumstances, many trainers are unable to adjust their style and see things from the learner's perspective; they simply attempt to explain the same principle a second time.

Neurolinguistic programming suggests that if people believe they cannot implement something, then they cannot. If they say things are different in their environment, then they are. As trainers we need to be more flexible to adjust to that perspective.

EXERCISE 6.3

If you are not convinced by the proposition that "If it's difficult for a learner, then it is difficult," try the following exercise. Examine the diagram in Figure 6.3. If you were asked to divide it into four areas of equal size and shape, your answer might look something like the diagram on the right.

Now try to divide the diagram on the left into *five* areas of equal size and shape.

This is a task that many people find difficult, even impossible. About 10 percent of the people we have shown this to find the puzzle extremely easy—yes, easy.

Have another look at it. Are you sure you don't know the answer? (You'll find the solution in Appendix 2.)

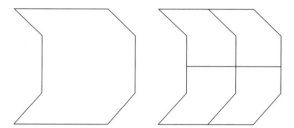

FIGURE 6.3. FIVE SHAPES PUZZLE

As Margaret explained this principle to Toula, she reminded her of the incident in the safety course when Toula was explaining kinetic lifting techniques.

"I remember," said Toula. "George was complaining that they couldn't use kinetic lifting techniques on those gas bottle pallets because they have two levels. He couldn't see the benefits of the lifting technique, not only to the company but to himself as well. He was not being open minded. I hate it when people do that. Nobody else said anything and if they had agreed they would have said so."

It was clear that Toula still felt upset about George's apparent obstructions to her lesson on lifting.

"Well," Margaret went on, "this principle is about that very kind of incident. George's perspective was that he couldn't do it your way. This principle asks you to acknowledge that if George cannot see it your way, you need to see it his way and seek a compromise or a different understanding of his position."

"At the time I was of the opinion that he may well have been right. Perhaps he couldn't use the lifting technique in that circumstance. What I witnessed, though, was your own resistance to George's perspective being as strong as you say his was. What I also saw was that it seemed to me that that one incident biased George against a lot of other things you said. I also think others might have agreed with him. I think the next principle is also applicable to the situation with George," Margaret concluded.

2. The Path to Comprehending the Patterns of Others Is to Seek Rapport, That Is to Meet Them in Their World

Rapport is meeting others in their world, trying to understand their needs, their values, and their culture and communicating in ways that are congruent with those values. You don't necessarily have to agree with their values, simply recognize that they have a right to them and work within their framework, not against it.

> "I know about this one," said Toula. "Do you remember how Janice introduced herself as a smoker? Well, as you know I don't smoke and I really detest it. I knew, though, that I wouldn't establish a rapport with Janice, or the others for that matter, by explaining how much I dislike smoking and how I find it hard to comprehend why anyone would want to take it up."
>
> "Instead I said, 'How long have you been smoking? How do you feel about the non-smoking trend these days?' Neutral questions such as these acknowledge her right to smoke and allow her to express her opinions freely. In this way I was 'meeting her in her world' without having to agree with her position."

EXERCISE 6.4

How might you respond to these statements made by learners in a way that meets them in their world?

(1) I hate this stuff. It's such a waste of time.
(2) Everyone says that. It makes me sick.
(3) I can't do it.
(4) This is all theory.

(See Appendix 2 for suggested responses.)

> Margaret and Toula had stopped for coffee. As they boiled the water Margaret said, "You see, by working harder at seeing things from George's world, you would have established a better line of communication. You might have found a solution together. At least George would have been more willing to hear your ideas on the issues. There are two other relevant principles here. The first is that the measure of effective communication is in the response you get, not the intent with which it was sent."

3. The Measure of Communication Effectiveness Is in the Response You Get, Not the Intent with Which It Was Sent

This principle implies that if you say something that upsets a person, it is irrelevant that you intended no harm. Effective communicators adapt to this principle in at least two ways. First, they actively avoid offending others by thinking about what they say before they say it. They follow the advice that it is better to keep your mouth shut and *appear* a fool than to open your mouth and *prove* it. Second, they are sensitive to the nonverbal signals that they receive in response to their communication.

"You may not have meant to resist George's point of view," Margaret explained to Toula, "but he saw it that way and so that is what it was. You may not have meant to treat his perception as irrelevant but, again, if he saw it that way then that is what it was."

4. Individuals Have Two Levels of Communication— Subconscious and Conscious

We must pay more attention to the subconscious because it often contains the most valuable information. It is quite common, for example, for learners to say that they understand something you have explained and yet remain confused. They may not tell you that they are confused for a number of reasons, such as they don't want to appear stupid. Despite their conscious message that they do understand, they will often tell you subconsciously that they are confused by exhibiting such telltale nonverbal signals as a furrowed brow or even shaking their head instead of nodding.

To pay more attention to the subconscious, you need to observe the extent of "congruence" in learners' communication. For example, when they say yes but shake their head instead of nodding, they are sending conflicting signals rather than congruent ones. You can respond by saying something like, "Perhaps I haven't made it really clear; you still seem a little confused." Check their response and be alert for congruence again.

Margaret continued and Toula looked more and more intently at her. "You said that 'nobody else said anything and if they had agreed they would have said so.' Well, I was watching them and I saw a lot of nonverbal signals that suggested they agreed with George. You see, people don't always say everything that is on their minds. Many times they will keep things to themselves, but that doesn't mean they aren't communicating with you. As you learn more about NLP, you will learn to understand more and more of that subconscious communication. As an example, you haven't said anything to me for a while, but I sense that you are still thinking a lot about what I am saying."

"Actually," Toula said, "I've been thinking that I really blew it. There is so much to think about when you are training that trying to pay attention to subconscious communication seems impossible. Perhaps I'm not cut out to be a trainer. I think I failed."

"There are a few more principles that I think are relevant to the incident with George," said Margaret.

5. There Are No Failures—Only Outcomes

Instead of saying "this failed," we should say "this was not the outcome I intended." After all, even some of the outcomes that you might describe as the worst failures may create a flash of personal realization, or the "a-hah" factor, as you suddenly realize a significant learning outcome.

Since NLP is largely about the ways in which certain language conditions us, we should avoid telling ourselves we are failures. If we say it often enough, we will be. Sometimes we set our goals with perfection in mind. Perhaps it is better to value the process of discovery that learning affords us rather than perfect outcomes. We may not achieve the perfect outcome, but learning may still have occurred, and the discovery process is itself an outcome that is not a failure.

6. Present Behavior Is Always the Best Possible Available Behavior

When someone says, "I could have done better," the truth is that given the circumstances, the desired outcome, and the available resources, this person did the best he or she could.

In education situations, when learners say they "could have done better" or that they "can't do something," we can respond in ways that promote their self-confidence and self-esteem by keeping this principle in mind. We could say, for example, "You did the best you could in the circumstances and in that particular state of mind. What will you do differently if the same thing occurs again?"

We can also respond more effectively by employing the skills of the "As. . .If" strategy and resource states. These skills (or skill patterns) are explained later in the chapter.

"When we agreed to look at what was troubling you in your training, we knew that there was something to improve on," Margaret consoled Toula. "The fact that we found what it was is not a sign of failure. It is merely an outcome. The beauty of it is that now there is a way to explore improvements. You did the best with the skills you had at the time. You have been successful in many things and now have a chance to extend yourself. Don't look at that as a failure but as an opportunity."

"Similarly, George does his best with his available behavior. He may have expressed his problem better, but the fact is that he did it in the best way he knew given his current communication skills, his mood, and the circumstances at the time. You might have been able to respond with the "As. . .If" strategy. But I'll explain that later. For now, think about how these next few principles apply to you and George."

7. Resistance Only Comes About as a Result of Inflexible Communication

When learners display resistance toward the educator, it is usually as a result of the inflexible way the educator has presented the information. For example, many people will resist information that is stated as an unchallengeable fact by a facilitator. If the educator rephrases the message or empathizes more with the learner, then the resistance will be diminished.

Learners, too, may be inflexible in the way they receive information. In other words, their own processes of generalizing, deleting, and distorting govern their communication and perceptions. Perhaps they are not challenging their own bias, assumptions, or preconceived ideas? If you can encourage them to do this more often, then the resistance will be less of a problem. One way to do this is to facilitate "critical thinking" exercises early in a program. Critical thinking is a process whereby assumptions and mindsets are examined and questioned. It is this process that provides the foundation for real change.

EXERCISE 6.5

Critical thinking exercises can take many forms, but activities designed around multicultural awareness are usually a good source. For example, try hawking and spitting into a cup in front of a group of people and watch the reaction. It will generally be one of utter disgust. Then blow your nose with a handkerchief and ask how they feel about that. They will typically greet this behavior with much more acceptance. Immediately thereafter ask someone to shake your hand, the one that you just used to blow your nose, and he or she will cringe away from you. This exercise always generates lively debate about cultural norms that are seldom challenged and raises some interesting questions about critical thinking.

Another source of critical thinking exercises is the daily paper. Headlines and their associated stories provide many examples of biased thinking and the way the populist view of things can be ratified inappropriately by poor reporting. One of our classic examples is a story of "Japanese disaster tours." The reporter told of tour buses of Japanese tourists who traveled to disaster sites taking photos after the San Francisco earthquake in the late 1980s. The tours were enraging Americans who found the tours ghoulish. A critical appraisal of the story might, however, reveal to the reader that the Japanese groups stood out because they were not Caucasian and, since Japanese tourists travel in groups as a rule anyway, the tours would be hard to miss. On reflection, we realize that if we were touring San Francisco at the time of a major world event such as this, we probably would have visited some of the sites too and even taken photos (and we certainly don't regard ourselves as ghouls). However, since we would probably be alone, and would look native to the casual observer, we would not be noticed and therefore no story would be written about us. What the story did was reinforce, or perhaps create, a stereotype about the Japanese that would validate the bias of any reader who was predisposed to feel that way. This story has provided us with many insightful sessions on critical thinking and the way our resistance to rational thinking is thwarted by the messages we receive and the way we perceive them. For a further discussion on critical thinking, see Brookfield (1987).

8. The Best Information About Someone Is Provided by His or Her Behavior

What people actually do is more important and powerful than what they say they'll do. You can look at this from two perspectives. On one hand, what you do as an educator will have more meaning for learners than what you say you will do. Earn their trust and respect by modeling what you regard as appropriate behavior. In other words, the old proverb holds true—actions do speak louder than words. From another angle, learners' actions are more powerful and meaningful than what they say they'll do.

Avoid judging people by their words. Instead, ask them to clarify their behavior, keeping in mind principle number 9.

EXERCISE 6.6

Consider questions like these the next time you are tempted to judge someone based on his or her behavior.

Have you done that before? What happened when you did?

What alternative ways have you tried in the past? What happened with those?

What alternative approaches do you think might exist? What would happen if you tried those?

9. The Intention of All Human Behavior Is Positive

Even some of the most aggressive behavior may be a cry for help or attention. This principle is similar to principle 1. Your perception of people's behavior is only a representation of the reality. It suggests that you should suspend your judgment of someone's behavior until you have considered the possible positive intention. Your response should then be based on the notion that the person had a positive intention in mind (perhaps subconsciously) and if you have truly come to value the principles outlined here, you will find that you have more success at managing what often appears as unacceptable behavior.

EXERCISE 6.7

Review the following examples and suggest a possible positive intent that could be involved in these situations.

Examples	Possible Positive Intent
Learner disagreeing strongly with you.	
Someone frequently coming late to class.	
A learner who dominates the discussion.	

(See Appendix 2 for suggested answers.)

"I think I'm getting it," said Toula. "What you're saying is that George's inflexibility was a result of my inflexibility in communicating my ideas to him; I judged George and decided that I didn't like him based on what he said about my ideas on kinetic lifting." Margaret smiled but said nothing.

"Also," Toula continued, "George may have had a positive intent with his behavior. Perhaps he was really asking for help by saying that my ideas wouldn't work. Maybe he really wanted some other ideas that would work."

"By George, I think you've got it!" Margaret said with a shout. "I still have a few principles to discuss with you though," she added.

10. The Value of People Is Constant; the Value of Behavior Is Open to Critique

This principle is about mutual respect: if you learn to truly adopt it into your own value system you will be more able to establish a rapport with learners. Again, it is about withholding judgment about people and questioning only their behavior.

Margaret reminded Toula of another incident that affected the safety program. During the introductions at the start of the program, Peter, one of the learners, would occasionally turn to the person next to him and speak quite loudly even while another person was introducing himself or herself. The fellow's behavior seemed quite rude and inconsiderate, and Toula could see others in the group becoming quite agitated. In fact, Peter's behavior was so disruptive that Toula took an instant dislike to him.

She tried to keep an open mind, but he continued his behavior for the next two hours. Not all the time, but every ten minutes or so he would be at it again.

Toula shot a few disapproving glares at Peter. Still this behavior continued.

His behavior affected her so much that at one point when he said something she responded with "Yes, well we've all heard quite a lot of your opinions, Peter. I think we should let someone else have a say." That certainly shut him up.

Margaret was observing this, however, and decided that Toula should have reacted differently. During the coffee break, she made a suggestion to Toula.

Acting on this advice, Toula quietly approached Peter while the others were distracted. She asked if he would mind withholding his comments until the other person had finished speaking. He was immediately apologetic and he confided in Toula that he was deaf in one ear and partially deaf in the other and at times didn't realize that others were speaking. Now it was Toula's turn to be apologetic.

"I was so embarrassed," she said to Margaret as she recalled her feelings at the time. "I thought he was being so rude that I really didn't like him."

Margaret replied, "That is what this principle is about. We really should suspend our judgment of people and talk to them about their behavior. Every person is entitled to dignity and respect, and if we remember that we will have much more success communicating with them, even about sensitive issues. By being able to explore Peter's behavior, we were then able to move him to where he could see everyone clearly and would know if anyone was speaking. By suspending our judgment of him as a person, we resolved the situation much more successfully than we might have if we just reacted to our dislike for him because of his behavior."

"Yes, I can see that now," said Toula. "And by the way, I really liked your idea to move everyone to new seats so that the others wouldn't think that we were moving Peter because he was disruptive. I could see that they were reacting to him like I was, and that was a great way to deal with that sensitively."

11. There Is a Powerful Connection Between the Way the Mind Affects the Body and the Way the Body Affects the Mind

This is an essential ingredient of NLP. It is the basis of most of the skills and skill patterns described later. Another way of expressing this is to say that what we think will affect our biological processes. Have you ever been late for something important and become so anxious about it that your pulse raced, you broke into a sweat, and even began to tremble slightly or fidget about in your seat? That's an example of this principle at work. By thinking anxious thoughts, your biology changed, causing you to perspire and your pulse to quicken.

The reverse is also true. For example, a person who is trim and fit may also be confident and self-assured. If a person gains or loses too much weight, he may come to regard himself as unattractive and become depressed and self-conscious, even to the point of losing all confidence. His body has eventually affected his mind. Other examples are explained below. Try them on a group and see the reaction.

EXERCISE 6.8

To see this connection in practice, read the following paragraph to a group. Use your tone to effect. Speak softly and in a relaxed tone at first and suddenly raise your voice for the last line.

> Imagine you are driving along an open road. It is a bright, sunny day, warm but not too hot. The cool breeze is flowing through the window across your arm, cooling your skin. The landscape is rolling grassy plains dotted with animals and flowering trees. As you imagine this view, try to feel the steering wheel in your hands and the contours of the seat you are in. Look around the car, see the dashboard, and look in the rear-view mirror. The road is clear in every direction and you are feeling great. Try to visualize yourself in this scene. Now look around the car again, see the dash, see the seat next to you, look in the rear-view mirror and *see a police car with flashing lights.*

Can you see the change in state created by the simple sight of a police car? People's whole persona changes. For some people, adrenalin flows, perspiration begins to come out of their pores, and even their breathing may change. Many people will have similar reactions to a real police car, especially if, momentarily, they think the police want them to pull over.

EXERCISE 6.9

Ask people to stand and relax. Then ask them to turn their heads and fix on a place in the room that is as far around as they can see without turning their shoulders. Now ask them to turn to the front again and close their eyes. Tell them to imagine they can turn their heads 360 degrees without any effort at all. Ask them to feel the way their muscles would feel if they could do that. Repeat this exercise several times as people imagine themselves in various settings. Each time ask them to visualize the setting and to try to feel the way their muscles would feel if they could do this without the slightest effort. Next, ask them to open their eyes and turn again to find the farthest place they can see. Many people report that they can now see farther. The explanation is that they have conditioned their bodies to go beyond the limitations they had previously programmed.

EXERCISE 6.10

Ask everyone to look at their feet and try to feel depressed. Now tell them to try to feel depressed while looking up at the sky. Again, many people report a mood change simply from looking up.

EXERCISE 6.11

Get a volunteer to lift you up. (Choose someone fit and strong.) Stand naturally and ask him or her to lift you from the ground. Then ask him or her to lift you a second time, but this time, just before the lift, try to mentally "dump" all of your body weight into your feet. Visualize it all simply dropping like a lead weight straight into your shoes.

Ask the person to compare the two lifts.

"Understanding this last principle is really important to helping you learn and use the skills that are an integral part of NLP," Margaret explained to Toula.

"Imagine the power your training would have in lifting skills, for example, if you were able to help people understand the effect their thinking has on their ability. In a way, a person's ability to lift correctly is affected by his or her attitude toward correct lifting and the attitude is affected by the ability. If you were able to create a positive attitude toward it, perhaps doing it correctly would follow, and vice versa. Think about the principles we have discussed over the weekend."

Then Margaret gave Toula a small book with the title, *NLP Skill Patterns*. "Have a look at the stuff in here, too. It explains the skills of NLP I'd like to talk to you about. After the weekend we'll talk some more."

Toula took the book home and read it three times. Since it was brief, she was able to really give some thought to the eleven skill patterns contained in it.

NLP Skill Patterns

There is a distinctive set of skills that go with the principles of NLP. These skills are a part of the behavior patterns we use to help us make sense of the world. These patterns are useful tools that demonstrate how we process information. They can help us to detect and utilize the patterns in people with whom we communicate. As you will see, you already make use of most of them in natural ways. The power of NLP is simply to make a conscious effort to use them to help learning.

1. Representational Systems

Every experience we have engages our senses in a variety of ways. We see, hear, feel, taste, and smell all at the same time; we absorb input from all of these senses simultaneously. However, as we learned earlier, we delete some of this information to help us comprehend what is going on around us; we distort some of it and we make generalizations about it. These rules can strongly influence the way we make sense of the things we take in via our senses. For example, as you look at the diagram in Figure 6.4 you are seeing a representation of a train.

As a result of your representational systems impacting on this figure, it is possible that you are also "seeing" some things surrounding the train that match your patterns of what goes with trains. Also, you may be "hearing" the sounds of the train as it hurtles along the track; you may "smell" the locomotive fuel; and you may "feel" the wind as it rushes by.

FIGURE 6.4. REPRESENTATIONAL SYSTEMS

How you represent this picture as you process it is a clue to your individual representational system. The way you have processed this picture is unique to you. There's unlikely to be another person on the planet who has the same representation of this picture as you have.

The way you have processed this information, with the mental images, sounds, feelings, and smells, is often referred to as processing with "modalities." The modalities are referred to as visual, auditory, kinesthetic, digital, and gustatory/olfactory states. The concept of modalities, or representational systems, is one of the most commonly discussed issues in NLP.

The way each person represents things, as we have shown here, is a result of patterns like others we have described. Your patterns will indicate a preference for the representational systems that you tend to make the most use of. Some of us are more comfortable and successful communicating visually and need, for example, to draw a diagram in order to describe the workings of a machine part. When you use the visual representational system, you redraw the picture in your mind. When you use the auditory representational system, you will pay a lot more attention to things like tone of voice and combinations of speech. Likewise, in this representational system, you will be more comfortable explaining how the machine part works and be equally comfortable hearing how it works. When you try to recall the information using the auditory representational system, you will "replay the tape" of what you heard.

When you use the kinesthetic representational system to describe the working of a machine part, you will be more likely to recall your sensations of touch and you may need to play with the actual part of the machine or use a working model in order to really understand how it works.

Another issue associated with modalities is the way our words give clues to our preferred representational system. For example, several people who have experienced the same event, like a robbery, may describe it differently.

Person A, who is highly visual, may represent the robbery by saying, "The robber was wearing a big black motorcycle helmet. It was like new because it was very shiny. He was taller than that sign over there; I noticed it when he was next to it."

Person B, who is highly auditory, may represent the robbery by saying, "All I heard was him shouting at everyone. A couple of people screamed and then everything went quiet as if we were waiting to hear his instructions. I could hear that he was nervous because his voice was kind of quivering."

Person C, who is very kinesthetic, may represent the robbery by saying, "Boy, was I ever scared. I felt like I would collapse. The minute he walked through that door I knew he was here for action. It felt like he was ready to pull that trigger any minute."

Person D, who is digital, may represent the robbery by saying, "The offender entered via the front door and demanded money from Teller C. These are the facts as I know them."

Person E, who is very gustatory/olfactory, may represent the robbery by saying, "The whole thing left a bitter taste in my mouth. The person smelled a bit like feta cheese and his taste in clothes really stinks."

These preferred representational systems also have an impact on the way people learn. Consider the following checklists to help people improve their visual, auditory, and kinesthetic potential.

Visual

A visual learner likes pictures, diagrams, graphs, and pictorial representations of the spoken word. Learning is enhanced by improving the visuals with the use of color, patterns, and adjustments to brightness and the size and depth of field (multi-dimensional). Visuals prefer to read than to be read to. They are good at copying visuals and recall detail better than people who have a different preferred modality.

Auditory

An auditory learner likes the spoken word. Learning is enhanced by improvements to sounds such as changes to volume, rhythm, pitch, and speed. Auditories like to repeat things back as a means to understand them. They will learn well from listening and cope better with spoken messages than with written ones.

Kinesthetic

A kinesthetic learner learns best by doing. Kinesthetics like getting their hands on things and trying them out. They like movement, action, being entertained, and having a fun experience. They like closeness and touch better than people of other preferred modalities. Generally speaking, they are also very good creatively as they are able to imagine things that do not exist.

Yet another distinction to be made in the issue of modalities is that of input, storage, and output. In other words, we may receive and absorb information visually, for example, but process it and pass it on to others kinesthetically.

Naturally, all of us use all of the representational systems at various times, but NLP modalities suggest that we have a preference. Grinder (1991) suggests that out of a class of thirty people, on average, twenty-two will be able to comfortably move from visual to auditory and then to kinesthetic communication styles. However, between four and six will have a strong preference for one of the styles and will be less able to understand unless you communicate in their style. Grinder calls these people translators. Another two to three will have other factors influencing their communication that might be described as "constraints." An example would be if they have just come from an emotionally draining experience. In order to tap into the modalities of learners, we need to understand how they learn best. The preceding descriptions of visual, auditory, and kinesthetic styles give some generalizations about how people learn. However, this may be extended to include other representational systems such as digital, taste (gustatory) and smell (olfactory). Further explanation of modality and its relevance to training is discussed in Chapter 7.

2. Submodalities

Submodalities describe the strength of a preferred modality and also the qualities of the modalities in which we communicate. As stated earlier, we communicate using all modalities but the qualities of the way we use them can be quite different from person to person. One of the differences is the clarity of the visuals we can imagine in our minds. Some people can "see" a clearer picture in their minds than other people. Likewise, some people can "hear" a clearer replay of the "tapes" in their minds, while others are able to sense the feeling and texture of things from memory more clearly.

The suggestion is that we as trainers can help to adjust the sensations people have by rearranging the intensity of the modality. For example, when telling stories or giving examples, we can attempt to make images brighter, dimmer, more colorful, or farther away. We can try to adjust mental sounds by adding imaginary background music or noise in the learners' minds, making the sound louder or quieter or more melodic and rhythmic. We might also try to adjust kinesthetic sensations by putting more texture to the sensation or emotion in the way we describe feelings.

We might also benefit from the concept of submodalities in the way we try to help people comprehend what we say. For example, if people are having trouble understanding what you say, you might try adjusting the modality or changing the representational system you are using altogether.

3. Constraints

There are many personal and social constraints that also affect our representational systems. These constraints are manifested in our language and gestures.

An example that many trainers can identify with is the different meanings that are attributed to the word "teacher." Some trainers have come to detest the word in its application to what they do. They have come to regard it as indicative of highly structured authoritarian delivery of facts. For others, it is a word that simply describes a person's role in the process of helping other people to learn. Each meaning has a different representation for the word based on the social constraints that people have placed on its meaning. These social constraints are also evident in what we have come to know as "body language." We sometimes interpret a person's gestures based only on what we have been told by others that these gestures represent.

For trainers it is important to understand that for everything we do and say, these social and personal constraints mean that the way our actions are perceived by others is influenced by their own representation of our actions and words.

4. Anchoring

Have you ever heard a pop song from your childhood and been transported back in time—feeling as you did then, visualizing the environment of the day? What about smelling a particular aroma that creates the same kind of feelings or visions from your past? The smell of your grandmother's perfume, the clinical aroma of a hospital, and the smell of baby powder all create powerful memories for many people. This is anchoring. You have "anchored" certain memories to these sounds and smells.

When we apply NLP to education, we often attempt to anchor people to sights, sounds, smells, and physical space to help them recall things. In this way, we can increase their ability to recall certain things by simply replaying the anchor. For example, if a trainer could get a learner into a motivated state, play a certain musical piece while the learner was in that state, and reinforce that several times, when the trainer later played the same piece of music it might recreate the same feelings of motivation.

Similarly, we often subconsciously anchor people to unpleasant feelings without realizing it. For example, if your training room is used for long, boring, and aggressive staff meetings, there is every likelihood that people are anchored to unpleasant feelings they have experienced in those meetings. Then, when they enter the room for a training course, those same feelings may return.

You can anchor people to music by playing a set piece every time they enter a room. The piece you choose should be congruent to the mood you want to create. "In the Mood" by Bette Midler (EMI) and "Love Is in the Air" by John Paul Young (Sony Music) are both good for an up-tempo mood, and baroque music is good for a relaxed mood. See the section on "Sound, Song, and Music" in Chapter 7 for more ideas.

Another way to use this process in a training activity is to anchor certain behaviors to particular parts of the room. In Figure 6.5, the various parts of the room are labeled according to the behavior or action the trainer will exclusively carry out in that part of the room. In this way, trainees will soon learn that when the trainer moves to the left side of the room, for example, he or she will be turning control over to the group who will be allowed to have more to say because, on this side, debate is encouraged.

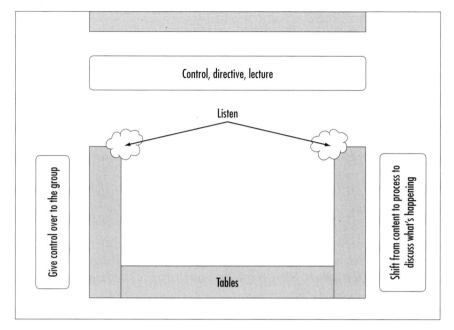

FIGURE 6.5. ANCHORING PEOPLE TO AREAS OF THE TRAINING ROOM

5. The As...If Strategy

Many people respond to new demands by saying "I could never do that" or "I'm not a very good operator." The As...If strategy is a technique that helps overcome this barrier. Whenever a person says, "I can't," the facilitator responds by saying something like, "That's okay. Lots of people feel the same way. But *if* you could do it, how do you think you would begin? How would you stand? How would you hold the lever? How would you feel as you began if you were an expert?" In other words, "Pretend as if you could do it anyway. I know you say you can't, but just pretend."

Often, people overcome their own subconscious barriers with this technique because they can be shown that they can do it. As they begin pretending, they find that some of their reasons for being unable to perform were irrational.

6. Congruency Among All Senses

When we communicate, it is common for our verbal message to be quite different from our nonverbal message. For example, when we want to tell our boss (or someone in power) about something he or she is doing that we dislike, our verbal communication sends one message but our nervous laughter and fidgeting sends quite another (and our subconscious signals are as powerful as our conscious signals). Because of this, the receiver often gets an unintended message, such as, "I'm not really serious."

The subconscious messages we send are more reliable than the conscious messages, since people often shroud their true feelings in politeness or hidden agendas. For example, the breathing patterns or posture of a person can often tell you about his or her true state. Calibrating your awareness to a person's subconscious messages can be a powerful tool for understanding him or her. As a trainer, you will often get signals from these sources that indicate the level of permission to proceed or not to proceed along certain avenues of the process with learners. For example, if they are uncomfortable about volunteering for a role play, changes to the rate of their breathing, changes in skin color, and posture shifts will indicate this reluctance. You are likely to see some or all of these clues: shallower, faster breathing; reddening of the complexion; hesitant movements; and glancing around at others.

Excellent trainers will work hard to maintain congruence in their own messages. They will send nonverbal messages that match what they say. Many trainers work hard at establishing a rapport, for example, and then spoil their hard work by having lunch away from the group, as if to say, "I'm not really your friend." This subconscious signal is often more powerful than all the verbal statements to the contrary.

7. Positive Language

The next skill in the NLP framework is the ability to use positive terms: to say what is possible rather than what is not possible; to ask people what you want them to do, not what you do not want them to do. For example, a trainer might say, "Please do not speak during this activity." To be more positive, the trainer could say, "Please keep silent." It is a minor change but encourages people to see the trainer in a positive light. Someone who speaks in negatives can create difficulties for himself or herself when trying to establish a rapport. (*Note*: Accelerative learning practitioners may refer to this as a part of affirmation, as we have done in Chapter 7.)

EXERCISE 6.12

In the following list there are a number of common negative expressions. Some of them you may even use yourself. Try to find a positive expression that may be used as an alternative.

1. We have a problem.
2. This is going to be difficult.
3. That's impossible.
4. We've got a lot to do today.
5. We can't go to lunch until one o'clock.
6. I've told you before not to. . . .
7. You don't understand.
8. You never. . . .
9. This isn't very interesting, but we have to do it.
10. You probably won't have a chance to apply this for months, but. . . .
11. I know you think role playing is like acting, but this won't be like acting.
12. I know last time we had role plays it was difficult, but today it won't be difficult.

(See Appendix 2 for suggested answers for 1, 2, and 3.)

8. States

The term "state" is used to describe the combination of mind/body actions that creates a mood or feeling in us. Many trainers will attempt to create a relaxed state in a learning environment because research has shown that learning is enhanced when the brain is in its relaxed state. There are many ways of creating this state; one of the most common is through the use of relaxing music and relaxation exercises early in the learning event. However, it is also possible that you want to create an excited state. This can also be done with music but the type would differ. It might also be created by the way you greet people and what happens in the first few minutes of a session.

States may be created by subconscious anchoring, such as shown in Exercise 6.8 (visualizing a police car). Negative feelings about being pulled over by a police car have created the anchor that changes your state when you see a police car—even an imaginary one.

Many trainers we have met do not say a word to learners as they arrive but prefer to hide in the corner until they are "on." What kind of subconscious message does this communicate? What kind of state does it create? Imagine the difference if you greeted people individually as they arrived with a warm handshake and a welcome, saying something like, "I hope you get a lot out of the day. I'm going to be doing my best to make it a really worthwhile day for you."

9. Resource State

A resource state is a state of mind or mood in which people feel that they are capable of anything or of some specific purpose. Many athletes use this technique to convince themselves that they can win.

Often we identify learning with negative feelings, and when we engage in learning we are anchored to negative feelings or a negative state. Helping people to get into a resource state can dramatically alter the way they feel about learning. This can be done in many ways and is only limited by your creativity in anchoring.

EXERCISE 6.13

One of the more interesting (and dramatic) ways to access a resource state is to anchor people to a "circle of excellence" through the use of visualization and music. This technique requires learners to visualize an imaginary circle on the floor in front of them (they do this with their eyes closed). While they visualize the circle, the trainer has them recall all of the feelings of being, say, excited. They stand in an excited way, they say things to themselves that they would say if they were excited, and so on. Meanwhile, music is quietly playing in the background. The trainer generates more and more images and feelings of excitement as the music gets louder. His or her voice builds the excitement by getting louder and faster until, finally, everyone steps into their circles and they continue to visualize the feelings while in the circles. With reinforcement over time, people become anchored to excitement with this music and their imaginary circle of excellence. Replaying the music can recreate the feelings. Anchoring these feelings to the circle means that, eventually, all they have to do is visualize the circle, step into it, and they will be excited. This technique is successfully used in coaching people to confront the new, the different, and the complex.

EXERCISE 6.14

Another way to access a resource state is to have people pretend that they are geniuses. Ask the group to stand the way a genius stands, think the way a genius thinks, write the way a genius writes. Call this their "genius state." Again, reinforce it by having people "get into their genius state" every now and then. Imagine the power of the state when, for example, the group is taking a quiz; when they get to question ten, instead of a question, it reads "True or False—You are a genius and will easily pass this quiz."

10. Sensory Acuity

It is important for you to develop an awareness of the nonverbal messages people send, sometimes subconsciously. For example, changes in skin color, such as blushing, can tell you a lot about the way a person is reacting to your communication. A person can communicate messages in other ways (through, for example, perspiration, breathing, speech modulation, and even laughter), and the truly skilled communicators will be aware of this and adjust their own communication accordingly.

11. Training Style and Modality Flexibility

One area to consider in the applications of NLP in the training room is that trainers tend to convey information in their dominant modality. If you tend to use visual representational systems, you tend to train using that mode most often. Likewise for auditory and kinesthetic representational systems.

Flexible trainers can adapt to the three modalities so that there is the best chance of people understanding and connecting with what they are saying. One way to discover your own preferred training modality is to get some feedback on your training. You can do this by using the following exercise.

EXERCISE 6.15

One way to determine the blend of auditory, visual, and kinesthetic representational systems in your training is to give the following diagram (Figure 6.6) to a colleague. His or her job is then to observe you and the style of your delivery. If you are "outputting" in a visual mode, for example, by drawing on a board, using an overhead transparency, or speaking in visual terms, the observer should mark a tick in the visual component of the diagram. He or she marks the diagram in this way throughout your session. The number of ticks in each segment will indicate how your representation system is outputting.

You can do this yourself by videotaping a presentation and reviewing the tape with the diagram ready.

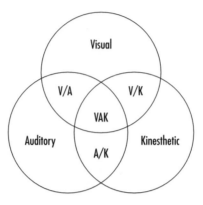

FIGURE 6.6. TRAINING STYLE AND MODALITY FLEXIBILITY

Toula returned to work after reading *NLP Skill Patterns* all charged up and raring to go. She talked with Margaret about how she might practice some of the skills and decided the first attempt rightly belonged with day two of the safety awareness course. George, Peter, Debbie, and the others returned for a follow-up program to reinforce their first day's training. Margaret sat in again to see how things went.

Inevitably, George mentioned the impossibility of using the lifting techniques with the gas bottle pallet. Toula sensed the others tense up, waiting for her reaction. George went slightly red as he said it.

This time Toula said, "If there was a way to lift safely while loading the gas bottle pallet, what would it be, George?"

George replied that he needed a simple lifting device. Toula asked more questions using her skills of rapport: "Tell me more about such a device." George explained it and others chimed in. Eventually, it was decided that they could make such a device in the machine shop without much cost at all. Margaret agreed to discuss the matter at the next management meeting as long as George was willing to come and present his ideas. "Of course I will," said George.

Margaret was thrilled with Toula's early venture into the world of NLP. After the program she called Toula over and said how pleased she was. "I told you it would help," she said to Toula. "It was more than helpful," said Toula, "it was a miracle."

Summary

In this chapter we have explained that NLP is not in itself a skill but rather a framework of communication issues that begins with a set of principles and includes a collection of skill patterns. Understanding NLP is an important beginning to using these principles and skill patterns.

To take the first steps on the path to more successful communication with others, you need to detect and utilize the clues people give you about how they pattern information. You should explore the clues that indicate the way you and others make sense of experience. These clues may be found in many ways, including the use of representational systems that incorporate visual, auditory, and kinesthetic modalities.

NLP can be a powerful tool if used with integrity. By adopting the values and skills associated with NLP, you will be able to create a better rapport with others and, as a consequence, develop a more fulfilling learning environment.

Bibliography

Andreas, S., & Faulkner, C. (1996). *NLP: The new technology of achievement*. London: Nicholas Brealey.

Bandler, R., & Grinder, J. (1975). *The structure of magic, Volume 1*. Palo Alto, CA: Science and Behavior Books.

Bandler, R., & Grinder, J. (1976). *The structure of magic, Volume 2*. Palo Alto, CA: Science and Behavior Books.

Brookfield, S. (1987). *Developing critical thinkers*. San Francisco, CA: Jossey-Bass.

Grinder, M. (1991). *Righting the education conveyor belt* (2nd ed.). Portland, OR: Metamorphous Press.

Jensen, E. (1988). *Super teaching: Master strategies for building student success.* Del Mar, CA: Turning Point.

Kamp, D. (1996). *The excellent trainer: Putting NLP to work.* Aldershot, England: Gower.

Laborde, G. (1987). *Influencing with integrity.* Palo Alto, CA: Syntony.

Lewis, B., & Pucelik, F. (1990). *Magic of NLP demystified: A pragmatic guide to communication and change.* Portland, OR: Metamorphous Press.

7

THE POWER OF ACCELERATIVE LEARNING

This chapter uses an A to Z mnemonic to list twenty-seven ingredients and "how to's" of accelerative learning.

"Accelerative learning is about creativity, finding one's true self and quality communication."
LARISSA KAMINSKAYA

Gems Mined from These Pages

- A majority of what people learn is absorbed subconsciously.

- Accelerative learning is not a package.

- All learners have the ability to enhance and amplify intelligence.

- Sound activates and accounts for 85 percent of the brain's energy.

- To be a trainer in accelerative learning, you should live accelerative learning.

Delivering the Emperor's Message

Rene Vichtez had just been given the opportunity of a lifetime. She had been asked to present at the industry's prestigious biannual conference. Excited by the offer, Rene started to plan and to dream about how to make her session both informative and memorable.

Rene had been given ninety minutes to cover the critically important area of implementing workplace learning. One discipline that she was keen to experiment with was accelerative learning, especially exploring music, telling stories, and using metaphors. However, this was risky given that accelerative learning had yet to receive mainstream acceptance with many of the people who would be attending the conference. Some of these people would be quick to call accelerative learning "a fad," "too unconventional," or "the flavor of the month."

Scared by the thought of being rejected by her peers, Rene spent several agonizing hours weighing the consequences of presenting this emerging technique. The more Rene thought about her fear, the more she realized that developing skills in accelerative learning was just another part of personal growth. Rene gained great confidence and strength from recalling many past experiences in which learning hurdles had been overcome by trial and error. Thus the decision was made over a glass of port one chilly evening that this opportunity would be Rene's debut in using accelerative learning.

Rene thought long and hard about what the major themes of the talk should be. One theme was that workplace learning must have the total support of all human resource and business systems in order to be successful. As Rene often says, "Bad policies and bad systems contaminate learning. It is very important that all people review and improve policies and systems on a regular basis."

In the past, Rene had tried to communicate her message with an overhead transparency and a best-practice example, but in Rene's honest opinion the major importance of this key point had never really "sunk in." With this in mind, she decided to make an extra special effort to use accelerative learning to help design an experience that would more vividly anchor this key point into people's long-term memories.

Given that the content of the ninety-minute session was already committed to other important themes, Rene could only allow five minutes on this specific message. So her training challenge was set. How could this message be communicated with impact using accelerative learning? Rene went about collecting some ideas and strategies to help achieve the desired objective within the time available.

A week later, while Rene was lying in bed one morning, she flashed back to the famous chariot race in the motion picture *Ben Hur*. Rene wondered, "What was it that made this scene so memorable?" After pondering for a few minutes, Rene yelled out, "It was the chariot and the wonderful team of horses. Each horse knew its role. They all pulled in the one direction and worked in total synchronicity with one another and with the driver." Rene's face lit up with excitement because, for the first time, she had found a powerful metaphor to communicate the message that human resources and business systems must pull together in one direction if workplace learning is to achieve meaningful results within organizations.

Excited by the prospect of designing an accelerative learning experience around the metaphor of the Roman chariot, Rene went about exploring the design options. Within a day, she had decided on a guided visualization of a Roman chariot using background music from *Chariots of Fire*.

The next afternoon, Rene spent three hours writing and speaking aloud a story that conveyed the message of "teamwork and alignment" in total synchronicity with three-and-a-half minutes of inspiring music. While rehearsing, Rene already knew that this technique was something extraordinary.

The following week, Rene did a test run of the guided visualization with a group of peers and received some important feedback regarding the ending, the verbal delivery, and the volume of the sound from the stereo. Accepting the feedback, Rene went away and finalized a story entitled "The Emperor's Messenger."

The long awaited day had arrived and the presentation was going according to plan. Around fifty minutes into the session, it was time for Rene to deliver the accelerative learning story of the emperor's messenger. Before beginning this rehearsed piece, Rene led a short physical stretching activity, followed by some very pleasant and peaceful yoga breathing. To do so, Rene began by saying, "Two of the most important things to do in all learning is to prepare your body and your mental state. Just as an athlete stretches and breathes before an event, it is good for us to become athletic learners and to stretch and breathe before conducting the next important activity."

Rene then asked the people to close their eyes, make themselves totally comfortable in their chairs, and to breathe normally.

"With your permission, I would like to conduct a short and powerful activity." Sensing that the mood of the room was both curious and receptive, Rene started to tell the following story of the emperor's messenger to the music of *Chariots of Fire*.

"We're going on a journey through time. You are leaving this training conference on this beautiful Tuesday and we are traveling through the 19th century, the 18th century, the 15th century, the 10th century, the 5th century, to the year 10 B.C."

"You are standing in a village, a Roman village, on a beautiful, clear spring day. As you stand in the village, you hear the bellow of a trumpet echoing through the valley. That sound announces the approach of the emperor's messenger's chariot."

"Excited, you begin to walk up the hill that overlooks the village. You start to run to see what is happening. As you run, you feel the breeze in your hair, you smell the spring flowers, you hear the rustle of the wind in the trees. As you reach the top of the hill, you gaze on the road and see a trail of dust coming toward the village. As you look and look, all of a sudden you see the emperor's messenger's chariot. A golden chariot, pulled by four beautiful chestnut horses—all working as a team, all in total synergy. What power! What strength! What grace!"

"Then you notice that the chariot begins to slow as it comes toward the village. As it enters the village, people close in and surround the chariot. The chariot stops. The horses remain motionless. The emperor's messenger stands, holding a scroll, and delivers a message of hope, joy, and prosperity for the years ahead. The crowd disperses, feeling empowered and hopeful for the times ahead."

"As you hear the music fade into the background, you realize it is time to leave this special place, knowing that you can return any time you wish."

As Rene said these final words, the volume of music was gradually lowered until not a sound was heard. Allowing a few seconds of total silence, Rene said, "Thank you. When you are ready, I would ask you to slowly open your eyes and make yourself accustomed to your surroundings."

Giving the group a few more seconds, Rene then asked the participants to pair up with one another to discuss the meaning of the story. After a further minute, she encouraged feedback.

Having heard a wealth of insightful comments from the group, Rene said, "To me the emperor's messenger's chariot provides an important symbol to us. Like the chariot, if we are to be successful in implementing workplace learning, all of the business and human resource systems need to pull in one direction. We cannot afford to have a renegade horse on the chariot. Likewise, we cannot afford to have a performance-management system, or a staff-selection system, or a job-design system that does not inspire and abide by the values of quality learning in the workplace. We need to deal with messages that contaminate discovery and innovation in the workplace. This means having a team effort among the various arms of the human resource and business planning processes to ensure that workplace learning is delivered. Otherwise, the message of workplace learning will never be received." With that, Rene began the remainder of her session.

During the next few days of the conference, many people came up and privately thanked Rene for the whole session. The words that most stuck in Rene's mind were said on the last day of the conference. A total stranger came up to Rene and said, "I enjoyed your session yesterday. I loved your emperor's messenger's chariot story. I could use that in my organization, not just to explain how workplace learning is created but also to highlight the importance of teamwork and synergy in project management, strategic planning, and change management."

Rene knew at that instant that taking the risk and the time to deliver the message through the medium of accelerative learning had been worthwhile. This was because Rene's session had been four days ago and yet to the stranger the session seemed a more recent memory. Given that this person had been to at least ten other sessions since Rene's presentation, the comment was truly remarkable.

For Rene, no further proof was required. The field of accelerative learning had created a training miracle.

The Exciting Frontier of Accelerative Learning

People in many walks of life are constantly seeking original ways to learn more effectively. Currently, the field of accelerative learning is supplying many new answers to these challenges. Whether improving the capacity to learn or improving the ability to train, accelerative learning is helping people in all corners of the globe to be more confident about learning, expand their potential for change, and enhance their quality of life.

During the past decade, we have observed and heard some truly remarkable stories of people who have embraced and succeeded in applying accelerative learning. On a personal level, we have observed people of all ages and backgrounds become champions of their own discovery and growth through a better understanding of how and why they learn.

In saying this, we do recognize that achieving results from accelerative learning takes substantial practice and perseverance. From our experience, it is far healthier to view accelerative learning as a powerful stress-free technique that employs whole-brain thinking and multisensory presentation to assist people to learn more efficiently and to improve continuously. In fact, on many occasions, accelerative learning may not result in faster learning (that is, accelerated) but will result in people remembering more easily and for longer periods.

Unlocking the Key to the Subconscious Mind

Accelerative learning recognizes the power of the subconscious mind and uses this to supplement conscious thought. Much of the merit of accelerative learning comes from the recognition that much of what people learn is absorbed subconsciously. For example, do you remember a story or a cartoon or television series that you loved as a child? What was it and how does it make you feel? The associations, connections, and feelings that you are now recalling have been stored and generated by your subconscious mind.

Training often fails because the methods utilized are designed to influence conscious thought only. Figure 7.1 shows the comparative difference between conscious thought strategies and the vast power of the subconscious. The way to reach the subconscious is by employing some of the strategies shown in the lower half of this figure, such as harmony of form, color, rhythm, rhyme, and movement.

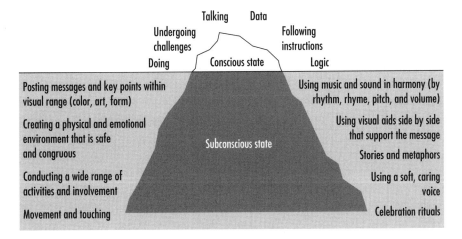

FIGURE 7.1. ACTIVATING SUBCONSCIOUS LEARNING

This activation of the subconscious was a very strong ingredient of Rene's visualization of the Roman chariot in the story "Delivering the Emperor's Message." Rene's methods included the following:

- Music and harmony—*Chariots of Fire* with pitch, vocal intonation, and rhythm;
- A visual—overhead transparency;
- Involvement—pair discussion;
- Breathing—to create a relaxed state; and
- Metaphor—to connect the feeling of the story to the message.

The implications of nurturing the subconscious become more and more important when one considers that information is processed by the subconscious mind prior to being received by the conscious one. If the subconscious mind rejects the data or is confused or dislikes the feeling of what is being shared, the capacity of the conscious mind to absorb new information, resolve challenges, or to undertake actions will be inhibited. The reason for this sequence is that the travel route to the subconscious mind is shorter. When a new thought, fact, or logic is being considered, the subconscious mind will consider, or possibly even filter, the information first.

Another issue suggested by Figure 7.1 is how the visual, auditory, and emotional anchors of the subconscious mind can dramatically affect the the learner's desire and receptivity. For example, if a learner is not feeling safe, he or she will most likely not tune in to what is being taught. By caring for the needs of the subconscious first, a trainer is more likely to create a mindset that is open to new learning.

Where Did It All Start?

Much of the origin of accelerative learning is attributed to the work in the 1960s of Professor Georgi Lozanov, an experienced psychiatrist and psychotherapist from Bulgaria. Lozanov taught foreign languages to both the conscious and subconscious minds using the power of positive suggestion. Lozanov called this science of suggestion "suggestopedia." A good modern-day example of suggestopedia is the powerful associations made on music videos and television commercials through strong visual images, emotive words, music, and rhythm. This is the reason we remember the words of a pop song or the logo or jingle of an advertisement with little conscious effort, yet struggle to remember a list of historical facts or dates.

Not surprisingly, Lozanov's language classes were taught by linking new material with music, the arts, motivational therapy, affirmation, breathing relaxation, vocal intonation, drama, role playing, and different speech patterns. It is claimed that students in Lozanov's foreign-language classes learned five times faster, with as much as 50 percent more retention, than those in comparable programs.

Since Lozanov's original work, the domain of accelerative learning has expanded worldwide with many different techniques and strategies. As a result, modern doctrines of accelerative learning have become increasingly more blurred, interconnected, and holistic in nature.

A to Z of Accelerative Learning

The following twenty-seven principles (see Figure 7.2) provide an overview of the building blocks of accelerative learning. Using the mnemonic of A to Z, including two contributions for the letter "M," a wide range of doctrine, ingredients, and strategy is discussed. For example, a person making a castle wall from building blocks can create countless designs and uses. Similarly, accelerative learning provides countless options and solutions to each training challenge. The only real limit is on our creativity.

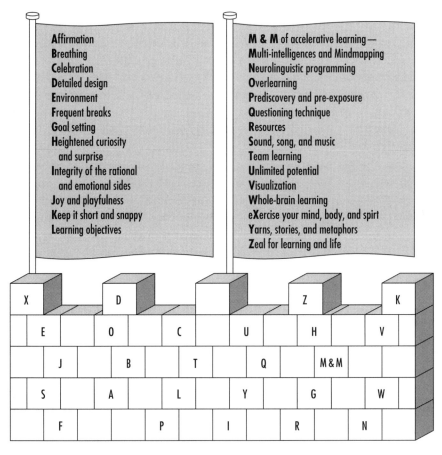

Affirmation
Breathing
Celebration
Detailed design
Environment
Frequent breaks
Goal setting
Heightened curiosity
  and surprise
Integrity of the rational
  and emotional sides
Joy and playfulness
Keep it short and snappy
Learning objectives

M & M of accelerative learning—
Multi-intelligences and Mindmapping
Neurolinguistic programming
Overlearning
Prediscovery and pre-exposure
Questioning technique
Resources
Sound, song, and music
Team learning
Unlimited potential
Visualization
Whole-brain learning
eXercise your mind, body, and spirt
Yarns, stories, and metaphors
Zeal for learning and life

FIGURE 7.2. A TO Z OF ACCELERATIVE LEARNING

Gaining Full Value Out of the A to Z Mnemonic

Before the twenty-seven building blocks are discussed, it is imperative that four important guidelines are understood.

Guideline Number 1

The twenty-seven fundamentals of accelerative learning are not all inclusive, hence the blank blocks in the castle wall in Figure 7.2. There are indeed many other doctrines, philosophies, and skills that could easily be included on top of those to be discussed. It is therefore essential that these principles be seen as only the start of your discovery, not the end. Accelerative learning should be seen as a rapidly growing and expanding field of possibilities and not as a set package. For example, in the case of the story "Delivering the Emperor's Message," Rene could have designed literally hundreds of different accelerative learning sessions that would have achieved the same learning objective. The guided visualization to the music of *Chariots of Fire* was only one of those options.

Guideline Number 2

When studying and applying each of the building blocks, be wary of becoming "hooked" on the techniques and fanfare of accelerative learning and neglecting the application. Remember that accelerative learning is about getting results for the learner. Before conducting or participating in any accelerative learning experience, take some time to reflect on the learning objectives and competencies being sought.

Guideline Number 3

The A to Z of accelerative learning has been written primarily for an audience of people training others. However, there is no field of human endeavor that could not benefit from the applications of these fundamentals—whether a person perfecting the art of swimming, a housekeeper speaking Chinese, a team leader coaching an employee, a trainer leading a strategic planning meeting, or a consultant writing a chapter for a book. As one of our most treasured colleagues, Glenn Capelli from the True Learning Centre, East Perth, says, "In its simplicity, accelerative learning is really about identifying true learning."

Guideline Number 4

Before designing accelerative learning, a trainer should recognize that high-leverage results take an extraordinary amount of time and effort to create. For example, for someone to prepare a three-and-a-half minute visualization, as described in "Delivering the Emperor's Message," it would not be uncommon for him or her to invest at least one full day to prepare, practice, and perfect the material.

Be sure to invest your and other people's time wisely. Start on the most important goals first. Then establish high-quality learning partnerships that support and consolidate your efforts. Be sensitive to building the confidence of the learner in using the techniques.

The result of your efforts will be that people who participate in your accelerative learning activities will remember material much longer than if they had learned through traditional lecturing methods.

Now let the A to Z begin!

A = Affirmation

Maintaining an optimum learning state requires constant reinforcement and subtle suggestion through the use of positive language, reassuring self-talk, and supportive feedback. Learning to speak positively and rephrase negative thoughts is a fundamental skill of accelerative learning.

As discussed in Chapter 6, trainers need to turn language around from expressions such as, "Let's now do a little activity" to positive expressions such as, "Let's now do a short and powerful activity."

The key to maintaining the momentum of the learning process is to create a "yes" mode in the learner. Learning occurs best when perceived barriers are identified, strategies are developed to confront and overcome them, and a positive suggestive state is maintained. This activity is particularly challenging when people bring preconceived notions or negative views of their learning potential into their learning experience. Positive affirmation ensures that learners have an opportunity to feel success and progress, thereby creating a positive self-image and positive beliefs. Given the power of the subconscious, this is best activated by emotive appeal rather than pure logic. This is illustrated in Table 7.1.

TABLE 7.1. WAYS OF STIMULATING A "YES" MODE

Learners to themselves	Write down and achieve goals; recall past learning experiences that the learner found very positive; see, hear, and feel progress.
Learner to learner	Design activities and rituals during which people share positive information and feedback with each other; encourage teamwork, mentoring, peer coaching, and recognition.
Learner to role models/ best practices	Talk, watch, or listen to the best. (This supplies the evidence that learning can achieve desired results.)
Learner to trainer	Ask people to demonstrate and contribute to the learning; have people show physically that they have learned (e.g., nodding their heads or putting their hands up to signal "yes").
Trainer to learner	Role model a commitment to the learner's welfare; demonstrate what is expected by exhibiting the competencies that are required of the learner.

B = Breathing

The most therapeutic and refreshing activity that can be promoted during a learning experience is relaxed deep breathing. The regular intake of oxygen aids clear thinking, feeds the brain, and reduces anxiety as well as providing an opportunity to relax and think creatively.

Accelerative learning is vitally linked to the capacity of a person to remain calm and focused. Quality breathing is the best medium for reaching this desired mental and physical state. It is a wonderful strategy in all situations. Whether for a professional basketball player shooting a three-point basket in overtime or a motorist fixing a fan belt in rush hour traffic, being centered and relaxed is essential.

Part of this demand for quality air is attributed to the complexity of the brain. It is estimated that the brain contains 100 billion neurons and the possible connections that these neurons can make are more than the known number of atoms in the entire universe. This places extraordinary demands on the brain; even though it comprises only 2 percent of the total body weight, it requires 20 percent of the oxygen intake.

With this in mind, one of the most important skills that a trainer can demonstrate and coach is the ability to relax using the full oxygen intake. Tai Chi and Yoga provide thousands of activities that increase people's circulation and energy capacity.

As displayed in Figure 7.3, another such activity is teaching people the importance of breathing from the stomach area. This activity can be simply introduced into any learning process and is ideal for settling the nerves of both the learner and the trainer. It can be done safely either in a standing or sitting position.

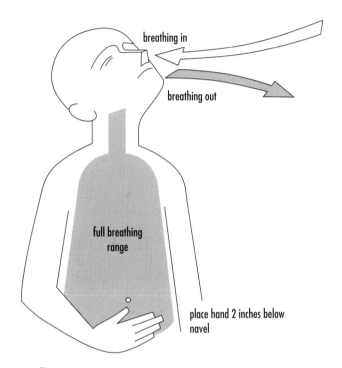

FIGURE 7.3. STOMACH BREATHING

Stomach breathing involves eight steps.

1. Sit or stand up straight and raise the chin so that there is a good airway.
2. Place the palm of one of your hands on your stomach approximately two inches below the navel.
3. Breathe normally (i.e., in through the nose and out through the mouth).
4. Slow down the rate of breathing and lengthen the time it takes to exhale. Focus on peaceful and deep breaths.

5. Observe or feel the rise and fall of your stomach area (close your eyes if this helps).
6. Listen to the whistle of the air as it enters and leaves your body.
7. Feel the stomach rise and fall at least ten times.
8. Practice regularly, anywhere, at any time.

In addition to self-maintenance, the quality and pattern of breathing provides one of the best signals to the trainer of the quality and impact of the learning. If, for example, a learner quickly changes his or her breathing to shorter and higher patterns, it is quite likely that the person is becoming stressed or that there is a lack of permission for what is being said or performed. When this occurs, the trainer needs to review the current situation, context, or approach and make some change so that the learner is breathing normally as quickly as possible. This can be done in a number of ways, including asking people to take a different body position, clarifying a person's view on the matter being discussed, leading an energizer, or simply taking a deep breath ourselves, thereby promoting the same response in others.

C = Celebration

One of the easiest fundamentals to apply in accelerative learning is to encourage celebration. There are essentially two ways to celebrate: the first is orchestrated and the second is spontaneous.

Orchestrated Celebration

A trainer can include rituals in which people either share their discoveries or reward themselves or others for reaching a milestone within any program. To be useful, these orchestrated celebrations should be exciting and inspirational and should clearly profile what has been assimilated. The importance of these rituals should not be underestimated; they engage the conscious awareness of achievements, but also anchor the subconscious feelings of well-being. Carefully planned, they can be a major asset to the accelerative learning process.

Warming people up to celebration is very important and should begin as early as possible in the training process. Remember that celebration is often neglected in workplaces and on training courses and will be new to a lot of learners. It does take time for people to be able to celebrate unconditionally. So it is important to begin the norm of celebration as early as possible in the learning process.

Celebration rituals can vary from simple sharing of learning results to more innovative and fun examples like the following:

- team presentations, demonstrations, and dramatization;
- course newsletters;
- award ceremonies;
- plays, puppet shows, poems, or songs based on the themes of the learning;
- quizzes based on the rules of a sport (e.g., soccer test or baseball match) or television shows (e.g., "Wheel of Fortune" or "Jeopardy");
- art shows;
- video production;
- group and individual presentations; and
- closing dinner parties.

Spontaneous Celebration

As the name suggests, spontaneous celebration occurs in the spirit of the moment. It could be a learner sharing an experience or people being allowed to think and talk about their learning successes. For this to occur, both the trainer and the learner need to create and build a climate in which support and acknowledgment are the norm rather than the exception. For example, if an employee comes up with an idea to improve workplace performance during a training session, he or she should be encouraged to share this idea immediately and then be praised for effort and initiative.

D = Detailed Design

Even though the field of accelerative learning has seen much change over the past forty years, going far outside the domain of Lozanov's original suggestopedia framework, there still remain a number of fundamentals that seem to be consistently followed by trainers who demonstrate accelerative learning. Much of this commonality of approach has arisen through a better understanding and acceptance of the way in which people learn.

Accelerative learning normally comprises excellent structure in three key areas: (1) preparing the learner, (2) presentation, and (3) application of learning. The ingredients of each of the three areas follow:

1. Preparing the Learner

- Welcome people to a safe and supportive learning space.
- Set up a training space with peripherals (relevant visual aids, equipment), warming music, and greetings for the learner.
- Provide positive suggestions and clear learner benefits for the upcoming process.
- Establish curiosity and interest for the upcoming process.
- Describe the big picture and structure of the program.
- Prepare the learners by relaxing them and asking them to put aside all outside distractions. (A breathing exercise might help to do this.)
- Establish clear ground rules.
- Seek the learners' permission to ensure that they wish to fully participate in the process.
- Clarify logistical and administrative requirements.

2. Presentation

- Present the material in small, digestible chunks.
- Link the material to real-life examples and past learnings.
- Dynamically present information using multisensory delivery.
- Encourage and coach people to become resourceful and self-directed in their learning.
- Create a low-stress and high-challenge environment in which success can be gained if efforts are invested. This could be called generating calm stimulation or peaceful excitement.
- Tell stories and give information in harmony with appropriate music that both energizes and stimulates curiosity.
- Present new information in harmony with music that relaxes people for effective learning.
- Use an array of learning methods to communicate your messages to the learners' brains. Seek to make as many connections as possible on the key points.

3. Application of Learning

- Conduct celebration rituals that affirm new competencies in the ways discussed earlier.
- Correct mistakes and highlight progress immediately in a supportive way by thanking learners for their efforts and then asking them how they feel they could improve further in the future.
- Provide a number of choices for how people can undertake practice and review.

- Allow flexibility and choice in the pacing, delivery, and assessment of the material.
- Consider how resources such as availability of coaches and reference manuals could be used to support learning on the job.

E = Environment

The emotional and physical environment is a major contributor to promoting learning at both the conscious and subconscious level.

A number of *emotional* considerations have already been discussed. These include establishing a rapport and making people welcome, creating a "yes" mode, managing a low-stress and relaxed state, encouraging learner empowerment, and carefully choosing vocabulary and body language.

In the *physical* environment, the following elements support better learning:

- good air flow and plenty of natural light;
- a non-smoking environment;
- portable and comfortable furniture;
- carpeted rooms (and accompanying improved acoustics);
- a wide collection of music for different moods;
- a number of positive statements and posters on the walls at varying heights;
- a division of the room into different locations: for example, a discussion area, a learning resources corner, relaxing space with coffee table books;
- fresh clean water and high-protein nibbling food on the table;
- puzzles and board games; and
- an aromatherapy burner (essential oils in a vaporizer—rosemary, lemon, and basil to promote alertness; lavender, juniper, and sandalwood for calming; eucalyptus, sage, and peppermint for energy).

F = Frequent Breaks

Learning is not an endurance event! Scheduling regular breaks aids recall and resilience. Rose (1985) and Jensen (1994) both suggest that a five-minute break every thirty minutes is probably optimum. This five minutes means a complete break from the topic at hand. As discussed in Chapter 5, depending on the mood and energy level of the learners, it may also be appropriate to conduct an energizer to stimulate receptivity to the next phase of the learning. The best energizers in this scenario would normally involve a combination of novelty, teamwork, involvement, body stretching, and/or deep breathing.

Frequent breaks also give learners a few minutes to deal with issues or needs that may be interfering with the current learning patterns. For example, some learners may need a few moments to make a note of key points arising from previous material. However, if this is happening regularly, it may indicate that the trainer needs to allow more time during the normal session for summarizing the material.

The impact of breaks can be assisted by the following:

- providing spring water, fresh fruit, nuts, raisins, and other dried fruit, low fat cheeses, and/or herbal teas or decaffeinated beverages in a special location away from the training area;
- playing cheerful, bouncy, high-energy music;
- placing a cartoon on the overhead projector for reflection or running a short video energizer (these are commonly available by training video distributors); or
- having an outside area for stretching and getting some sunlight and fresh air.

If lunch is being provided, opt for a light lunch with plenty of protein rather than carbohydrates such as a heavy pasta. Protein meals include fish (tuna and salmon), lean meat, chicken, and lentil burgers. People should be encouraged to have a walk around for at least ten minutes after the meal. After the break has elapsed, welcome people back on time with a "thank you" gesture such as a group stretch, playing some welcoming theme music, or just a simple smile and a "thank you."

Frequent breaks and lots of variation are the keys to maintaining interest and energy. Skillful management of breaks can add vitality to any program and can result in better outcomes.

G = Goal Setting

The commitment to realistic, challenging, and measurable goals is an integral part of personal growth. Goal setting requires the skills of adaptability, coping with ambiguity, and having a clear focus of one's personal mission and dreams. Learners can be held accountable, either individually or collectively in teams, for achieving and demonstrating progress toward their outcomes.

There are a number of ways in which a goal-setting process can be improved. First of all, ensure that adequate time is given to people at the beginning of the program to set their goals. Second, supply time, resources, and coaching on setting goals and reviewing progress. Third, coach people to feel that they own their goals already and that all they need to do is to remain calm, focused, and committed to their learning to achieve their aims. Finally, highlight the point that goals are not carved in stone; they can be changed.

People need to concede that the goal itself is only the secondary benefit of setting aims and outcomes. What is most important is that people learn new skills and expand their capabilities as a result of pursuing the goal.

Helping People to Set Goals

The following questions can help individuals set learning goals. These can also be easily adapted for teams.

- Why is this goal important to me?
- What's in it for me?
- How will I feel when I reach my goal?
- How will I go about reaching my goal?
- What resources can I call on to help me achieve my goal?
- What can I do in the next week to start toward my goal?
- What is my timetable?
- What are my milestones?
- How will I celebrate progress?
- Who else will directly benefit when I achieve this goal?
- Who else wants me to achieve this goal?

H = Heightened Curiosity and Surprise

The unpredictable, the novel, and the different should be encouraged during an accelerative learning experience. Creating anticipation stimulates the learner's receptivity. Whether this be by painting a picture of an upcoming learning event with a personalized letter of introduction or by rearranging the office furniture for a positive coaching session, regular attempts need to be made to encourage ongoing receptivity in a low-stress environment.

Examples of additional ways of stimulating interest include the following:

- Make connections between past, current, and future activities and relate them to learning objectives and benefits.
- Let the learner have a taste of what is going to happen (i.e., talk about it, demonstrate it, read a story, or show a brief video).
- Quote testimonials from others who have done the training.
- "Plant the seed" regarding upcoming activities (e.g., "On Thursday, you will get a chance to operate a 'lunar module' during the outdoor learning segment.")
- Create a theme for the day. For example, on day three of a five-day program, you could ask people to wear their loudest shirts or blouses to the program.
- Say to people, "Remind me at one minute past ten and I will tell you about. . . . " It is amazing how much anticipation and fun this simple strategy can create while also helping you with your time management. Reward the person or persons who remind you.

EXERCISE 7.1. STIMULATING INTEREST AND CURIOSITY

How might you raise interest and curiosity for:

- a session right after a lunch break?
- an upcoming presenter?
- a session that is perceived as dull?
- a recall session?

I = Integrity of the Rational and Emotional Sides

Valuing the importance of both the linear (rational) and the nonlinear (emotional) sides of the human spirit is integral to the success of accelerative learning.

Accelerative learning should provide a holistic approach to change and personal growth by actively supporting positive affirmation, promoting celebration, and allowing the free expression of feelings and thought.

Real learning can begin when learners are able to express their aspirations, fears, and successes without feeling embarrassed or patronized. Furthermore, the expression of these feelings must be acknowledged openly as a legitimate, natural, and essential part of personal growth. It is only when people positively question and review their beliefs that there will be a genuine opportunity for change.

As will be discussed in "W = Whole-Brain Learning," trainers need to accept that people have natural preferences in the way they learn and express themselves. It is therefore essential that no learning style or method be seen as superior to any other.

J = Joy and Playfulness

A special characteristic of an accelerative learning experience is that it must be enjoyable. Stress should be reduced by conducting activities that are safe and challenging. The trainer needs to instill confidence and self-esteem by reinforcing key principles and by giving learners plenty of opportunity to apply or remember what has been taught. The best learning environment is one in which people are encouraged to experiment, to take risks, and to make mistakes in order to discover and progress. Whether the activity is conducting an outdoor learning experience, solving a puzzle, reading new content to music, creating a poem of the day, doing a case study, or developing a checklist, it all should be done in a supportive and collaborative way.

One of the great opportunities in learning is to allow "the child within" to express itself. Adults can improve their learning potential by letting go of the code of conduct that dictates how and what they learn and by looking for the fun and enjoyment in learning. If the word "fun" creates an image of children playing, maybe the adult needs to replace that image with one of people looking for the practical, the rewarding, and the entertaining. An awareness of the beauty and energy of learning needs to be discussed and experienced.

K = Keep It Short and Snappy

Scheduling short, powerful sessions is a key rule of accelerative learning. Breaking well-designed material into short and snappy chunks will aid effective recall. Having more beginnings and endings enables the trainer to incorporate greater versatility into the training, while allowing the learner a chance to reflect on past learning before the next chunk of material is presented.

It is common for some trainers to conduct fifteen-minute sessions with breaks in between, particularly when complex new material is involved. Remember that the goal of accelerative learning is efficiency and that this is significantly aided by having the material broken into small digestible parts.

L = Learning Objectives

Accelerative learning, like all training, should be about achieving desired learning and not about providing a show or performance of training techniques.

Whether the outcome is knowledge, a skill, or an attitude, people must have the confidence that the training is helping them achieve the competency they require. The ultimate long-term measure of the success of accelerative learning in the workplace will be the improvement of business performance as a consequence of the training.

To help learners successfully achieve learning objectives, a trainer must be aware of the relevant past experiences and competency of each learner. If a person already has the competency required, he or she should not be forced to participate in the accelerative learning experience. In this regard, it is imperative that each learner be given a choice of what to do. Choices include leaving the course or remaining and making oneself available as a mentor, coach, learning resource, or as an observer of a planned activity. Alternatively, the person may choose to undertake some other self-directed activity that enhances competency in a similar or different area.

When preparing the accelerative learning material, the trainer or instructional designer needs to be actively involved with the client or learner in the identification, production, and assessment of learning outcomes.

For further information on competency-based training and the management of self-directed learning, see Chapters 3 and 4 respectively.

M&M of Accelerative Learning: Multi-intelligences and Mind-mapping

As with a packet of M&Ms®, accelerative learning provides a wide range of colors and options from which to draw. Two of these options are (1) understanding and embracing multi-intelligences and (2) using mind-mapping to assist recall.

M = Multi-intelligences

Pathfinding work in *Frames of Mind* by Professor Howard Gardner (1985) expanded contemporary thinking and paradigms about human intelligence. This work and the subsequent publications *Seven Ways of Knowing* (1991) and *Seven Pathways of Learning* (1994) by David Lazear have provided trainers with a number of important tools and considerations when undertaking accelerative learning. Gardner (1985) defines intelligence as "the ability to solve problems and fashion products that are of consequence in a particular cultural setting." Gardner goes on to say, "Problems range from creating an end to a story, anticipating a chess move, to repairing a quilt. Fashioning products ranges from developing specific theories, musical compositions, to organizing a successful political campaign."

David Lazear (1991) states that Gardner's research has "blown the lid off" the previous views of intelligence. Four findings support this view: (1) human intelligence is more multifaceted and broader than was generally accepted in the past; (2) learners have the ability to enhance and amplify intelligence; (3) people can change their intelligence; and (4) intelligence can be taught.

The implications of these findings for creating training miracles are immense. When people begin to understand that they are multi-intelligent and unique, it provides the learning process with almost limitless potential. If, for example, a learner is struggling to recall or apply an idea, the concept of multi-intelligence can provide a framework to expand the discovery options for that person.

With this in mind, trainers need to service and adapt to at least seven areas of multi-intelligence when designing, delivering, and assessing learning. The application of these findings is potentially transformational, particularly when trainers are allowed to consider and use the full range of learning options available to them.

Gardner's seven areas of multi-intelligence can be best remembered by using the memory aid of "SLIMBIL." Take a minute to read "The Story of SLIMBIL" in Box 7.1.

Box 7.1

The Story of SLIMBIL

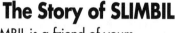

SLIMBIL is a friend of yours.

SLIMBIL is a multi-intelligent individual who loves to learn and understand reality.

You have already met SLIMBIL in many places including at work, at school, on holidays, in the parking lot, and at the movies. You even came face-to-face the last time you looked in the mirror. In fact, you meet, or you are with, SLIMBIL wherever you might go.

SLIMBIL is also very clever. SLIMBIL can repair cars, fly a kite, make chocolate mousse, complete tax returns, perfect your favorite cocktail, and develop a checklist for superior customer service. With so many diverse abilities, you might say SLIMBIL is not just intelligent but multi-intelligent.

Actually, to be truthful, SLIMBIL exists in all of us. SLIMBIL is not just one person; SLIMBIL is part of the make-up of every human being.

So, as a trainer and learner, make sure that you marvel at the unique strengths and capacities of each SLIMBIL you meet. Learn to support each SLIMBIL as a beautiful, unique, and multi-intelligent learner. Remember that SLIMBILs are more than just intelligent, they are multi-intelligent.

Even though SLIMBIL's name is a symbolic way of remembering seven areas of multi-intelligence, it is suggested that SLIMBIL may offer many other talents yet to be recognized. In addition to being spacial/visual, linguistic, intrapersonal, musical, bodily kinesthetic, interpersonal, and logical/mathematical, SLIMBIL is also known to be very positive, intuitive, and spiritual. This is evidenced by SLIMBIL's being able to relax while also having a wonderful sense of inner strength and peace.

But for now the name of SLIMBIL will have to do.

Source: Adapted from a presentation by Mark Reardon Learning Forum/Supercamp at the International Alliance for Learning Conference, Boston, Massachusetts, April 1993. Reproduced with permission.

The Seven Areas of Multi-intelligence in SLIMBIL

Taking SLIMBIL as a central character in our understanding of multi-intelligence, we will now explore seven dimensions of intelligence.

S STANDS FOR SPATIAL/VISUAL

Spatial/visual intelligence is related to the sense of sight and the ability to form images and pictures in the mind. A person with a high "S" intelligence can use the following techniques, which play to his or her strengths, to learn:

- Create a mind map
- Make a diagram, chart or illustration
- Create a mental video documentary
- Color, highlight, underline
- Look for the big picture
- Create interactive imagery
- Take photographs or make films or posters
- List key elements
- Paint, draw, and sculpt
- Navigate and find his or her way
- Visualize outcomes, objects, and actions from different viewpoints

L STANDS FOR LINGUISTIC/VERBAL

Linguistic/verbal intelligence is an ability to explore different ways of expressing language and is stimulated by the spoken word. A person with a high "L" intelligence can use the following techniques, which play to his or her strengths, to learn:

- Read a story or case study and develop a sequel
- Listen to a story or poem and discuss it
- Learn the meaning of a new word each day and practice using it
- Make a speech on a topic about which he or she has a great deal of interest and excitement
- Keep a journal and write reflections about events from the day
- Create a script or play
- Question what is being said
- Write on a memory map
- Use humor
- Articulate thoughts on an issue
- Create a mnemonic
- Verbalize in his or her head

I STANDS FOR INTRAPERSONAL

Intrapersonal intelligence involves an excellent understanding of self. A person with a high "I" intelligence can use the following techniques, which play to his or her strengths, to learn:

- Detail preferences for thinking and feeling
- Step back from a situation and examine himself or herself as a third person
- Experience and apply holistic approaches to life
- Describe a sense of mission or purpose for actions
- Concentrate
- Use language, music, art, dance, symbols, and interpersonal communication to express inner and private thoughts
- Create own learning plan and sequence
- Write down what is already known
- Investigate a subject and then decide on the significance of it for him or her
- Seek feedback or analyze work methods
- Take control of his or her learning
- Commit to stretching his or her abilities and reaching higher levels of self-awareness

M STANDS FOR MUSICAL/AUDITORY

Musical/auditory intelligence includes such capacities as the recognition and use of rhythmic and tonal patterns and sensitivity to sounds from the environment, the human voice, and musical instruments. A person with a high "M" intelligence can use the following techniques, which play to his or her strengths, to learn:

- Write a song or jingle
- Use background music for study or a presentation
- Use music to stimulate or relax as desired
- Be sensitive to different sound frequencies
- Maintain a rhythm when working
- Use tone to change emotional states

B STANDS FOR BODILY KINESTHETIC

Bodily kinesthetic intelligence is the ability to use the body to express emotion, to play a game, or to create. A person with a high "B" intelligence can use the following techniques, which play to his or her strengths, to learn:

- Demonstrate and practice
- Show what he or she knows
- Act out/role play
- Make a model or conduct an experiment
- Walk around and discuss the problem
- Be in tune with the body performance
- Integrate mind and body
- Develop excellent motor coordination

I STANDS FOR INTERPERSONAL

Interpersonal intelligence involves the ability to work cooperatively in a group as well as being able to communicate verbally and nonverbally with other people. A person with a high "I" intelligence can use the following techniques, which play to his or her strengths, to learn:

- Work/revise/discuss with a partner
- Plan how to teach to someone else
- Seek joint outcomes and resolve conflict
- Learn from case histories
- Communicate both verbally and nonverbally
- Empathize with diversity of values, feelings, fears, anticipations, and beliefs
- Participate in team discussion
- Notice moods, temperament, motivations, and intentions

L STANDS FOR LOGICAL/MATHEMATICAL

Logical/mathematical intelligence has been traditionally acknowledged as a major intelligence in education. Learning methods are often associated with what we call "scientific" or "logical" thinking. A person with a high "L" intelligence can use the following techniques, which play to his or her strengths, to learn:

- Define by listing in a logical sequence
- Look for a pattern or concept
- Analyze into parts, step-by-step
- Create a system to solve a problem;
- Compare, contrast, measure
- Create a flow chart
- Build up a case history
- Conduct an experiment

- Make objective observations and, from the observed data, draw conclusions, make judgments, and formulate hypotheses
- Observe and understand details as part of a general pattern
- Recognize patterns to work with abstract symbols such as numbers and geometric shapes

EXERCISE 7.2. APPLYING MULTI-INTELLIGENCES

Select a short topic (no more than a one-hour presentation) that you have traditionally found difficult to train or coach in an interesting and exciting way.

Topic _____

Given the need to address multi-intelligence, which activities could you include for each of the seven intelligences?

S

L

I

M

B

I

L

How would you structure them into your material?

Time	Key Point	SLIMBIL Category	Aid/Equipment

Using the questions raised in Exercise 7.2, the following lesson plan was developed for a fifty-minute presentation on overcoming career burnout.

The client was a large power company located in a major capital city. The audience was made up of predominantly blue-collar employees in the 40–55 age group.

TABLE 7.2. LESSON PLAN FOR OVERCOMING CAREER BURNOUT

Time	Key Point	SLIMBIL Category	Aid/Equipment
0–2	What is career burnout?	Group discussion (Interpersonal, Linguistic)	Whiteboard
2–4	Group mime: Take up the body position of a person who is in burnout. How does that feel?	Bodily kinesthetic	
4–6	Group mime: Take up the body position of a person who has overcome burnout. How does that feel?	Bodily kinesthetic	
6–8	Define career burnout.	Read notes (Visual, Linguistic)	Course notes
8–14	Write down when you believe that you have been burned out.	Self-analysis (Intrapersonal)	Course notes
14–20	Highlight the seven ways to overcome burnout (draw icons from Exercise 12.3).	Mind Map (Visual)	Flip chart, paper, colored pens
20–25	Ask each learner to list a range of thirty-minute activities that he or she could do in each of the seven categories shown on his or her mind map.	Visual, Intrapersonal	Course notes
25–30	Group sharing.	Discussion	
30–38	Describe your one-month vision for better managing career burnout. Complete one of the following seven activities to explain how you would best describe yourself in one month's time.	Interpersonal	
	1. Draw what you will be doing more of.	Spacial/Visual	
	2. Describe in fewer than twenty words what you will be doing more of.	Linguistic	

TABLE 7.2. (*continued*)

Time	Key Point	SLIMBIL Category	Aid/Equipment
	3. Take a deep breath and then consider the impact that managing burnout will have on your life.	Intrapersonal	
	4. (a) Describe music and sounds you will hear more of. (b) Describe the songs you will sing or hum to more.	Musical	
	5. While stretching, consider what you will be doing more of. How will you walk when you have successfully managed burnout?	Bodily kinesthetic	
	6. Talk and listen to one other person about his or her vision in overcoming or managing career burnout.	Interpersonal	
	7. Allocate a total of 100 points for all of the activities you wish to undertake to overcome burnout. For example, you might distribute your 100 points among nine practical ideas. A score of 30 points for one activity would indicate a higher desire to use this option compared to another activity to which you only assigned 10 points. This would then leave 60 points to be allocated to your remaining ideas.	Logical/Mathematical	
38–45	List a five-point action plan for the next month.	Logical/Mathematical	Course notes
45–50	Open forum.	Discussion (Interpersonal)	

M = Mind-mapping

Mind-mapping is a mighty and robust tool that assists learners to access and recall information more effectively. The popularity of mind-mapping has increased dramatically in recent times with people from many walks of life exploring applications such as note taking, decision making, and project management. Whatever the application, creating mind maps is much more than just an accelerative learning tool, it is a productivity tool.

What Is Mind-mapping?

Mind-mapping can be defined as a "whole brain" method for taking notes, planning, and brainstorming. It is whole brain because it connects the right and left sides of the brain in the processing and storage of information. People who use mind-mapping quickly find out that it can significantly improve the recall of information and stimulate creativity and comprehension of thoughts and feelings. It also saves time because less time is used to recall and access information.

For people to reap the full benefits of mind-mapping, they should express their own creativity. For example, if a number of students are using mind-mapping to summarize a lecture, it would be common to see each person produce his or her own unique mind map.

Mind maps need not be produced only on notepaper. They can be created just as easily on different media including flip-chart paper, whiteboards, and computers.

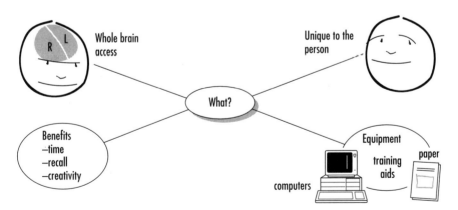

FIGURE 7.4. MIND MAP OF "WHAT IS MIND-MAPPING?"

Why Does It Work?

The benefits of mind maps are not surprising given that they integrate the rational, logical, linear left brain with the playful, spacial, nonverbal, and big picture right brain. As a consequence, mind-mapping encourages greater flexibility, enjoyment, and spontaneity than would be possible using traditional left-brain methods such as taking notes on lined paper in a single-color pen.

Many people may see mind-mapping as nothing more than doodling, but, in fact, when it is employed effectively and confidence grows with the technique, mind-mapping provides an expansive, exciting tool for many situations. For example, project planning by mind-mapping could connect ideas about what is to be done, how it will be done, why it is important, who should be involved, when the key milestones are, where the activities will be undertaken, and what the resource considerations are.

In addition, mind maps could be used to explore the hierarchy of thinking related to building and connecting ideas, creating "to do" lists, collecting and grouping ideas prior to writing or speaking, weighing the pros and cons of an idea, networking via electronic mail, or as a visual or memory aid.

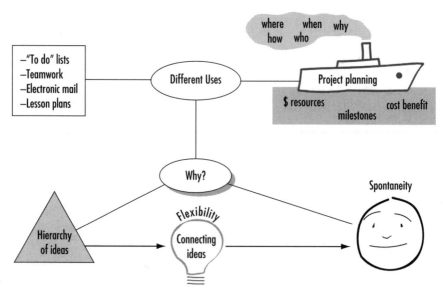

FIGURE 7.5. MIND MAP OF "WHY" DISCUSSION

How to Draw a Mind Map

As discussed, there is no set way to draw a mind map. The shape and characteristics of it will be determined by the learning style of the people involved, the time available, and the topic in question. For example, some people love highly colorful and pictorial mind maps while others find connecting vocabulary with an occasional symbol is sufficient for effective recall and application.

A guiding principle, however, is to start with a rough sketch of the blanket structure for the issue under consideration and then to let your creativity run wild. After you have developed a sense of the material to be explored, redraw the mind map.

Allow yourself the luxury of being bizarre and unusual. Remember, it is not a drawing competition. It is about you being able to process and remember effectively.

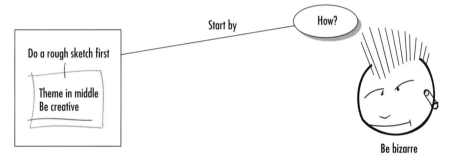

FIGURE 7.6. MIND MAP OF "HOW" TO START

The hows of mind-mapping can be described under the headings of writing style and layout.

Writing style. The way words can be used on a mind map can vary. Options include adjusting the size, using abbreviations, and employing 3-D images.

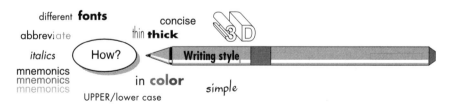

FIGURE 7.7. MIND MAP OF "HOW" TO VARY WRITING STYLE

Layout. Many authors and trainers in accelerative learning suggest that a mind map should start with a large bold theme in the center of the writing or computer surface. From there, a wide range of thoughts and feelings can be expressed in a number of ways.

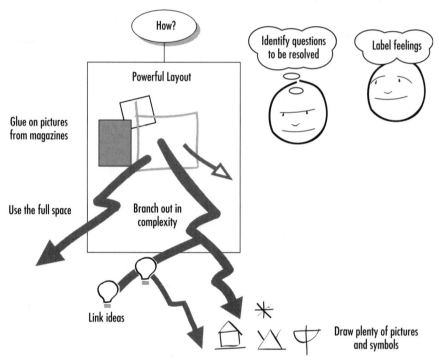

FIGURE 7.8. MIND MAP OF "HOW" TO USE LAYOUT POWERFULLY

What If You Feel Uncomfortable?

As with most new or different methods, it takes time and practice to develop confidence mind-mapping. Much of the resistance to doing mind maps comes from past experiences that we may have had at school or at home where drawing and doodling were often seen as undesirable. To benefit from mind-mapping, both the trainer and the learner must be prepared to lead from the front. As with driving a car, unless you are prepared to release the emergency brake and put the car into first gear, you will never travel anywhere.

We suggest that everyone have with them as permanent companions a notebook and some colored markers. Alternatively, a laptop computer, crayons, or different grades of lead pencil could suffice.

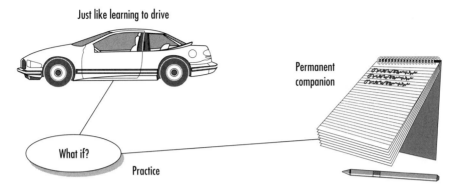

FIGURE 7.9. MIND MAP OF "WHAT IF" DISCUSSION

A full mind map of what has just been discussed is shown in Figure 7.10.

N = Neurolinguistic Programming

As discussed in Chapter 6, neurolinguistic programming provides an excellent communication framework in which to create training miracles. A trainer who has insights into NLP will have an enormous repertoire of principles and skills that will positively influence his or her capacity in accelerative learning. Skills may be in such areas as anchoring, congruency, and matching delivery methods to people's modality preferences.

In addition to the determination of an individual's modality and submodality preferences, NLP can give trainers vivid information about how their communication may be received, stored, and output by learners. For example, a trainer who is demonstrating a preference for visual, auditory, or kinesthetic modality could be observed in one of the following ways:

Visual

A visual trainer will work in a neat and color-coordinated training room that is well-organized. Materials will be stacked or shelved by size, color, or some similar ordering system denoted by the look of the material. Boards are visually pleasing, and the use of color is a definite feature. The trainer will have a preference for displaying information visually. The trainer is usually neat, tidy, and color-coordinated as well; for him or her, appearance is a priority.

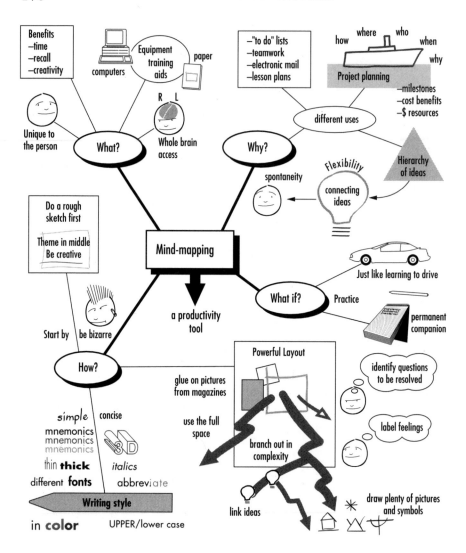

FIGURE 7.10. MIND MAP

Auditory

An auditory trainer uses group discussion and dialogue methods more often than other trainers. Music is commonly used. People with dominant auditory preferences tend to repeat things that others have just said to them. They usually dress in harmony with the attire of others.

Kinesthetic

Kinesthetic trainers work in training rooms that appear very busy and hands-on. They love to display participants' work, and you'll find examples posted on the walls and on the desks. The trainers themselves have a comfortable appearance and dress according to how they feel.

EXERCISE 7.3. EXPLORING TRAINERS' STYLES

1. List the names of past or current trainers who you believe are good examples of dominance in each of the following categories:
   - Visual
   - Auditory
   - Kinesthetic
2. How would you sum up your style in the visual, auditory, and kinesthetic ranges?

To fully reap the benefit of modality for accelerative learning it is important to understand that people quite commonly receive, store, and output information with a different mix of modality patterns. For example, an individual may input with a major preference for auditory, then store information with visual, auditory, and kinesthetic preference. When requested to output during some form of assessment, this person may prefer to use a combination of auditory and kinesthetic.

As a trainer, it is therefore important to recognize the idiosyncrasies of modalities. To be successful in applying the concept of modality, trainers need to adapt their training styles and assessment methods to engage a full array of modality and submodality preferences. Sticking to one style of communicating may suit some learners but will certainly be incompatible with others.

O = Overlearning

Quality learning is all about practice and application. To be successful, there must be numerous and varied ways to revise and assess progress. Common overlearning methods include team quizzes, peer revision of visual aids, team mind maps, and learning contracts.

Trainers should always identify the major themes for each of their training programs and ensure that the key messages are being learned in a multitude of ways. In one three-day program on leadership, seventeen different training methods were used to reinforce a major theme of trust and trustworthiness. These training methods included a lecture, a trust walk, visual aids with relevant affirmations, group discussion, role plays, a case study, a video, a team learning exercise in which learners created a checklist on how to develop trust, visualization, a self-awareness activity using questionnaire feedback, reading articles, reading a poem on trust, trust falls, a team quiz, telling stories on trust, developing an action plan for increasing trust back on the job, and singing a song about trust. All of these techniques served to build a foundation for overlearning that strengthened the level of trust and trustworthiness in the group.

In his book entitled *Accelerated Learning,* Rose (1985) recommends the following six-step process to support recall of facts or skills and overlearning:

Step 1. Immediate rehearsal of new facts or skills within the short-term memory span. Include review and feedback processes with activity.
Step 2. Review after 10 minutes. (5-minute review)
Step 3. Review after one day. (5-minute review)
Step 4. Review after one week. (3-minute review)
Step 5. Review after one month. (3-minute review)
Step 6. Review after six months. (3-minute review)

Rose claims that this schedule can dramatically improve recall. For example, four reviews can increase the percentage of material remembered to 88 percent.

EXERCISE 7.4. THE A TO O OF ACCELERATIVE LEARNING

Let's apply the principle of overlearning and see if you can remember the A to O of accelerative learning already discussed in this chapter.

Close this book and on a blank piece of paper recall as best you can the A to O of accelerative learning.

Exercise 7.10 contains a further learning sheet on the A to Z of accelerative learning.

P = Prediscovery and Pre-exposure

Prediscovery and pre-exposure are increasingly being seen as essential components of accelerative learning. The less familiar people are with the content of what is to be learned, the greater the need to instill familiarity or excitement or to condition them to the upcoming experience.

Prediscovery

Prediscovery is commonly called prework. During this phase, the learner undertakes activities such as reading, answering questions on a case study, rehearsing entry-level competencies, taking a self-scored quiz, listing learning needs, and selecting some "work in progress" to bring to the training.

Asking people to undertake prediscovery activities has a number of benefits, including the following:

- Establishing a common base for the program;
- Preparing the learner for what will be expected;
- Securing a benchmark to assess improvements in learning;
- Saving time during the training;
- Obtaining evidence of commitment and raising the energy of the learner toward the program; and
- Sending out a clear signal that the trainer and the learner are serious about the learning experience.

Pre-exposure

Pre-exposure sets the scene and engenders enthusiasm for the upcoming program. Skillfully managed and packaged tactics such as personalized welcoming and congratulation letters, direct contact by phone, meetings beforehand with the trainer, and involvement of the learner in the design, delivery, and evaluation strategies can add significant interest and energy to the learning experience.

Q = Questioning Techniques

The art of asking questions is the cornerstone of accelerative learning and of creating training miracles in general. It is the ability to ask and answer quality questions that will dictate the impact of a learning experience.

Good questioning skills include the ability to:

- probe learners for their needs;
- access experience or expertise;

- leave the space open for people to think further on a question or challenge;
- expand horizons and encourage confidence and creativity; and
- use silence and change of pace to promote thinking and expression of feeling.

Let Your Fingers Do the Talking

A very popular and powerful questioning technique used to help break through the language barrier was developed by Bandler and Grinder (1979) and then by Laborde (1983). This method provides a decisive way to determine people's real needs or intentions when they communicate. Think of the last time you felt you understood what someone had said only to find out later that you were each thinking along different wavelengths. This method provides a strategy to surmount the "fluff" that often occurs when people miscommunicate.

The method employs both of your hands as learning aids. As shown in Figure 7.11, your right hand is known as the "recognition" hand and your left hand as the "response" or "fluff-busting" hand. When these two are joined together, you have a ready-made tool to recognize, and deal with, possible miscommunication. In this way, a person can use his or her hands as a "decoder" for statements that may be unclear or unspecific. That is, he or she may recognize the symptoms of fluff on the one hand (right) and respond by fluff-busting with the other hand (left). Table 7.3 further explains the relationship between recognition and response.

Each digit of the right hand recognizes a particular type of phrase or word and responds by asking a key question stored by the corresponding finger on the left hand.

TABLE 7.3. HOW THE FINGERS ON EACH HAND EITHER RECOGNIZE OR RESPOND

	Recognition	Response
Thumbs	Too much, Too many	Compared with what?
Index fingers	Noun—person/place	Who or what specifically?
Second fingers	Verb	How, specifically?
Third fingers	Should/Shouldn't	What would happen if you did?
	Must/Mustn't	What will cause or prevent this?
	Can/Can't	
Fourth fingers	Absolutes or generalizations	Always? Are you sure?
	Always, Never, Everybody	Never? Are you sure?

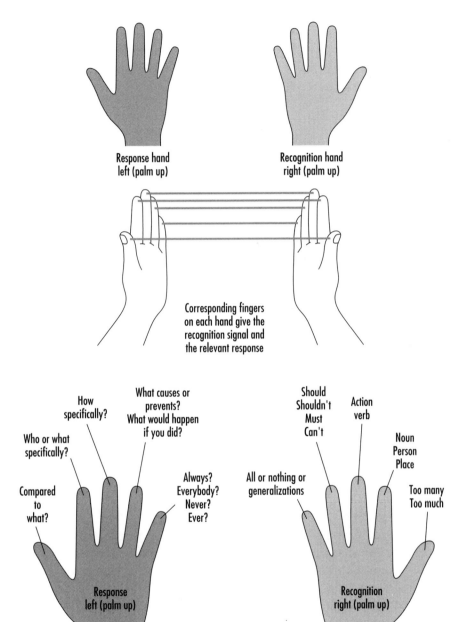

FIGURE 7.11. LET YOUR FINGERS DO THE TALKING

EXAMPLE OF "FLUFF-BUSTING"

Thumbs
Recognition: "This program is *too expensive, too long,* and *too boring.*"
Response: "Compared with what?"

Index fingers
Recognition: "I don't like *role plays.*" (noun)
Response: "What, specifically, don't you like about role plays?"
Recognition: "The *people at work* won't agree." (noun)
Response: "Who, specifically, won't agree?"

Second fingers
Recognition: "This *wastes* my time./This is a *waste* of time." (verb)
Response: "How, specifically, does this waste/is this a waste of time?"
(*Note:* Be flexible in your recognition of nouns and verbs and in the responses you give. Common usage may be different from correct grammatical usage.)

Third fingers
Recognition: "I *can't* implement this on the job."
Response: "What would happen if you did?" or "What prevents you from implementing this?"

Fourth fingers
Recognition: "This accelerative learning *never* works."
Response: "Never? Are you sure? In every situation?"

R = Resources

Accelerative learning encourages the development of resourceful people by the sharing and exchange of information sources. Suitable resources, in addition to the trainers themselves, include books, videotapes, audiotapes, mentors, interactive CD-ROM, past examples, teams, best-practice demonstrations, guest presenters, key contacts and organizational resources, on-line and CD-ROM databases, and technologies such as facsimile, teleconferencing, and telephone. You can use colored paper to identify your materials according to priority: white for high priority, pink for medium priority, and yellow for supplementary materials.

To reap the full benefits of learning resources, time should be allocated so people can reflect on, experiment with, and apply the information at their own pace. This will encourage the full use of the resources while also endorsing their value. However, most of all, it will encourage people to pursue their own self-directed learning agendas.

The trainer can assist the process by helping clarify learning objectives and providing some guidelines on where and how the information could be obtained. Finally, the quality of the learning process can be improved if people agree to share the outcomes of their discoveries with one another. The better the exchange of information, the higher the leverage of the accelerative learning experience.

For more information on how discovery is undertaken through the use of resources, see Chapter 3 on self-directed learning.

S = *Sound, Song, and Music*

The full use of sound, song, and music in learning is still undiscovered territory. Since Lozanov's original work, people such as Tomatis (1991), Campbell (1992), and Swartz (1991) have provided important leadership on how sound, song, and music should be used for accelerative learning. To explore this issue we have listed some of their key recommendations and findings. We have also included some of our recommended music choices.

Sound

- Sound energizes the brain. People who are placed in a soundless environment can quickly become lethargic because the brain lacks stimulation.
- According to Tomatis (1991), sound accounts for 85 percent of the electrical energy of the brain. Sound is conducted through our ears as well as through our bone structures. Since sound has such a powerful impact on the energy and vitality of the brain, it is important that it is used to nurture learning.
- People who have major hearing impairment lose 35 percent of their capacity to energize their brains.
- The right ear picks up information and the left ear picks up emotion and tonality. Individuals with dominant left ears will often experience learning difficulties when the learning is predominantly information-based. Trainers should always review and periodically change seating arrangements within training venues. This

reduces the likelihood of participants being stuck for indefinite periods on the "wrong" side of the room. For example, individuals working on computers who hear the trainer's instructions and data through the left ear, which has a stronger bias for emotion and tonality, should be given the opportunity to move to the other side of the room so that they can hear the trainer's instructions through the right ear.

- There is a difference between hearing and listening. Listening is the active ability, intention, and desire to tune in to certain sounds. People who tune out can hear but choose consciously or subconsciously not to listen. Chapter 6 refers to this process of tuning out as "deletion."

- Different languages have different frequency ranges, so people's ability to hear and absorb sounds will depend on the listening range of the individual and the capacity of the left ear to tune in to tonality.

- The full magic and wonder of the human voice should be explored. As shown earlier in Figure 7.1, the capacity to unlock the subconscious mind can be heavily influenced by the tonality, speed, rhythm, loudness, pitch, diction, and nasality of your message.

EXERCISE 7.5. VOICE EXERCISE

Take ten deep breaths as suggested in "B = Breathing." Repeat the phrase "Goo Gah, Gee Gah, Gay Gah, Gi Gah, Go Gah" five times. On the first occasion start with a very soft whisper and then raise your volume slightly each time to reach your normal speaking voice by the fifth recital.

EXERCISE 7.6. RAISING YOUR ENERGY LEVEL

Instead of having a stretching break, conduct a sound energizer for yourself and your learners. This can be done by repeating aloud the vowels of the alphabet, from a low to a high pitch. It is best if you do this standing up.

Song

Singing provides a powerful medium to access the subconscious, emotive mind, as well as the conscious, logical one. There are various ways you can use song to stimulate the learner. These include the following:

- Creating your own words and melody to sing to;
- Creating the words and singing to an existing melody; and
- Singing the words along with the actual music.

Singing can be used to celebrate, to acknowledge the integrity of feelings, or just to have fun. It is a wonderful closing gesture for a training course. The words and feeling can help provide both a special meaning and an anchor to the material that has been discussed.

Music

When music is used effectively, it is a wonderful bonus to an accelerative learning experience. Music can do the following:

- Implant information into the long-term memory;
- Create the mood for effective learning;
- Maintain attention and focus concentration;
- Relax the listener and induce comfort;
- Expand creativity and imagination; and
- Provide an emotional anchor with which the trainer can change the mood.

General guidelines for music include the following.

- Use pacing, patterning, singing, moving, dancing, and mood and tempo changes to stimulate learning.
- Use your voice as a musical instrument by adjusting your pitch, volume, and pacing. Use a soft, caring voice to create an atmosphere of empathy.
- Amadeus Mozart was one of the best composers of stimulating music because so much of his music engages a wide range of sound.
- The Lozanov approach uses music very effectively by paying particular attention to "active concert" and "passive concert" music. Active concert generates vitality, energy, productivity, and enthusiasm (around eighty beats per minute and above). Passive concert generates a soothing, relaxing mood ideal for studying (around forty to sixty beats per minute).
- Active and passive concert music can also be used for welcoming, for inspirational music, for sound breaks, and to inspire imagery and creativity.

Recommended music choices are presented in Box 7.2.

Box 7.2

Recommended Music Choices

Active Concerts

Tchaikovsky: Piano Concerto No. 1 in B flat minor, Op. 23
Mozart: Violin concertos Nos. 2, 3, and 5, Eine Kleine Nachtmusik KV525
Beethoven: Piano Concerto No. 5, Op. 73—"The Emperor"

Passive Concerts

Vivaldi: Winter of the Four Seasons
Pachelbel: Canon in D
Handel: Water Music Suite—Horn suite in F major. Fa majeur. F-dur

Welcoming Back from Breaks

"In the Mood" by Bette Midler
"Welcome Back" from the TV show "Welcome Back Kotter"

Energy Breaks

The Commitments original motion picture soundtrack, MCA by various artists
"Drums of Passion: The Beat" by Batatunde Olatunji
"I'm So Excited" by the Pointer Sisters
"Walking on Sunshine" by Katrina and the Waves

Stretching Activities

"Don't Worry, Be Happy" by Bobby McFerrin
"Higher and Higher" by Jackie Wilson

Great Favorites

"Watermark" by Enya
"Olympic Experience," EMI Classics by various artists
Merry Christmas Mr. Lawrence original motion picture soundtrack by Ryuichi Sakamoto
Strictly Ballroom original motion picture soundtrack by various artists
The Mission original motion picture soundtrack by Ennio Morricone
Power of One original motion picture soundtrack by Hans Zimmer

Gaining Licence to Use Music

Any use of copyrighted music in a training course is classified as a public performance and is deemed unlawful unless approval has been given to do so. It is the direct responsibility of the organization to ensure that it has obtained permission for the use of copyrighted music in a training program.

For inquiries: Australia and New Zealand—Australian Performing Rights Associations; United States—American Society of Composers, Authors and Publishers; Hong Kong—The Composers and Authors Society of Hong Kong Limited; South Africa—South African Music Rights Organisation Ltd; United Kingdom—Performing Rights Society Limited.

T = Team Learning

Team learning has been, and still remains, the lifelong best friend of accelerative learning. Teams provide the necessary synergy to help people achieve their learning goals through the exchange of diverse views and experiences.

Because of the importance of team learning, accelerative learning activities should include as much group exchange and dialogue as possible. Teamwork is quite simple given that most learning activities are already suited to exchange, creativity, and dialogue. The dynamics of team learning can be enhanced by the following:

- Invest time early in the training for people to discuss and feel the qualities of successful teamwork.
- Form people into a series of core teams that will take responsibility for their own discovery during the learning. Give each team the opportunity to establish its own team learning goals, form its own team identity, and determine a method to evaluate its own progress.
- Use high technology, such as teleconferencing, electronic mail, and telecommuting, to bring together learners who may reside in different places and time zones.
- Establish teams that are balanced and, where possible, heterogeneous (i.e., seek diversity in gender and mental, occupational, and cultural backgrounds).
- Coach people to focus initially on the content of discussion and then on the finesse of managing the team dynamics.
- Ensure that team learning remains a collective responsibility.

- Structure accelerative learning rituals for team celebration and evaluation.

EXERCISE 7.7. ACTIVITY FOR TEAM LEARNING

When working with, for example, a new product specification sheet or a new policy statement, apply the following steps:

1. Decide on your learning objectives and create an assessment process.
2. Form, for example, four learning teams.
3. Select four segments of the material to be examined and assign one to each team.
4. Ask group members to study the material individually for approximately three minutes. They may make notes or use highlighters to identify key points.
5. Allow each team's members three minutes to talk and compare among themselves.
6. Ask each team to select a coach. For ten minutes the team helps the coach develop a process to teach the material.
7. Rotate each coach around to the other teams. Thus, if there are four teams, there will be three rounds of learning. Each round will take ten minutes. Each team will therefore benefit from three coaching sessions on a previously undiscussed policy or product.
8. Implement the agreed-on assessment process.

U = Unlimited Potential

Trainers need to believe passionately that each individual brings his or her unique chemistry and potential into a learning experience. True and unlimited learning can only occur in an environment in which the capacity of people to create learning miracles is recognized. Only then can the trainer's self-awareness, inspiration, and trust allow people to reach their true learning potential.

Facilitating accelerative learning necessitates a balance of good structure, trust, flexibility, and patience. People must be given time to reflect and assimilate critical discoveries as they are contemplated and practiced. It is essential that the trainer listens to and cares for the learner in an unconditional and supportive way.

V = *Visualization*

Visualization allows the learner to bring to life the material being discussed and to make positive connections to new material being examined. There are many areas in which visualization can be used, including the following:

- Recalling a past experience;
- Projecting into the future—for example, imagining yourself using a new skill;
- Expanding options and horizons;
- Formulating milestones and goals;
- Engaging in the feeling of success;
- Making sense of new material;
- Relaxing; and
- Motivating and inspiring.

The best visualization allows the learner to feel, see, touch, smell, taste, and hear messages associated with the experience. The correct choice of music can also aid the visualization.

EXERCISE 7.8. ENGAGING YOUR LEMON SENSES

To highlight the power of visualization, undertake the following activity.

Take five deep breaths. Slowly breathe out any tension and anxiety that you may have stored up in your body and mind.

Place one of your hands out in front of you with the palm turned upward. Imagine that in this hand there is a beautiful, yellow, cool lemon. Raise the lemon to your nose and smell the fragrance; then rub the chilly and moist lemon against your face. As you look to your side you can see your best kitchen knife and your cutting board. Place the lemon on the cutting board and slice it in half with the knife. Pick up half of the lemon and bring it up to your mouth and bite it as hard as you can.

When you have completed this exercise, write down your feelings and thoughts on the activity.

Visualization can be a carefully scripted story (e.g., "Delivering the Emperor's Message") in which learners are given greater opportunity to choose where they are and what they do in their visualization. Alternatively, it may be unscripted. For example, a trainer may say,

"Please recall your favorite holiday spot. Where is it?" during a relaxation activity or "What does your desk normally look like?" during a time-management course.

A visualization can be disassociated or associated.

A *disassociated* visualization is when you view yourself. For example, you see yourself playing against your favorite tennis player at a grand slam event. You watch the game as if you were a spectator in the grandstand.

Associated visualization is when you actually experience the sensation of an act or skill. For example, you imagine rallying with your favorite tennis player in that grand slam game. Here you have to shift your attention to moving, balancing, and stroking the ball to outwit your famous opponent. This cognitive shift in thinking from disassociated to associated visualization is a vital link in the coaching process; imagining that you are hitting the tennis ball is better preparation for a tennis game than watching from the grandstand.

W = Whole-Brain Learning

Accelerative learning must be designed, delivered, and assessed within the framework of the whole brain. In other words, as introduced in the discussion on mind maps, learning should engage the full spectrum of the left and right brain.

In this regard, trainers must adapt to the learning style of the individuals rather than waiting for the learners to adapt to them. For example, a trainer who regularly teaches in a highly emotional and passionate way may inhibit and frustrate a learner who prefers a more logical and rational approach. To avoid this, trainers should use a multitude of different learning methods. This way the trainer is less likely to lose or not to connect with someone for an entire experience.

Two authors who have provided some powerful insights in meeting this challenge are McCarthy and Herrmann. In her book, *The 4MAT® System,* Bernice McCarthy (1987) details an eight-step model that includes learning styles, teaching, and left and right brain considerations. As shown in Figure 7.12, a trainer should consider structuring activities using a discovery process of experiencing, watching, conceptualizing, and doing, therefore increasing the chances of activating learning within a whole-brain framework.

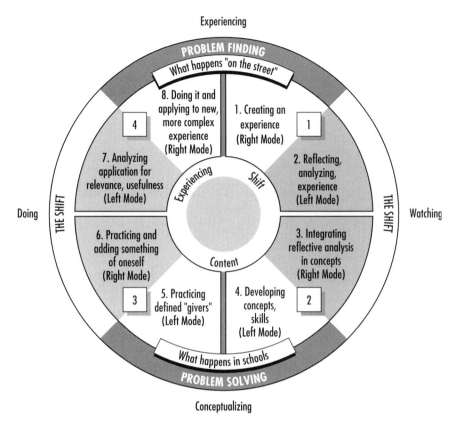

FIGURE 7.12. WHOLE BRAIN QUESTION WALK AROUND

Source: McCarthy, B. 1987. *The 4MAT® System: Teaching to Learning Styles with Right/Left Mode Techniques,* Excel, Barrington, Illinois. Reproduced with permission.

Similarly, Ned Herrmann, in his book, *The Creative Brain* (1990), has developed a model that explores whole-brain thinking and learning diversity. Herrmann recommends the design, delivery, and evaluation of whole-brain learning in a four quadrant brain model.

As shown in Figure 7.13, at the trainer's disposal is a wide range of training and learning possibilities within the brain preferences of facts, form, feelings, and fantasy.

X = eXercise Your Mind, Body and Spirit

To maintain the creativity and energy necessary to design, deliver, and assess using accelerative learning, the trainer must invest in self-nurturing activities that energize his or her own mind, body, and spirit.

Cerebral

A Facts **Learns by** thinking, by working with ideas, logic, needs, facts and theories, builds cases **Responds with** formal lecture, case discussion, textbooks, programmed learning, behavior modification	**D Fantasy** **Learns by** self-discovery, constructs concepts, values intuition, is concerned with hidden possibilities **Responds with** experiential, experimental, visual, aesthetic, individual, and involved learning
B Form **Learns by** testing theories, values, structure and process, oriented to skill attainment through practice **Responds with** structure and sequence, textbooks, case discussion, programmed learning and behavior modification	**C Feelings** **Learns by** listening and sharing values and intuition, works for harmony, integrates experience with self **Responds with** experiential learning, sensory input, movement, music, people-orientated cases, group interaction

Left Brain (left side) — **Right Brain** (right side)

Limbic

FIGURE 7.13. WHOLE-BRAIN TEACHING AND LEARNING CONSIDERATIONS

Source: From *The Creative Brain,* copyright 1989, 1990, Ned Herrmann/Brain Books. Appendix E, with permission from the author, Ned Herrmann, and the publisher, Brain Books of The Ned Herrmann Group.

At times, conducting accelerative learning can be very draining, so it is essential that realistic goals are set. Never underestimate the time required to prepare and structure powerful learning activities. Take the time out to celebrate personal milestones as they are achieved.

Trainers are often guilty of spending all their time helping others without taking time out to recharge their own batteries—even your car needs a checkup every few months. Your body never lies and your learners will realize if something is astray.

Remember that you are number one and that your chances of creating miracles with your learners and yourself will depend on how you look after your mind, body, and spirit. This will be explored further in Chapter 12.

Y = *Yarns, Stories, and Metaphors*

In Australia, the tradition of telling tall stories or yarns has taken on almost legendary proportions. Of course, passing down oral history via stories is a common trait in cultures all over the world. Accelerative learning acknowledges the power of these yarns and stories and encourages their use as a means of adding power to key learning points. Adding metaphor to the yarning equation allows a new dimension in creativity to be realized. It can help add important clarity, symbolism, and meaning to learning.

A good story is short and engages the whole group. The storyteller uses eye contact but avoids gazing at one individual for an extended time. Avoid long explanations in the story. Let your voice be an instrument. When using music, fluctuate your voice's pacing, resonance, tone, and energy to mirror the emotion of the story. Tell the story as if you are performing a dramatic reading at a concert. The best stories are often your own. Keep a record of experiences you have had; when you share the truth the story will have greater meaning. Your story will be all the more memorable if it has drama, suspense, inspiration, emotional stimulation, and appropriate humor.

A metaphor is a way of naming or describing that is not to be taken literally. For example, when we say "A mighty fortress is my God" or "A land of milk and honey," we do not mean it literally. Another example is when we say, "You can't make an omelette without breaking a few eggs" to express the idea that we need to make sacrifices in order to get what we want.

A metaphor can be extended to become a story that expresses an idea (e.g., the Roman chariot metaphor in the story told by Rene in "Delivering the Emperor's Message").

Metaphors can also help learners make connections and see patterns or relationships between two ordinarily different ideas. For example, as a flower needs to bend with the breeze, so an accelerative learner needs to bend and sway and adapt to the challenges. To make a metaphorical story from this, we could create a story about a flower bending with the breeze in order to survive and grow. The story would be told perhaps as a response to a discussion about inflexibility in learning.

Games and experiential activities can also be very powerful metaphors for real life. (See Chapters 5 and 10.)

EXERCISE 7.9. GENERATING WONDERFUL METAPHORS

1. Forced Relationship

Create two lists like those shown below. One list is of concrete terms and the other is of abstract terms. Form subgroups and ask learners to blend the two by forming sentences from the core " . . . is like . . . because. . . . " Taking turns, each subgroup member chooses a term from the concrete list and completes the first part of the core. The next person chooses a term from the second list. A third person then completes the sentence.

Concrete Terms	Abstract Terms
An ashtray	Religion
A bouncing ball	Love
Sunset	Hate
A blanket	Morale
A newborn baby	Growth
A cup of tea	Wealth
A ferry	Childhood
A fur coat	Expert advice
A swimming pool	Intuition

For example, one response might be "A blanket is like expert advice because it makes you feel warm, safe, and secure."

This exercise can easily be adapted to connect concepts in a training program. If the ideas in the concrete list are substituted with concepts such as customer service or total quality, you can then create metaphors that can be used and reinforced throughout the program. For example, "Customer service is like love because it is about a lasting relationship."

2. Dictionary Method

Begin by choosing the item you wish to create a metaphor about—let's say learning.

Ask a person to choose a number between 1 and 1,300 (the number of pages in your dictionary) and turn to that page in your dictionary. The next person is asked to choose a number between 1 and 20. Count down that many definitions on the page that you have turned to. Let's say numbers 620 and then 8 are chosen. In our dictionary, that leads to the word "lens." Our metaphor might be "Learning is like a lens because when we focus on the needs of the learner we are more likely to see better results."

Z = Zeal for Learning and Life

Your leadership and passion for learning is contagious!

Clearly, when we expect others to learn, we must role model the appropriate behaviors. For someone to train in accelerative learning, he or she should also live accelerative learning. That way he or she will be better able to confront any challenge with integrity.

Your zeal for learning must be a tangible thing. It must manifest itself in your behaviors and actions as a trainer and as a person. Tangible ways to give weight to your sincerity, integrity, and congruence include the following:

- Showing resource books, videotapes, audiotapes, and articles you have collected;
- Demonstrating your skill and role modeling the attitudes that you believe are important;
- Sharing your successes and failures in learning;
- Being prepared to try new things, enjoy, and stretch yourself whenever possible;
- Quoting why, how, and where you learn;
- Seeking new learning and personal growth in all aspects of life;
- Removing all negative self-talk;
- Sharing and learning perspectives from a wide range of people (e.g., children, people from different backgrounds);
- Rigorously seeking out a wide range of mentors; and
- Always looking for the positive intention of people.

EXERCISE 7.10. LEARNING SHEET ON THE A TO Z OF ACCELERATIVE LEARNING

List the A to Z of accelerative learning ingredients.

A	N
B	O
C	P
D	Q
E	R
F	S
G	T
H	U
I	V
J	W
K	X
L	Y
M&M	Z

Summary

The expanding field of accelerative learning provides people with a medium to transform the way they feel and think about themselves and a range of ideas and methods to improve the way they learn—in the same way that Rene combined the use of the metaphor of a Roman chariot and the music from Vangelis' "Chariots of Fire."

The A to Z of accelerative learning provides the building blocks that can help mold and create possible training miracles. As advances in technology, human understanding, and learning continue, so will the chance to find new territory in this exciting field.

In the future, the only limitation to the application of accelerative learning is our imagination and our desire to experiment. The full potential of accelerative learning is yet to be realized.

Bibliography

American Society for Training and Development. (1992). *Info-line series: Basics of accelerative learning.* Alexandra, VA: Author.

Bandler, R., & Grinder, J. (1975). *The structure of magic, Volume 1.* Palo Alto, CA: Science and Behavior Books.

Bandler, R., & Grinder, J. (1976). *The structure of magic, Volume 2.* Palo Alto, CA: Science and Behavior Books.

Bandler, R., & Grinder, J. (1979). *Frogs into princes.* Moab, UT: Real People Press.

Buzan, T. (1993). *The mind map book.* London: BBC Books.

Campbell, D. (1992). *100 ways to improve your teaching using your voice and music.* Tucson, AZ: Zephyr.

Deporter, B., & Hernacki, M. (1992). *Quantum learning.* New York: Dell.

Frischknecht, J., & Capelli, G. (1995). *Maximizing your learning potential: A handbook for lifelong learners.* Dubuque, IA: Kendall/Hunt.

Gardner, H. (1985). *Frames of mind.* New York: Basic Books.

Goleman, D. (1995). *Emotional intelligence: Why it can matter more than IQ.* London: Bloomsbury.

Herrmann, N. (1990). *The creative brain.* Lake Lure, NC: Brain Books.

Hermann, N. (1996). *The whole brain business book: Unlocking the power of whole brain thinking in organizations and individuals.* New York: McGraw-Hill.

Jensen, E. (1988). *Superteaching*. Rancho Cucamonga, CA: Turning Point.

Jensen, E. (1994). *The learning brain*. Rancho Cucamonga, CA: Turning Point.

Jensen, E. (1995). *Brain-based learning and teaching*. Rancho Cucamonga, CA: Turning Point.

Laborde, G. (1983). *Influencing with integrity*. Palo Alto, CA: Syntony.

Lazear, D. (1991). *Seven ways of knowing*. Palatine, IL: Skylight.

Lazear, D. (1994). *Seven pathways of learning*. Tucson, AZ: Zephyr.

Lozanov, G. (1979). *Suggestology and outlines of suggestopedy*. New York: Gordon & Breach.

McCarthy, B. (1987). *The 4MAT® system: Teaching to learning styles with right/left mode techniques*. Barrington, IL: Excel.

Oka, M. (1994, June). Accelerated learning—Fact, fad or myth? *Human Resource Monthly,* pp. 6–10.

Rose, C. (1985). *Accelerated learning*. New York: Dell.

Rylatt, A. (1994). *Learning unlimited: Practical strategies and techniques for transforming workplace learning*. Sydney: Professional and Business Publishing.

Swartz, R. (1991). *Accelerated learning: How you learn determines what you learn*. Durant, OK: Essential Medical Information Systems.

Tomatis, A.A. (1991). *The conscious ear*. New York: Station Hill Press.

White, J., & Day, K. (1992). *Aromatherapy for scentual awareness*. Brighton-le-sands, Australia: Nacson & Sons.

Wycoff, J. (1991). *Mindmapping*. New York: Berkley Books.

8

SUCCESSFUL ROLE-PLAYING TECHNIQUES

This chapter explores techniques to improve the use of role playing, including a practical model to ensure that the role play achieves high-quality learning outcomes.

Gems Mined from These Pages

- A good role play is engaging, energizing, and builds confidence quickly.

- Trainer leadership is the most important factor in overcoming resistance.

- Always gain people's permission before stretching them.

- Role playing is about application, not about winning an Academy Award.

- A role play has tremendous versatility.

"Quality is never an accident; it is always the result of high intention, sincere effort, intelligent direction and skillful execution; it represents the wise choice of many alternatives."

WILLA A. FOSTER

No One Told Me That Terry Was Coming!

Rob sat politely during the first morning of the annual two-day supervisor training course. Every now and then he shifted slightly in his seat. Something was clearly on his mind.

"Nice training venue overlooking the sea," Rob thought, "but what a waste of my time! Honestly, I should really be back on the job organizing my staff, not sitting here, bored out of my brain. The last time I went on one of these training courses the trainer raved on about theories and played mind games all day. All I got out of that program was a numb backside. Surely the CEO could have sent someone else on the course. Maybe Toni or Hilda should have come—they're young and green. I am too old for this sort of stuff. Anyway, I will be retiring in ten years."

During the coffee break Rob found out that Personnel had hired an external trainer named Chris Gombrich for the next two-hour session on staff motivation. This immediately brought back memories of past training experiences for him. "I bet the trainer will talk about Maslow and Hertzberg," he confided to a new acquaintance. "Then we will see a video or, worse still, we will contemplate our navels for a while. After that, hopefully, we can have lunch by the pool. I just pray that I can last that long without upsetting somebody or falling asleep. Anyway none of these so-called training experts has to deal with the world's laziest person—my Terry. Let's see how this Chris Gombrich changes my life today. I won't be holding my breath waiting."

As the less-than-excited Rob walked back into the room after coffee, he noticed that Chris Gombrich has changed the furniture around. The twelve chairs were now arranged in a horseshoe formation. The tables were nowhere to be seen. On the walls was a series of posters that had quotes and headings to do with motivation and coaching. After greeting the attendees, Chris proceeded to give a twenty-minute overview of the modern principles of motivation.

"The words are different from past courses, but still I hear nothing new or earth shattering," reflected Rob. "I've never yet heard anyone offer a good idea about how to motivate that no-good Terry who works for me," he thought to himself.

At that instant, Chris looked over at Rob, paused, and asked with a pleasant smile, "What would you add to what has been said so far?"

Feeling slightly rebellious, Rob said, "Sounds nice in theory but none of this stuff will help me motivate my Terry."

Chris replied, "Tell us about Terry."

"Well," Rob said, "Terry has been working for me for about six months, but I can't seem to get any decent work output." Chris looked around the group and asked whether it was okay with everyone to discuss this issue for a while. Everyone agreed. Rob then asked that everyone keep the ensuing conversation confidential.

Over the next fifteen minutes, the training group went about building a common understanding about Terry. The discussion covered age, personality, interests, and work history. Interestingly, the rest of the group made some suggestions and raised questions that Rob found useful. The discussion focused on those characteristics that the group found particularly challenging.

As the group agreed on the common ground, Chris wrote the key facts on the board at the front of the room. For example, everyone agreed that Terry could either be male or female; however, for Rob it was all too clear that Terry was a 38-year-old male.

Next, Chris placed an empty chair at the front of the room and asked for a volunteer to be the character of Terry. Steve quickly jumped up and sat in the empty chair. The group, with Chris's support, went about coaching Steve on "Terry's" body language and mood. Over the next ten minutes, the role of Terry started to unfold in front of the group.

Chris asked the group to determine a simple on-the-job situation in which they would need to motivate Terry. The group accepted Rob's suggestion that Terry should be asked to check the accuracy of a management report. This was particularly relevant to Rob because a week earlier he had made that same request, and Terry still had not done the task.

Chris moved another chair opposite to the one in which Steve was sitting. He asked Rob whether he would be prepared to relive the experience that he had with Terry on the job some days before. Chris made some small additions to the furniture, including bringing in some extra props such as tables, in boxes, paperwork, and a telephone. Rob sat down as he had during the initial discussion on the job, but this time, instead of Terry sitting opposite him, he saw Steve, who was role playing Terry.

Rob began by trying to motivate Terry the same way that he had done previously. As the role play began, the group quickly suggested that Rob needed to ask rather than tell Terry what to do. Rob did not quite understand this point, so Rema jumped up and sat in Rob's chair and showed Rob what was happening from her perspective. Rob found this feedback quite amazing and could now see and hear what was meant by asking rather than telling. He was amazed that his telling approach could have the effect on someone that the group was now revealing.

Over the following ten minutes, Rob continued to fine tune his approach based on group feedback. Chris occasionally stopped the activity and got others to swap with Steve so that they could participate more actively in the role-training experience. For Rob, it did not seem to matter who was playing the role of Terry because he was getting enormous value out of the opportunity. He continued practicing until he felt confident.

After spending about thirty minutes at this, Chris became aware that Rob was feeling a lot more proficient and so stopped the activity. He checked that everyone was feeling relaxed and comfortable and then split the group into three small clusters. In these subgroups, the participants developed lists of practical tips that were learned from the activity.

Two days later Rob was back on the job applying what he had learned in a discussion with the real Terry. What Rob tried in the work situation went perfectly.

When the recall day for the course arrived a month later, Rob could not wait to tell the rest of the group of his success. To Rob's complete surprise, a number of other people also made significant discoveries and insights from the same activity. The trainer then led a similar but more advanced activity—this time exploring the issue of coaching someone who had recently missed out on a promotion.

The day after the course Rob returned to the workplace. As a group stood around during a coffee break, Terry came up to Rob and asked, "How did the course go yesterday?"

Rob replied, "It went fantastically well! It is the first time I felt I have learned something from a training course." Terry nervously replied, "Yes, I must admit that I am enjoying working here a lot more since you started doing that course." Rob thanked him for the feedback and invited him to sit and join him for coffee. As he sat down, Rob felt overwhelmed. "Who would ever think that I would be sitting down talking to this guy. What a miracle!"

Making Sense of the Role Play

A role play can be defined as a training method in which people act out roles or characters within a scenario according to either scripted or unscripted instructions. The best role plays depict actual behaviors that address learning needs. These behaviors should enable people to practice the range of knowledge, skills, and attitudes that are required in real life.

A good role play is engaging, energizing, and allows fast confidence growth. Role plays should provide immediate and powerful insights into attitudes that need to be changed, as well as providing opportunities to explore the impact of behavior on oneself and others. For example, in "No One Told Me That Terry Was Coming!," Rob developed an increased capacity to motivate an individual named Terry. Similarly, a learner in a customer-training course may practice calming down an angry customer by portraying competencies such as establishing rapport, using assertiveness, listening actively, and seeking and obtaining mutual agreement. However, the greatest opportunity for using the role-playing method lies in workplace coaching during which people can learn and practice key competencies as they are raised.

The benefits of a role play include the following:

- Allows learners to practice skills in a safe learning environment;
- Provides a chance to revisit past behavior to confront challenges;
- Allows the exploration and practice of new behaviors;
- Provides an opportunity to gain feedback on verbal and nonverbal behavior; and
- Promotes new ideas, strategies, and values to improve performance.

Dealing with Role Play Resistance

Like all training strategies, the role play is not without difficulties. One of the major obstacles to the success of a role play is the resistance of learners to the technique. The following story may help explain how this can be overcome.

The Lessons from the Eagle

It was a brisk and windy morning as the eagle and two young eaglets looked over the vast inland plain from the relative safety of their nest high in the mountains. Today was a very special day. Today the two eaglets would have their first flying lesson. Pensive and nervous, they waited for the strong and proud eagle to start.

For what seemed an eternity, the eagle gazed out on the plain respecting and admiring a group of seagulls performing the wonder of flight as they made their way to the bay. Without making a sound, the eagle shifted its attention to three water buffalo roaming along the river bank and then to the faint shrieking of the water birds in the swamps below.

The atmosphere at the nest was filled with pride and hope. Calmly, the eagle turned to the two eaglets and said, "You may think today is about flying. Well, today is more than just that. Today is about giving yourselves the freedom and the choice to resolve one challenge and to begin another." With the flickering of an eye, the eagle calmly stood back, took a deep breath, and leaped out toward the plain. The two eaglets watched in awe as the eagle soared and played in the sky.

After a few minutes the eagle returned to the nest. Taking another deep breath, the eagle smiled, reached out, and clutched the two eaglets under the safety of its wings. The eagle took the two learners to a tiny rocky outcrop overlooking a small valley. Placing the eaglets down, the eagle sensed that the learners had suddenly become tense and apprehensive. The eagle then paused and asked in a quiet and caring voice, "What would you both like to say?"

The two eaglets looked at each other nervously, until one finally replied, "This flying looks impossible. I will never be as good as you. Since I heard yesterday that I was going to learn I have been having terrible nightmares." The other eaglet continued by saying, "I tried to fly all last week. I hurt my wing falling down. I don't think I've got what it takes."

The eagle said reassuringly, "When I was learning I felt the same way. You see, flying is just like any other role of our lives—the same as searching for food or coaching, it takes time to learn. Flying is not about passing or failing or indeed about perfection. It is about discovering who you are and who you need to become to get where you want to go. Now let's go through the key principles of flying."

For the rest of the morning the eagle coached the two eaglets, starting with the four key principles of relaxing, ensuring speed, taking a straight and flexible body position, and seeking enjoyment. Next the eagle slowly led the eaglets through the specifics of each of these principles. In each case, the eagle demonstrated and the eaglets practiced. After a while, the eaglets were practicing jumping off the rocky outcrop onto the ground a few inches below them. The eagle encouraged the eaglets to take more risks but, most of all, to have fun. On several occasions the eagle left the eaglets unsupervised to discuss and revise the material they had learned. When the eagle returned, the eaglets were rewarded with some fresh and juicy lizards.

For the next few days the lessons continued. Each day the challenges became slightly more difficult. There were, of course, times when both of the eaglets and even the great eagle made mistakes. However, everyone saw this as a natural part of the coaching process. As the eaglets' confidence grew, so did their skill. Then came the day that they had journeyed so far for. It was time to fly, and the eagle told them that the next day they would be flying from the nest high up in the mountains.

That night, the eaglets slept in the nest in the mountains, reassured that they had come a long way since that first tentative morning. The big day arrived; the land quickly began to warm under the splendor of the beautiful sun. Wonderful upward drafts began to drift from the vast land below.

The eagle gave the signal; then mentor and protégés stood back, took a deep breath, and soared toward the plain. Uncertain at first, one of the eaglets panicked. Almost immediately, the voice of the eagle came to mind, helping the eaglet remember

how to relax and renew the good body position they had practiced so thoroughly. After a few seconds, the eaglet's struggle was
replaced with the true magic of flight. For the next hour the three
danced in the sky and, finally, they reached the spot where the
water buffaloes were resting far below.

On reaching this spot, the eaglets screamed with pleasure
and joy and the eagle stood proud. Then one eaglet turned to
the eagle and said, "I now know how it feels to be free." After
a few moments, the other said, "I now look forward to the day
when I can coach."

On hearing this, the eagle turned with a tear in its eye and
flew out toward the sea.

"The Lessons from the Eagle" captures many of the positive coaching skills required to lead successful role plays. If you apply some of
the principles in the story, many of the causes of resistance can be
overcome. Let us examine some of the lessons to come out of the
story.

The first lesson is unquestionably the leadership of the trainer.
There is no doubt that the positive energy and belief of the trainer
are contagious. If a trainer is apprehensive about a technique, he or
she will show this either verbally or nonverbally, and this will dramatically affect the capacity of the learners to experiment and discover. The trainer needs to act with confidence and excitement about
the role-play process. Most of all, the trainer needs to communicate
with sincerity, openness, and compassion for the learners.

Second, the trainer will have to accept that some learners will need
plenty of structure and sequential guidance if the role-playing method
is to be successful. A powerful technique that addresses this need is
the behavior-modification technique. It offers trainers and learners a
methodology that helps remove much of the fear that comes from
apparently unstructured training activities. This method is summarized later in this chapter.

Finally, there is a long list of techniques that can make a big difference to learner involvement in role plays. However, before beginning
or asking for involvement, it is imperative that you get people's permission for their participation. Role playing is about empowerment,
not imposition.

Suggestions for Removing Resistance

- Warm up the group by giving it a less threatening activity to do first: for example, hold a small-group discussion.
- Describe how this skill will help in many situations.
- Sell the benefits of the technique.
- If the term "role play" is causing discomfort, call the technique something else such as "activity," "try out," or "skill practice."
- Perform a demonstration yourself—show them what is expected.
- Make the scenario as realistic as possible.
- Show genuine sensitivity and tact, listening to people's fears, suggestions, and expectations.
- Ask for the learners to make this activity one of the most positive learning experiences they have ever had.
- Keep the activities short and sharp.
- Run a short presentation session detailing practical tips before starting the role-play activity.
- Give clear instructions containing small steps and checklists.
- Stress that role playing is not about winning an Academy Award but that it is about making the attempt.
- Use music to set the mood for the activity (see Chapter 7).
- Allocate observer roles and regularly rotate people into different responsibilities.
- If you are using video equipment, introduce it in an earlier activity. Remove the pressure of the role-play ritual.
- Encourage deep breathing and stretching to help create a relaxed, supporting environment.
- Encourage celebration and create opportunities to practice and learn.

Designing Role Plays

There are three steps to designing an effective role play. Much of the upcoming discussion will be closely mirrored by material in Chapter 9 on designing and using classic case studies. This is particularly relevant in the area of writing good stories and scenarios.

Step 1. Identify a Clear Purpose

It is important to determine the objectives that will be learned or practiced during the training exercise. Even though some role-playing methods, such as role-training method, are heavily influenced by learner input, the final activity must be relevant to real situations and experiences. The role play, like all learning, should be competency-based, thereby ensuring that the activity focuses on learning outcomes.

Step 2. Developing a Scripted or Unscripted Story Line

Depending on the learning objectives, a role play can range in design from being heavily scripted to being completely unscripted. In the case of the scripted approach, learners are asked to behave in a clearly defined way. Conversely, unscripted role plays allow maximum freedom for a participant to behave as he or she would normally respond. The key differences, benefits, and disadvantages of scripted and unscripted role plays are outlined in Table 8.1.

TABLE 8.1. COMPARING SCRIPTED AND UNSCRIPTED ROLE PLAYS

Category	Scripted	Unscripted
Script	Defined by the trainer	Defined by learners
Events in the role play	Dependent on the story	More dynamic, depends on personality of learners and the way the role play unfolds
Behavior of players	Defined by the depth of the story and the experience of the author	Likely to reflect personal experience of participants
Level of resistance	Higher as a consequence of perceptions of "acting"	Less due to spontaneous behavior and natural feel of events
Outcomes	Easier to predict and debrief	Harder to predict—almost anything can happen
Transfer of learning	Can be high if well scripted and researched and if believable	Spontaneity can lead to more realism
Application of learning	Reflects a more structured response to a set situation	Creates a more flexible outcome strategy to unexpected situations

Step 3. Providing Clear Instructional Material

For a role play to be conducted effectively, each role player needs to be provided with a clear set of guidelines on how to perform his or her role. It is important that adequate instructional material is provided. When participants have had limited previous exposure to role playing, the instructional material will need to be more detailed. In addition, some participants will require a longer time to prepare for their roles.

Instruction briefing notes should also be written for the trainer. Material should include comments on anticipated outcomes, a lesson plan detailing key points, checklists for the observers, resources/people requirements, props and material requirements, time frames required for briefing and conducting the activity, and, finally, a list of recommended debriefing questions.

Conducting a Role Play

Having designed the material, the trainer needs to shift his or her attention to leading and conducting a successful role play. The following suggestions complement the earlier discussion on how to overcome resistance.

Step 1. Briefing

After arousing curiosity and interest in the upcoming activity, the trainer must clarify the learning objectives and time constraints and seek commitment on group norms and ground rules for the role play. The trainer needs to explain that role playing is a rewarding experience and must be taken seriously.

Step 2. Allocation of Roles

After outlining what is about to happen, the trainer must consider casting. Learners may initially be selected for roles based on observed personalities, work responsibilities, or their volunteering, or by picking roles and names randomly from a hat.

Time needs to be allocated for the clarification of the scripted or unscripted aspects of the activity. In this regard, the trainer should ask questions to ensure that everyone understands his or her role. This might include laying down the nonnegotiable rules. For example, a trainer may say to a person who is performing the role of a hostile customer, "In this role you can play the character any way you like (i.e., soft rule) but, remember, you must start by slumping on the counter (i.e., hard rule)." To assist in their preparation, people can be shown photographs or video clips of behavior on which the characters are based.

Step 3. Set Up the Activity and Atmosphere

The role of the trainer now shifts to that of a production manager. He or she must ensure that relevant and adequate props are available to help create the realism of the scenario. Props may include furniture, equipment, clothing, sound, and lighting.

Step 4. Overseeing the Role Play

Once the activity has begun, the trainer should intervene when the play falls flat or the roles are not being performed. The trainer should also ensure that the observers are attentive and learn from their observation and participation. Their attention may be maintained by providing clearly written and complete instructions.

Step 5. Debrief the Role Players and the Observers

Role plays can create a multitude of emotions and reactions ranging from euphoria to disappointment. The trainer must ensure that role players are taken out of character as quickly as possible and de-briefed. Debriefing necessitates that negative feelings or unrealistic views of a performance are dealt with prior to discussing any further issues or moving on to another topic. Debriefing should also include observers as it is often they who need the most support and attention.

An important component of the debriefing process is to get peo-ple to disconnect themselves from the role they were portraying. The quality of the learning arising out of the role play will be improved if this disassociation process is done well as it will aid better and more objective assessment of the issues that arise from the dynamics of the role play. For example, it is quite common for a person to become so involved in playing a role that he or she continues to take on the behavior or persona of the role being played well after the activity has finished. Another common occurrence is that people become so involved in "play-acting" that they lose sight of the learning issues. It is imperative that the trainer quickly gets learners out of their roles so that applications of the issues in the role play can be affirmed. In this way, the key principles are more likely to be transferred back to the workplace, where they belong.

Questions that assist the debriefing process follow.

- How do you feel you did in the role of "X"?
- What did you do well?
- What would you do differently next time?
- How do you differ from the role you played?

The trainer will be able to gauge whether the group is ready to move on by observing its nonverbal permission. For example, shorter breathing cycles and defensive body positions are clear indications that more debriefing may be necessary. When the debriefing is completed, trainers should have people return to their normal seats. Do not discuss other matters while people are still sitting or standing in an area where they performed the role play.

Step 6. Debriefing the Content of the Role Play

Time must be spent critiquing key points and behaviors that are to be carried out in real life. This includes listing the positive competencies that were learned. To achieve this, participants must be willing to accept positive feedback and to not struggle with everything that is being said. Video playback is a helpful tool in this process. The video can capture significant feedback on nonverbal behavior as well as providing greater awareness and insight into the role players' performances. For more information on debriefing, see Chapter 11.

Step 7. Conducting a Closing Ritual

Depending on the energy and the intensity generated by the role play, a closing activity may be required to help make a clean break before the next session. Examples of ending rituals include the following:

- Setting up small groups to list the key learning outcomes from the role play.
- Forming small circles of learners and giving each group a small ball or bean bag to toss around. When a person catches the object, he or she completes the following statement: "What I feel most like saying is. . . . " After thirty seconds the object is passed to another

person within the circle. The activity continues until all have had sufficient opportunity to share their feelings and thoughts.

Advancing Role Playing to Spontaneous Role Training

The story "No One Told Me That Terry Was Coming!" is an example of the more sophisticated role-playing method called "role training." The role-training method is often used in therapy training and counseling. It is ideally suited to most areas of interpersonal communication. Role training is often referred to as "a spontaneous role-playing method." Adaptations of role training can be highly scripted, with outsiders (trained protagonists) brought in to the training environment to participate in assigned roles. High-profile uses of trained protagonists include security and terrorist training.

Role training advances the concept of a role play in six ways:

1. It provides an opportunity to construct a relevant role play on the spur of the moment for the receptive trainer. This unrehearsed role play, if well selected and well briefed, will add power to a training or coaching session.
2. The scenario is created by the people undergoing the learning. The participants are thus able to script a scenario that is real and meaningful. The result is a more focused and accelerative activity that has greater practicality.
3. The activity will produce outcomes that will lead to better clarification of the roles or behaviors required in the workplace. For example, in "No One Told Me That Terry Was Coming!," the suggestions about what it takes to motivate someone like Terry were clear and directly transferable for Rob.
4. The observers play a more active role than often occurs in the traditional role-play methods. Observers can be instantly called on to show how to physically or emotionally deal with the situation being demonstrated.
5. Spontaneity is encouraged by pausing the activity at appropriate moments and discussing the behaviors, skills, and roles being demonstrated.
6. The skills, behaviors, and roles being learned can be tested and measured with greater ease in and out of the training room. For example, in "No One Told Me That Terry Was Coming!," Rob, as a result of the initial coaching session, went back to the job,

applied what was learned, and then discussed the application at a recall session. This subsequently led to a more advanced role-training session.

The Stage Management of the Role-Training Method

To achieve a positive result from the role-training method, the stage management of the role-training process must be tight. There are three key responsibilities involved:

1. the director;
2. the role players; and
3. the observers.

The *director* is normally the trainer; this responsibility requires a wide range of skills. These include the ability to:

- develop a framework and process to deal with the needs that arise;
- create or locate checklists, models, or formulas that can support people as they apply the skills;
- debrief people in often highly emotive situations;
- inspire people and engender discovery;
- organize logistics and people to achieve objectives; and
- facilitate learning and evaluate progress.

In regard to *role players* (sometimes called protagonists or auxiliaries) and *observers,* these functions are normally performed by the learners on a rotational basis. As discussed, they can also be performed by outsiders.

Ten Steps in Conducting a Role-Training Session

The role-training session requires the trainer to be in total harmony with the needs and wishes of the learners. To assist in meeting this aim, the following ten steps are suggested for conducting this role-playing method successfully.

Step 1. Sufficient Time Must Be Allocated

Determine whether there is sufficient time to undertake the role-training session. For example, a minimum of one hour is recommended to script and complete the simplest session.

Step 2. Warm Up the Participants

Warm up the participants and discuss the purpose of the role-training session in advance. In some cases a preliminary training session may be needed to highlight general knowledge and skills prior to starting.

Step 3. Identify the Theme

Identifying the theme is a vitally important stage of the process. Since the learners need to agree with one another on the common ground, the time required to identify the theme is far longer than for a normal role play. Typically, the trainer will use a flip chart or white board to brainstorm and reach consensus on the scene and situation. (*Note:* Take a minute to remember how Chris Gombrich performed this function in the story, "No One Told Me That Terry Was Coming!")

Confirm the following issues prior to beginning:

- What are the learning needs of the participants?
- Where and when did the situation occur?
- Who was involved and what was his or her contribution to the situation?
- What are the challenges or obstacles to be resolved?

Step 4. Clarify Key Characters

Obtain agreement on the behavior and background of the key players. Encourage people to coach one another on the personality and content issues required.

Step 5. Select Appropriate Role Players

Appropriate role players need to be selected from within or outside the group.

Step 6. Ensure There Is a Task to Examine

Ensure observers have a task to examine. It is important to do the following:

- Train the group in accurate observation;
- Assign tasks such as role identification and assessment;

- Invite active sharing; and
- Develop healthy group norms such as constructive feedback and sensitivity.

Step 7. Undertake Ongoing Assessment

Facilitate the role-training practice by undertaking an ongoing assessment of what is occurring. A number of techniques can be used to add power to this step. These include role reversal, intervention interviews, mirroring, doubling, modeling, and tag team—all of which are explained later in the chapter. At the end of the role play, be sure to debrief people's feelings before moving on to content.

Step 8. List and Discuss Appropriate Behavior

List and discuss the appropriate behavior and strategies demonstrated during the process. This exploration should link with material already discussed by the trainer in previous sessions or, alternatively, reinforce the issues learned during the role training just completed. This then serves as a stepping stone for on-the-job application and review.

Step 9. Conduct a Role Test

Conduct a role test by having the participants try out the learned behaviors in real life.

Step 10. Review

Review the role test at a recall session by identifying what occurred in real life. Depending on what has occurred, there may be a need to revisit or rescript another scenario.

The Potpourri of Methods and Tactics

Just as a potpourri dish contains a large array of wonderful fragrances and colors, the large number of techniques, methods, and tactics in role playing can produce an exciting blend of outcomes. In a very real sense, role playing has it own potpourri to discover. Depending on the combinations of ingredients used, there are a limitless number of potential learning outcomes.

As one reads the practical and theoretical background material on role playing, a wide range of terminologies become apparent. Figure 8.1 summarizes the methods, terminology, and tactics that we have found most useful. In many cases the jargon or description may differ, but in reality there may be no substantial difference in the intent or application of the method. So it is therefore important to double-check this when applying various role-playing techniques.

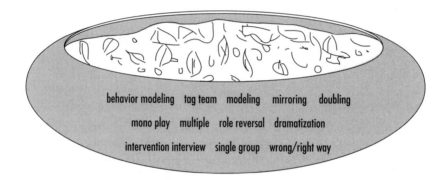

behavior modeling   tag team   modeling   mirroring   doubling

mono play   multiple   role reversal   dramatization

intervention interview   single group   wrong/right way

FIGURE 8.1. THE POTPOURRI OF ROLE-PLAYING METHODS AND TACTICS

The methods and tactics of effective role playing are explained below alphabetically.

Behavior modeling is a highly structured method that actively reinforces the positive behaviors required to perform a skill. Behavior modeling has been extensively used in training people to coach, to counsel, and to deal with conflict.

The six steps of the behavior-modeling process are listed below:

1. The trainer formally presents the essential core skills to be mastered.
2. The trainer presents a prepared video or dramatization that shows the essential core skills to be used. The participants are then required to state the core skills being exhibited.
3. Learners role play using the core skills discussed. This session is also often videotaped to provide feedback to the role players.
4. Feedback on performance is provided, including self-critique and feedback from other role players, observers, the trainer, and the video.

5. Participants draft a "learning contract," making commitments on how to apply skills outside the learning environment.

6. A follow-up session is used to reinforce and validate learned behaviors. Coaches and mentors are then placed "on the job" to discuss skill development with the learner using the structures developed. To support this process, mentors and coaches may learn core training skills.

During a *doubling* process, a third or fourth person is brought into the role play. As displayed in Figure 8.2, a third person may show one role player (first person) the perceived impact of his or her actions on another role player (second person). For example, when a tactic is used by the first person that is perceived as wonderful, the third person may stand silently with arms outstretched in an open and large posture. Less extreme postures will communicate feelings along the continuum from very bad to outstanding. The fourth person may do the same, but in his or her case, he or she is supporting the second person. As shown in Figure 8.2, if the actions of the second person are perceived to be very poor, the fourth person may choose to sit silently on the floor in a closed huddle.

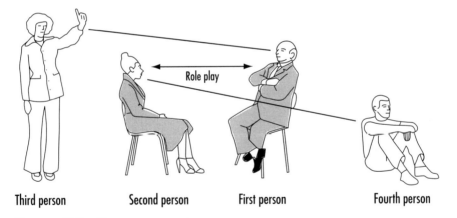

Third person   Second person   First person   Fourth person

FIGURE 8.2. DOUBLING IN ACTION

Dramatization involves people reading or playing out an actual script or story. This technique is addressed in more detail in Chapter 9.

An *intervention interview* is when the role play is stopped and the role players are interviewed for a short period of time. After a brief interview, the role play continues. Other terminology that is sometimes used to describe these interventions include "an aside" and "freeze-framing."

Mirroring involves inviting a participant to observe and mimic another person's role playing. The observer is asked to verbally or nonverbally comment on or demonstrate what he or she sees, hears, or feels is coming across. This mirroring process provides vivid information to the role players on how their behavior is being perceived by others. However, remember that observations are subjective. The person performing the mirror role is expressing his or her perceived reactions, which are subject to personal deletions, distortions, and generalizations.

Modeling is when group members show how they would deal with the role under discussion.

In a *mono play,* individuals demonstrate a range of characters and behaviors. An empty chair or a simple prop such as spectacles or a hat can be used to signal a shift in role. For example, an individual could practice a performance discussion by performing the roles of both the manager and the employee: first, he or she presents feedback and then he or she responds to the feedback. This technique enables people to consider the implications of their actions on others because they are on both the sending and the receiving ends of the communication cycle.

The *multiple* method is when small groups of individuals simultaneously act out the same role play, thereby actively involving all participants in role playing at the same time.

Role reversal occurs when individuals swap roles in the middle of the role play.

Single group is when one role play is undertaken in front of the larger group. Non-role players are assigned observer roles. This strategy allows the trainer to have more control over the learning process and allows more focused discussion on the learning objectives.

Tag team occurs when two people are assigned the same role. When a role player gets stuck on what to do, an assigned double can take over by making a prearranged nonverbal signal (e.g., tapping the current role player on the shoulder).

In *wrong/right way,* undesired behaviors are demonstrated and then followed by a demonstration of desired behaviors.

Summary

Successful use of the role-playing technique requires sensitivity to warming up the learners and then providing adequate support and coaching. When carefully designed and led, this method can add important leverage and insight to personal growth.

The versatility of the role-playing technique is particularly exciting when combined with other methods like role-training, behavior modeling, and mono role plays.

Bibliography

Eitington, J. (1989). *The winning trainer* (2nd ed.). Houston, TX: Gulf.

Pescuric, A., & Byham, W.C. (1996, July). The new look of behavior modeling. *Training and Development, 49*(2).

Pfeiffer, J.W., & Ballew, A. (1988). *University Associates training technologies: Using role play in human resource development.* San Francisco, CA: Pfeiffer.

Thiagarajan, S. (1996). Instruction games, simulations and role plays. In R.L. Craig (ed.), *The ASTD training and development handbook: A guide to human resource development* (4th ed.). New York: McGraw-Hill.

Van Mentts, M. (1983). *The effective use of role plays: A handbook for teachers and trainers.* London: Kogan Page.

9

DESIGNING AND USING CLASSIC CASE STUDIES

This chapter provides a wide range of suggestions on how to gain maximum benefit from the use of case studies: how to write them, introduce them, and process them more effectively.

"We will not solve problems using the same thinking which creates them."
ALBERT EINSTEIN

Gems Mined from These Pages

● Case studies help bridge the gap between theory and practice.

● The way a case study is undertaken is dictated by the learning objectives.

● Set clear expectations and ground rules.

● When structuring the case, use the ratio of 1 to 6.

● Trust the group to move the case study along.

Playing the Trump Card

It has been a challenging time for The Paradigm College, a newly formed adult-education institution. Over the past five years, academics and administrative staff have invested long hours to advance the credibility of this new, semi-rural distance-learning center.

Recently, the chancellor decided to introduce an international best-practice performance-management system into the college. She felt that such a system would provide an important focus on major business opportunities such as the new interactive multimedia packages on adult literacy and environmental protection. She also saw performance management as an excellent way of ensuring that sufficient resources were allocated to high-leverage instructional design, marketing, and learner support.

As part of the implementation strategy of the performance-management system, funding has just been allocated to conduct formal training on how to hold annual performance-review sessions. All academics and administrative staff have been told to attend.

When the department heads heard of the new performance-management initiative, there were mixed reactions. Chris from Business and Jo from Engineering were very supportive and excited by the prospect of increasing their profiles by identifying their successes. However, Pat from Social Science and Tony from Fine Arts were less optimistic. They feared that this performance-management system might lead to an invasion of their academic independence and a heightened expectation of achieving business outcomes at the expense of caring for students.

The personnel officer, Tricia Holst, was tasked with conducting the training and was aware of the diverse views of the academic staff. During the past month, she tried unsuccessfully to arrange a meeting among the various department heads. She reached a point at which she was at a loss as to how to gain the support of the people involved. She decided to use a notable external consultant to help her bring about the change.

The external consultant began the assignment by holding a series of on-site meetings with the department heads. Not surprisingly, Chris and Jo shared their optimism while Pat and Tony communicated their displeasure about the whole purpose and intention of performance management. The latter pair was also irritated by the fact that the system was "dumped" on them by the chancellor, without any consultation.

Having gathered data from a very informative and challenging on-site day, the consultant gained the agreement of the four department heads and the personnel officer to attend a special one-day seminar on the theme of "Performance Management Within Higher Education."

The day began at 9 a.m. with a general overview of best practice in performance management. The behavior of the staff during this first period of the program was very diplomatic, ranging from an occasional nod to a smile.

After morning coffee, the consultant's trump card, a case study, was played. Here the group of five was given forty minutes to read a case study and draft an action plan for implementing a performance-management scheme at a remarkably similar hypothetical educational institution.

The case study instructed the participants to reach consensus and draft a realistic and measurable twelve-month action plan. When it had finished, the whole group was to present its plan to the consultant.

When the briefing of the case was completed, the external consultant went away from the group and sat in a corner of the room, observing from a distance.

Immediately after the group discussion of the case began, the atmosphere in the seminar room became very tense. Pat stated, "Just like Paradigm, this hypothetical organization will meet resistance unless senior academics are involved from the start." Chris, on the other hand, did not see the value of protracted consultation. Chris's statement started a barrage of terse exchanges between him and Pat.

Observing this from the corner, the external consultant quietly came across the room and sat with the team. After a couple of minutes, he suggested that the group needed to be more conscious of listening to one another. The external consultant then mediated between the warring parties until the behavior of active listening was demonstrated. At that stage, the consultant rose from the table and returned to the corner seat.

As a result of the consultant's intervention and the case's relevance to Paradigm, the quality of debate and dialogue dramatically improved. Instead of arguing, the department heads listened to and explored the merits of one another's perspectives.

Once the case study and presentation were completed, the external consultant led an open forum on the relevance of this case to the group's own organization. Everyone agreed that the issues were nearly identical. The group then agreed to work hard in the afternoon to resolve the obstacles confronting the implementation of performance management.

From here, the day progressed with greater promise and momentum, and a draft implementation plan was drawn up for Paradigm by 5 p.m. Although the group recognized that more work was still to be done, there was now, at least, a general desire to seek out and find solutions to the challenge. The case study provided an important turning point for the quality and tone of debate for everyone involved. In many ways the playing of this case-study trump card provided a catalyst for real change. As Tricia said in the parking lot at the end of the day, "It was then that miracles started to happen."

What Is a Case Study?

A case study can be defined as a method in which learners examine a story that reflects real-life principles and situations. As a consequence, jargon, principles, symptoms, incidents, and supporting information should be familiar to the participants.

The case-study method originated at the Harvard Law School in 1869 and since then has become very popular in many training contexts including employee development and business strategy programs. In its simplicity, the technique of having people examine and consider the possibilities of a hypothetical scenario or story has been in use for thousands of years. Harvard Law School pioneered the skill of designing, writing, and presenting cases.

A case study builds a range of skills, including critical thinking, analysis, communication, interaction, and judgment, relevant to both current and future learning requirements. For this to occur, both rational and emotional elements of the human spirit need to be fostered. Whether it is a shop-floor employee exploring the key skills of team leadership or it is senior academics sharing their perceptions on performance management, the individuals should be given the opportunity to share their thoughts and feelings on the material presented.

The complexity and style of a case study will vary depending on the learning objectives and issues being addressed. Typically, a case study will contain a structure that includes information about facts, key people, and their feelings. The most common delivery format is a written one; however, more and more trainers are using video, live demonstration, and multimedia simulation. The advantage of these additional methods is that they better depict the dynamics and behaviors of the story.

Benefits of Case Studies

Successful case studies comprise the following benefits:

- Bridge the gap between theory and practice.
- Stimulate creativity and inspection of multiple solutions.
- Allow the review of real-life situations without the actual personalities being involved.
- Enhance understanding by reflection, discussion, and feedback.
- Highlight the fact that complex problems will often require a wide range of actions.
- Build presentation and communication skills by asking learners to present their views.
- Help to break down fixed attitudes, beliefs, and views.
- Facilitate a transfer of learning and behavioral change.
- Explore wider and more global issues, such as the design and implementation of policy.
- Enhance the skill of "red flagging" critical issues.

Steps in Designing a Case Study

As highlighted in the story "Playing the Trump Card," training miracles do not happen simply by chance. The case-study technique requires careful research, clever design, and excellent delivery. As you read these steps, keep in mind that many of the principles of conducting successful role plays also overlap here.

Step 1. Undertake Careful Research

The determination of whether a case study is an appropriate training technique should be based solely on whether the learning objectives will be best reached by using this approach. As a consequence, on-site research or discussion with the client or learner should be undertaken prior to beginning any design. Do not fall into the trap of running a case-study exercise without first identifying the learning requirements. A good case study requires clearly defined goals and well considered design before high-quality analysis and discussion can occur.

Although it is preferable to tailor your own material for a case study, there are commercially available products that may perfectly match your learning requirements. When choosing the commercial case, be careful to ensure that it meets your learning objectives. If you decide to amend the commercial material be sure to maintain the intention and flow. Don't underestimate the time and resources required to do this repackaging or refocusing job properly.

Step 2. Articulate Objectives

As previously discussed, the ultimate success of the case-study method will be contingent on how well the method is linked to the learning objectives in question. One of the pioneers in the field of learning ob-jectives was Benjamin Bloom, who compiled two pathfinding works entitled *Taxonomy of Educational Objectives: The Cognitive Domain* (1956) and *Taxonomy of Educational Objectives: The Affective Domain* (1964). Bloom grouped learning objectives into three categories, with each having its own sliding scale of complexity. The categories follow:

1. Psychomotor—essentially involving physical skills
2. Cognitive—thinking skills or intellectual ability
3. Affective—mainly concerned with values, attitudes and feelings

Bloom's work continues to provide inspiration to training and edu-cational thinking even though some forty years have passed. For ex-ample, in a more recently produced article, Romm and Mahler (1991) linked a planned approach for case studies to Bloom's framework. Taking the categories of cognitive and affective domain, Romm and Mahler made practical suggestions on how a case-study method could best be designed. Their framework mirrors the rising scale of com-plexity that exists within the Bloom model, while also recognizing that physical skill development is best performed by non-case-study methods such as hands-on practice and coaching. Based on the work of Romm and Mahler, the following suggests how learners could demonstrate measurable learning against Bloom's framework of the cognitive and affective domain.

Cognitive Domain (in increasing order of complexity)

- *Knowledge*—Learners should repeat facts or a body of knowledge relating to the case details.
- *Comprehension*—Learners should demonstrate an understanding (comprehension) of the case and the relationships between facts. They might, for example, have to differentiate between the important and unimportant issues. For this to be achieved, you may include some intentional "red herrings" to challenge the learner's ability.
- *Application*—Learners apply the knowledge that they have gained from the study by developing some form of action plan.
- *Analysis*—Learners dissect, identify, or group the material contained within the case into its component parts. For example, a student of company law may identify facts or precedents supporting a case.
- *Synthesis*—Learners draw conclusions from their analysis of the case. To synthesize their analysis of the legal case, for example, the learners should be asked to decide on the guilt or innocence of the parties in the case.
- *Evaluation*—Learners develop an assessment method for determining standards of performance. For example, a legal student may be asked to develop criteria that validates his or her verdict.

Affective Domain (in increasing order of complexity)

- *Receiving/attending*—Learners acknowledge or notice the feelings or reactions that the characters display within the case.
- *Responding*—Learners articulate their own reactions to the feelings of the characters within the case.
- *Valuing*—Learners express their own values associated with the feelings of the characters. This allows the exploration of personal values and biases regarding the scenario. For example, a learner might say of a character in the case, "She should feel that way." This learning objective was highlighted in the story "Playing the Trump Card" when the various participants associated their current feelings about Paradigm College with the hypothetical college.

- *Organization*—Learners modify the priority of their value system as they internalize the issues and feelings of the case. For example, a learner may say, "If I'm ever in that situation, I think I would change my strategy—listen first and then act." Or, in the case of "Playing the Trump Card," the personnel officer may have realized that the academic staff should have been consulted prior to the introduction of a new performance-management system.
- *Characterization of value*—Learners integrate the values and belief structures of the case into their own behavior.

Step 3. Determine the Best Method of Delivery

Having explained the learning objectives for the case study, it is important to then consider the best method available to achieve the results desired. In this regard, Romm and Mahler (1991) suggest five core learning strategies to structure case studies.

Core strategy number 1: *Individual processing of the case.*

Core strategy number 2: *Chronological group discussion.* Teams address a series of questions or logic within a prescribed time frame. The teams then explore a range of views on the case. This is particularly important when the case has a number of alternative outcomes.

Core strategy number 3: *Simultaneous group discussion.* Teams concentrate on different aspects or different questions pertaining to the case. The teams then feed back their findings through writing, role playing, or video.

Core strategy number 4: *Chronological group dramatization.* Individuals and teams dramatize the case rather than discuss it. During the dramatization, people experiment with various aspects of the case including acting out different endings and applying different solutions. The major benefit of playing out is that it helps learners internalize the facts, feelings, and emotions of the case.

Core strategy number 5: *Simultaneous group dramatization.* Teams play out a specified aspect or stage of the case. Like the chronological group dramatization, the teams play out the issues, but in this strategy they can only explore and dramatize one aspect of the case. Then they play out their material to the larger group or to a governing or coordinating committee.

Practical Tips

Considering the advantages of each of these five core strategies, it is evident that the results from a case study can dramatically improve when it is designed and used correctly. Some tips to remember are listed below.

1. Individual processing and group discussion are more conducive to the attainment of cognitive objectives than are those methods requiring dramatization.
2. Issues that require the expression and articulation of feelings (affective domain) are best served by group dramatization. Training programs involving awareness of group sensitivity and development of communication skills are better advanced by playing out the feelings and values rather than using more formal question-and-answer discussion sessions.
3. An open, chronological discussion seems to be more conducive to the attainment of low-level cognitive objectives such as receiving/attending and responding than are simultaneous discussions in which people are required to concentrate on only one aspect or perspective of the case.
4. If learners are allowed to explore freely through simultaneous discussions, then they are more likely to move to a higher level of the cognitive range, including synthesis and evaluation.
5. Chronological dramatization seems to be more conducive to attainment of low-level affective objectives, particularly when greater choice is given to the learners on what they will dramatize in their teams.
6. Playing out different aspects of the case before a larger group (simultaneous dramatization) seems to promote higher level attainment of affective objectives (organization, characterization of value). Each smaller group that presents is restricted to exploring a specific aspect of the case.
7. Experiment with and blend the five core strategies. As you combine or modify the approaches, new and exciting learning opportunities will be discovered.

Step 4. Develop the Story

Like a good book, a case study needs a story that grabs and holds the learner's attention. The situation should be described with all the color, drama, and life that you'd expect to find in a novel. The characters should be lifelike with real names rather than joke names. (See the following example.)

Another One of Those Days

Patricia was pleased with herself. "I'm actually going to be on time for the meeting for once," she thought. "Mobeen can't give me that look of disapproval this time. I've even got enough time for coffee before I go." She went to get her coffee and met Lee, whom she hadn't seen for a couple of weeks. She stopped to chat about his vacation and her plans for a vacation next month. After about five minutes she returned to her desk.

Before she sat down again, Steven approached her to ask for advice on a problem he was dealing with. She gave him her opinion and then realized that the meeting was due to start in a couple of minutes. As she stood to go she remembered that she was supposed to take the trainer's report with her to the meeting. "Now where did I put that report?," she asked herself. She started sorting through the stack of folders on her desk when a note that she had written caught her eye: "URGENT!!! Call Jo Murray ASAP on Monday morning." "Oh, no!," she thought, "I forgot to get back to Jo. I can't leave it any longer." Jo was furious enough on Friday when last they talked.

Ten minutes later she had dealt with an irate Jo but still hadn't found the trainer's report. The more she looked, the more depressed and panicky she became. She was already late for another meeting and as she searched through the clutter on her desk and in her filing cabinet, she discovered further unfinished work and pressing matters. She even found a proposal she was supposed to read and make a decision on two weeks ago, not to mention the stack of correspondence waiting to be answered.

Finally, she discovered the trainer's report caught up between two other reports she had started to read and make recommendations about. Whenever she started to deal with something, it seemed that something else suddenly seemed more urgent, so she usually found herself changing direction part way through.

> She hurriedly grabbed her report but in her haste she knocked the remainder of her coffee all over her desk and herself. It was the last straw and as she slumped back in her chair she thought, "Looks like another one of those days!"

As discussed in "Step 1: Undertake Careful Research," the basis of a good story is excellent on-site research and creativity. Determining where and how you undertake your research is an essential prerequisite to a good study. Where will you access the information? Will you interview people? Should you gather the information by observation, documentation, or through other information sources and media? Can you undertake the on-site research within your own organization or will you have to go elsewhere? What background data are you seeking to support the study and to what depth will you need to explain it?

After collecting information, you will need to sort through the data and relate the material you have researched to your objectives. From your preferred data develop a list of events, circumstances, and characters that capture a theme that will best draw out the learning objectives you are seeking. If you are developing a written case or a script for a video or multimedia package, make sure it is well-organized, clear, grammatically correct, and as lively as possible. The case study may also include quotes from key players, organization charts, financial statements, and abstracts of background reports to create further real-life imagery.

Write the case study as if the key players, or the organization, are actually experiencing the situation right now. This can be written in either first or third person. For example, "Jo said, 'I am concerned about Patricia'" (first person) or "Jo appeared to be concerned with Patricia" (third person).

Ensure that the background information includes feelings, actions, and key events. Life can be added to the study by including appropriate dialogue and an eye-catching beginning. Use names that reflect the nature of the community at large. This will include both male and female names (or names that are gender neutral such as Chris and Jo) and names from a variety of ethnic origins. However, if gender and background are relevant to the reality of the case, use specific male and female names. It is important to avoid names that reinforce inappropriate stereotypes (e.g., supervisors always having an Anglo-Saxon male name).

Your case should communicate an overall challenge, and all relevant information needs to be enclosed. In structuring the case, it is important to ensure that people will have sufficient time to undertake the activity. With this in mind, it is suggested that a ratio of 1 to 6 is a reasonable yardstick. That is, if the case takes five minutes to read and internalize, thirty minutes should be allocated for the learners to diagnose the case study and the trainer to debrief the material presented.

Have your case reviewed by both an experienced case writer and a subject-matter expert. For example, in regard to the case study "Another One of Those Days," an expert on time management may be appropriate.

Care is required when preparing material on highly sensitive and/ or political issues. Sometimes you may have to rework your material to ensure that there is no political fallout from the learning activity. In some cases, official approval may be required prior to use.

Case-study questions can be used to add extra focus to the learning activity. However, the questions should not telegraph the issues and principles before they are fully explored. Examples of good questions include the following:

- What are the short-and long-term issues to be considered?
- What are the assumptions of the key players?
- What should be done?
- What can be learned?
- What are the key factors?
- If you were Patricia in "Another One of Those Days," what would you say to Jo Murray regarding the urgent message?

Prior to formally conducting a case study in a training program, the trainer should conduct a trial run. The piloting of the material should include reviewing the designed material as well as physically conducting and reviewing the activity itself. After doing this you will be better prepared to make final amendments before implementation. The evaluation of the case study should examine whether the case material is sufficient, complete, accurate, realistic, and clear. Feedback from a trial run will determine whether the dynamics and learning objectives can be achieved through the material. Key factors will be whether the case study sparked the necessary interest and excitement and whether it led to constructive discussion and learning.

Conducting a Case Study

Having written the case study, you need to shift your attention to how the case study should be conducted. This process will be reviewed in five stages: preparation, briefing, diagnosis, debriefing, and maintaining a resource register.

Stage 1. Preparation

Before a trainer presents a case for diagnosis, he or she must take time to become familiar with the material. This is particularly important when the case is new or has not been used for quite a while. This task is easier if the comments and suggestions made by previous trainers or learners have been recorded in supplementary material attached to the case.

Sometimes the trainer may choose to supply preliminary information to the learners in the form of a lecture, a handout, or visual aids. This may help to enhance the quality of diagnosis. It is also important that the trainer acknowledges his or her own attitudes and biases before initiating a case. Often trainers can fall into the trap of letting their feelings and thoughts get in the way of other people's learning.

Stage 2. Briefing

The briefing process sets the tone for the learning process. It provides the learners with a clear indication of the ground rules and expectations required. Some of the common issues to be clarified follow:

- Stressing the overall focus of the case;
- Checking the familiarity of the group with the case-study method;
- Highlighting that a range of possible alternatives will need to be explored and that there is not a fixed answer; and
- Scheduling time for individual and team activity.

It is also useful to state ground rules before starting. Common ground rules include the following:

- The learners should listen to others and build on their ideas.
- Everyone should remain focused on the content of the case. Where assumptions are necessary, list them.
- The trainer will provide clarification, not answers.
- The learners must constructively challenge ideas and develop realistic actions.
- The case study should be undertaken in a spirit of openness, inquiry, and experimentation.

When outlining these ground rules, the trainer must sell the case-study method as important and the activity as a critical part of the learning experience. To do this, learners must be reminded of their learning responsibility and asked to treat the study seriously and industriously. The realism of the case study can be enhanced by asking people to present their observations and recommendations within reasonable real-life constraints and contingencies.

Stage 3. Diagnosis

Depending on the degree of experience of the group in using case studies, the trainer should be able to set the group to work on the material almost immediately. Normally, learners should read, listen to, or watch the whole case study and then go over the material once more before developing possible solutions or strategies.

During the diagnosis stage, the trainer should move quietly around the room monitoring that the ground rules are being followed. It is very important not to interfere and to trust the group to keep the activity moving. However, it may be necessary on some occasions to make some interventions to help the quality of review, debate, and dramatization. Reasons for intervening may be as follows:

- Reminding people of time requirements;
- Encouraging an even flow of communication among group members;
- Reaffirming that the trainer's role is not to provide answers;
- Channeling discussion back toward the learning objectives;
- Suggesting major avenues of inquiry that have been overlooked;
- Helping to eliminate premature trivialization of issues when the diagnosis has become badly sidetracked; or
- Dealing with frustration that some learners may be having with the case-study methodology.

Stage 4. Debriefing

As with all training techniques, the most important stage of the case-study delivery is the debriefing stage. It is here that the learning objectives are discussed or experienced before moving on to another activity. It is essential that the key learning points are summarized and that there is a clear linkage to the desired learning objectives. If the case study solutions are being formally presented or demonstrated by the learners, the trainer will need to hold a closing discussion to ensure that the necessary learning has happened. This should occur immediately following the completion of the case-study review by the participants. Sometimes emotions may reach fever pitch, so be careful to deal with these feelings prior to moving on to the next activity. Further skills and frameworks for dealing with such emotions are discussed in Chapter 11.

If the case study has been based on a real-life situation, it is sometimes practical to declare how the challenge was handled and what the actual consequences of the strategy were. At the end of the case-study activity, take time to thank the participants for their effort and commitment.

Stage 5. Maintaining a Resource Register

To gain maximum value out of the case-study method, we recommend that trainers maintain a record of their work and results with a particular case study. The goals of the resource register are to upgrade and maintain a ready reserve of case studies as well as to have a summary of key concepts, topics, and outcomes achieved. With some simple cross-referencing, either written or on computer, a trainer will be able to quickly remember past discoveries as well as select cases for future use when required.

It should be noted that this idea of maintaining a resource register can easily be adapted to other training techniques discussed in this book. To assist you to implement this idea, the following headings for a case studies resource register are suggested.

> ### *Title of Case*
>
> - Source of material or on-site research undertaken
> - Key theme of story
> - Major learning objectives
> - Process used to stimulate learning, including notes on
>   - preparation;
>   - briefing;
>   - diagnosis; and
>   - debriefing.
> - Comments on notable past experiences
> - Recommendations for the future

Summary

A case study is not the answer for all training requirements and can easily be abused if overused. But, if selected and conducted well, a case study will add value and substance to learning.

To be successful, the trainer must be skilled in identifying objectives and then structuring a meaningful story. The trainer must then be able to present the case study with integrity and conviction so that suitable discussion, reflection, and dramatization are engaged.

Bibliography

Alden, J., & Kirkhorn, J. (1996). Case studies. In R.L. Craig (Ed.), *The ASTD training and development handbook: A guide to human resource development* (4th ed.). New York: McGraw-Hill.

American Society for Training and Development. (1987). *Info-line series: Get results with the case method.* Alexandria, VA: Author.

Bloom, B. (Ed.). (1956). *Taxonomy of educational objectives: The cognitive domain.* New York: David McKay.

Bloom, B. (Ed.). (1964). *Taxonomy of educational objectives: The affective domain.* New York: David McKay.

Einsiedel, A.A., Jr. (1995, August). Case studies: Indispensable tools for trainers. *Training and Development, 49*(8).

Eitington, J. (1989). *The winning trainer* (2nd ed.). Houston, TX: Gulf.

Laird, D. (1985). *Approaches to training and development* (2nd ed.). Reading, MA: Addison-Wesley.

Niemyer, E.S. (1995, January). The case for case studies. *Training and Development, 49*(1).

Pfeiffer, J.W., & Ballew, A. (1988). *University Associates training technologies: Using case studies, simulations, and games in human resource development.* San Francisco, CA: Pfeiffer.

Romm, T., & Mahler, S. (1991). The case study challenge—A new approach to an old method. *Management Education and Development, 22*(4), 292–301.

ADVENTURES IN PARADISE

HOW TO ORGANIZE AN OUTDOOR LEARNING PROGRAM

This chapter explores the key issues of coordinating, rather than facilitating, an outdoor program. The ideas in the chapter can be used as a starting point for some low-risk outdoor program activities.

"You can discover more about a person in an hour of play than in a year of conversation."
PLATO

Gems Mined from These Pages

- Outdoor learning produces better results than traditional training.

- The method creates powerful metaphors for workplace behavior that leave lasting images imprinted on the minds of participants.

- The psychological and physical well-being of participants is critical.

- Choose a facilitator who has adventure expertise as well as educational experience.

- High-quality debriefing is central to the success of outdoor learning

Pegasus Learns to Fly with Stilts

Downsizing as a result of restructuring had created all sorts of new challenges for Pegasus Engineering. Pegasus had also hired a new general manager named Dennis Potter, and that meant some changes to policy and direction on top of the downsizing.

Nadia Borecki, the CEO of the company, was doing her best to coordinate all of the changes. She decided to send everyone to an outdoor team-building program to help bond them into a tightly knit unit. In particular, she had briefed the facilitator to highlight the issue of delegation, especially in respect to Dennis and the staff. She also explained to the facilitator that it would be useful to focus on feedback from Dennis to the staff since he was building a reputation for being critical and for making negative comments to them. Furthermore, he was known for not delegating, preferring to do everything himself. Nothing the CEO said seemed to have changed him so far.

Today was the second day of the program and everyone was nursing aching muscles from the exercises of the day before. An early morning hike would work out that stiffness, so everyone set off through the fog at 6:30 a.m. An hour-and-a-half later the fog had lifted and the sun was shining brightly. The group stopped for a rest on the bank of a shallow but fast-running stream. The sound of the water bubbling along over the stones was mesmerizing.

Without anyone knowing how he got there, the facilitator suddenly appeared on the far bank about five yards away. He called instructions to the others that they were to use the materials that were set on the bank to get everyone across the stream without anyone getting wet. The materials seemed to be little more than some dead tree branches and rope. The comedian of the group called out, "Hey, we're from Pegasus, aren't we? Let's fly across."

Dennis ignored this and, wasting no time, he began to lash the branches together. Meanwhile, a designated person in the group recorded the proceedings on video. Dennis was making a fair attempt at building a ladder and it soon became obvious that he meant to lay it across the stream. Some of the others tried to convince him that it wouldn't work, but Dennis replied that he was an engineer and that he knew what he was doing. The apprentice toolmaker began to help tie some of the branches together and soon others were lending a hand as well. Dennis began to get frustrated by the poor quality of the knots and took over from some of the people. "You're not letting us help you, Dennis," said Marie from Sales. "If you knew anything about knots, you'd be a lot more helpful," Dennis replied (and was captured clearly by the facilitator's video camera).

Suddenly, Dennis' secretary, Tanya, suggested stilts. "If we build a pair of stilts we could simply wade across," she said. Dennis just snorted. Others in the group gave it more thought. "I can use stilts," said Tanya. "I'll wade across. Then we can tie the ropes between trees on each side as handrails—put them under your armpits to keep from falling. If we make the foot rests high enough to keep everyone out of the water but still low to the ground, then we can all do it." Dennis panned the idea. "Anyway," he said, "if stilts were the answer, we wouldn't have been given so many long branches." He insisted they continue with the bridge. He was first to attempt the crossing. Subsequently, he was also the first to get wet when the bridge collapsed under his weight.

Later that day, back at the conference center, they watched the video. Dennis watched himself get wet all over again. The facilitator probed their approach to the problem and, in particular, Dennis' delegation and consideration of Tanya's suggestion about stilts. The facilitator asked about parallels to their work environment. Some team members brought up Dennis' delegation but, again, he refused to accept that he was in the wrong. Stilts would not have worked, he maintained. As the discussion continued, the facilitator played a segment of another tape that showed a group crossing with stilts.

It was a risky thing to do, and Dennis' immediate reaction was anger. He complained bitterly that the facilitator was just trying to make a fool of him in front of his staff. Much discussion followed. Eventually Dennis saw that Tanya's suggestion may not have been such a bad idea and that he should have given it more thought and listened more closely to her at the time.

After dinner that night the group played a short game. Dennis and Tanya were teammates. Dennis slipped back to his old ways once or twice, but when he did, Tanya said, "Dennis, you're forgetting the stilts."

At the close of the program, on the third day, the facilitator presented everyone with a small gift. Dennis was given a tiny pair of crudely constructed stilts mounted onto a wooden base.

Two weeks later, Nadia was in the office. She had heard all about the stilts incident and today she was listening to Dennis and Tanya in a heated discussion about Tanya's organizing a meeting for him. Tanya said at one point, "Dennis, you're forgetting about the stilts." Dennis immediately calmed down. He paused and said, "Okay Tanya, tell me your side of this again. I'll try harder to listen."

When Nadia heard this she yelled with joy, "It's a miracle!"

Why Consider Outdoor Learning?

The Pegasus Engineering example is the type of scenario you might confront in an outdoor learning program and illustrates the kind of outcome you might expect to achieve. Skilled facilitators are often able to create the level of profound learning that Dennis displayed in "Pegasus Learns to Fly with Stilts."

The result of the Pegasus experience is largely indicative of the reason why outdoor learning continues to emerge as a legitimate training method. It has been a component of military training for many years, but it has only more recently been associated with corporate training. It provides the opportunity to combine structured training with an outside environment that places people in unfamiliar settings. It can dramatically influence the excitement that learning holds for people and it contributes to lasting impressions that are remembered far longer and more deeply than images of a sterile classroom.

Some outdoor experiences can also be done indoors. However, many outdoor learning providers would argue that experiential learning methods carried out in a classroom do not achieve the same results as learning outdoors. If you compare a group of people sitting in a training room in a traditional two-day program using experiential activities with a group participating in a two-day adventure in which they are abseiling and using a flying fox and leaping across a ravine, it is generally argued that the memories of the latter will be more profound. As a result, the lasting memory of the event will leave a more permanent imprint of new behavior and skills. Because of this imprint, successful transfer of learning to the workplace happens almost by default. It's hard to forget that exhilarating moment when you overcame the fear of jumping off a cliff or experienced the support of your peers when you had to physically help one another across a muddy swamp.

The experiential argument now has some basis in research. The Corporate Adventure Training Institute (CATI—a nonprofit research center located at Brock University in Canada) is dedicated to conducting and coordinating studies on the effectiveness of adventure training. Using a validated Team Development Inventory (TDI) as an instrument for measuring effectiveness, CATI conducted several studies into the effectiveness of outdoor learning in developing teams. In one study CATI set out to determine whether outdoor learning about teamwork was more effective than learning done in a classroom. CATI studied three groups, each consisting of forty-two members. One was a control group that received no training. The second received classroom training, and the third received outdoor training.

The TDI was administered ten times: at three months, one month, and one week before the programs began; at the start and finish of the programs; and one week, one month, three months, six months, and a year after the programs ended. Changes to staffing levels meant that the numbers dropped to between thirty-three and forty by the end of the testing period.

As Figure 10.1 shows, the outdoor (or experiential) group experienced dramatically better short-term results than the classroom group and sustained a greater change for much longer. Even after a year, the results were almost 10 percent greater than those of the classroom group. These results show that the classroom group enjoyed short-lived learning, while gains from the outdoor/experiential group lasted much longer.

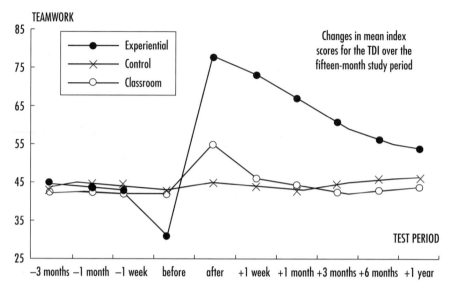

FIGURE 10.1. CATI RESEARCH RESULTS

Source: Corporate Adventure Training Institute (CATI), *Research Update No. 9,* Brock University, Ontario, Canada. Reproduced with permission.

These results are put forward to illustrate the strength of outdoor learning and the benefits that make it one of the most popular and growing methods of training today. There are also several other benefits over more traditional learning that are responsible for the growing enthusiasm for outdoor learning.

Innovation

Training practitioners, looking for new and stimulating ways to get their message across, often find that outdoor learning grabs the learner's attention and interest. "After all," many will say, "the messages we have to give them are things they've heard before: trust, cooperation, leadership, and the like. What we need to do is wake up their subconscious and keep these issues foremost in their minds. Strong imprints are what we need and this method can give us that!"

Lasting Images

The challenges involved and the extraordinary self-insight achieved by meeting them have been credited with creating such strong imprints on participants that they may never forget their experiences. Imagine someone used to office life in the city confronting and meeting the challenge of abseiling down a ninety-foot cliff, or workteam members, used to helping one another out on tasks like filing or assembly routines, having to physically help one another walk blindfolded through unfamiliar bushland or forest. It's easy to see how such activities would leave a strong imprint on the memory. Naturally, excellent facilitation is required to create a strong link between that imprint and the necessary learning outcomes so that the memory is connected to behavior change.

Enjoyment

There is common agreement that outdoor learning provides a good time. Even the most sedentary participant, one afraid of the physical challenges but who is given the choice to participate coupled with plenty of peer support, can have a good time. Almost any trainer will agree that learning should be enjoyable. This is one of the most significant reasons for the growth of outdoor learning though it can also be its weakness. Learning should be enjoyable, but some inexperienced practitioners forget the learning element and focus too much on the fun. A good balance is critical.

Unfreezing Formal Structures

Outdoor learning examines the formal structures and relationships in organizations and allows the unique strengths and abilities of all team members to emerge, in ways that other forms of learning cannot match. For example, imagine that a vertical slice of an organization is taken on an outdoor experience. In the usual workplace, hierarchical structures are difficult to examine because the pecking order is so firmly embedded in the subconscious. However, picture a situation in which the boss (who, let's imagine, is in his or her 50s and unfit) has to climb a thirty-foot wall with the assistance of a mailroom clerk whom others perceive as having no status in the organization. The physical help that the "lowly" mailroom clerk provides for the boss is a strong metaphor for the sort of support the boss should call on more often back in the workplace. Powerful debriefing of the experience can create an everlasting imprint of that new relationship and shake the embedded patterns of traditional top-down power.

Whole-Brain Learning

In Chapter 7, we explained the concept of whole-brain learning. Outdoor learning is a process that is congruent with our understanding of the way in which people learn best. In other words, the method engages the whole person in learning. People are physically, emotionally, and mentally involved. The process engages their logic in problem solving, their sense of order in planning how to approach the challenge, their emotions by confronting their fears, their reflections on feedback and their own behavior, and their imagination as they visualize possible outcomes. The powerful impact that some outdoor learning creates also affects the subconscious of learners because they may be learning a lot about themselves that they are unaware of at the conscious level.

Engaging Natural Learning Ability

There are two assertions we think are important to our total concept of training in the workplace. First, with very few exceptions, every person on this planet is a skilled learner, but each person doesn't necessarily utilize those skills during "formal" learning. Second, as trainers we need to foster lifelong learning in the workplace if we are to adapt to change.

Organizations, therefore, often have workforces of experienced learners who may not be applying this ability in the workplace. As trainers we need to help them do so. Outdoor learning is one process by which we can encourage that. In a sense, outdoor learning takes formal learning (oriented to hard business goals) into an informal setting in which people are drawn into natural behavior. We believe that this unity can help people realize that reflection and self-learning are legitimate learning processes and that they can indeed use their natural ability to learn in formal settings such as at work. When we can legitimize the value of lifelong learning at work, and when people commonly reflect on actions they take at work as part of a learning process, then we can truly say we have contributed to a miracle.

Box 10.1

Outdoor Learning at Merck, Sharp and Dohme

The use of outdoor learning at Merck, Sharp and Dohme was first introduced as part of an "Excellence in Management" program that focused on four critical areas of management: leadership, communication, managing change, and teamwork. Prior to the use of outdoor learning, management development had involved traditional classroom and on-the-job learning.

The Excellence in Management program was specifically designed to incorporate 40 percent classroom learning and 60 percent outdoor learning with groups of twelve managers operating in teams of six over a period of five days.

The design of the program focused on critical organizational issues related to leadership, communication, managing change, and teamwork. The outdoor learning exercises created challenges and problems that could not be replicated in the classroom. Outdoor activities were enhanced by the completion of a personality profile by each participant. The inclusion of this activity created greater self-awareness and aided in teamwork both outdoors and during classroom activities.

The high impact of outdoor learning created a lasting bond between participants that enhanced their performance during the program and, most importantly, was carried back to the workplace. Trust, support, respect, and loyalty were the values accentuated by the outdoor experiences. These values are evident when managers who have participated in the Excellence in Management program work in cross-functional problem-solving teams back on the job.

A key to the success of outdoor learning at Merck, Sharp and Dohme has been the design of the program and the utilization of the environment to stimulate individuals and teams to meet challenges that are different from those created by traditional learning. A combination of indoor and outdoor learning linked to organizational issues and personal development has proven successful both in generating excellent teamwork and in providing individuals with a highly motivational and memorable experience.

Including outdoor learning as part of training and development can involve additional costs; however, these can be offset by utilizing less expensive venues closer to the outdoor area. In the case of the Excellence in Management program, guesthouse accommodations in the Blue Mountains, west of Sydney, have been ideal.

After years of traditional methods of learning, staff members have taken to outdoor learning with great enthusiasm. The high acceptance has been demonstrated by the extremely low dropout rate. Maybe this is because we hire people who love a challenge, or maybe it's the opportunity to get out of the office and into the great outdoors.

Peter Philipson
Human Resource Development Manager
Merck, Sharp and Dohme
Sydney
Recipient of the 1995 Excellence in HRD in Training and Development Award from the American Society for Training and Development (ASTD).

Source: Merck Sharpe & Dohme (Australia) Pty Ltd. Reproduced with permission.

What Is Outdoor Learning?

Outdoor learning is a form of experiential learning that occurs outside the normal classroom environment and takes learners into a more informal learning environment. The same structures that exist for other forms of experiential learning are an important element of outdoor learning. Participants must be briefed, they must engage in an active learning experience, and they must be debriefed to draw out the salient learning points.

The outdoor component of the experiences can range from low-risk activities such as the team game "fifty up" to medium-risk activities such as the "trust walk," right through to such things as rappelling down a 150-foot cliff face or even scuba diving. (Examples of activities are outlined in Appendix 3.)

Outdoor learning is sometimes referred to as adventure learning. The essential difference between adventure learning and other forms of outdoor learning is the level of perceived physical risk. The greater the perceived risk in the learning experience, the greater the adventure for the learner.

In outdoor learning, participants are placed in unfamiliar settings and given physical challenges that are difficult to achieve without some danger (e.g., abseiling). Confronting this challenge and succeeding is the heart of outdoor learning. Another primary element is the combination of personal challenge and team support. Many outdoor learning programs involve group problem solving in which the entire group is responsible for achieving the task. The cooperation necessary for team members to support one another through some of the most difficult challenges many of them have ever faced is the key to building a more cohesive team back in the workplace.

The object of outdoor activities is to show that if you can meet the challenges you confront there, then the challenges faced in the workplace will pale by comparison and your behavior at work will mirror the success achieved in the great outdoors. The following components need to be considered whenever you are planning an outdoor program.

Goals

Like all experiential learning, outdoor learning must be based on clear goals and outcomes. There is little to be gained from an activity that explores group problem solving if this is not an issue that needs to be addressed. However, a program for a sales force in which each person confronts personal outdoor/adventure hurdles may be entirely relevant if the sales force is having trouble meeting the challenge of increasing sales budgets or overcoming fears of rejection or call reluctance.

Challenge and Unfamiliar Tasks

It is important to recognize that outdoor learning does not purposefully present physical danger. In fact, if anything, the reverse is true. Outdoor learning requires many precautions to guard against physical danger. An important component, however, is the perceived physical danger. Many people find it difficult to leap from a twenty-foot wall onto a trapeze, despite the presence of a safety line preventing them from falling if they slip. The point is that if you can get people to take the risk doing something they think they cannot do and they discover that they can, this can be translated with expert debriefing into their whole attitude about the way they manage others, the way they cooperate, and the way they approach life and work.

Discovery Learning

When people suddenly discover something long hidden or when they find something hidden after a frustrating search, they are often inclined to exclaim "a-hah!" Sometimes this "a-hah!" of discovery is a mental one, as when a learner suddenly realizes that he or she has discovered something meaningful. The "a-hah!" factor is one of the most significant components of outdoor learning. The activities are designed to help people discover something about themselves. This process of discovery learning helps to create lasting behavior change.

The intention is to place people in learning situations that make them forget their workplace roles. The activities then create an environment that brings out natural behavior. When this behavior is later debriefed, the mental "a-hah!" can almost be heard.

Metaphors for Workplace Behavior

When a manager in a muddy creekbed trying to help a receptionist crawl under a two-foot high cage through the slime forgets the moment and yells at the receptionist for poor performance, the manager may very well be mirroring workplace behavior. When it comes to the receptionist's turn to help the manager, he or she may feel inclined to let the manager fall just to get back at him or her.

It is these vignettes and the strong metaphors they invoke that outdoor learning is famous for. The hope is that the manager will never forget the feeling of falling into a quagmire rear-end first because he or she was not capable of helping others over hurdles that they found difficult. Next time the manager berates the receptionist for not taking a message perfectly, the fall in the mud may be brought up as a reminder of how appropriate feedback should be delivered. The strength of these metaphors is dependent on the skills of the facilitator. The facilitator must first re-create the events of the muddy creekbed back in the classroom (or discuss it while still in the field) and make the point about cooperation as well as engender a sense of trust and open communication that will exist back in the workplace. Otherwise the receptionist may not bring to the manager's attention his or her berating behavior.

These on-the-job replays are an integral part of the miracles that can occur in outdoor learning. As the manager and receptionist think back to their outdoor experience, the learning outcomes miraculously resurface to help reshape behavior.

Reflection

Outdoor learning is obviously about action. The activity creates a sense of fun and challenge, and the reflection on that action cements new learning. Purposeful outdoor learning programs have a strong component of personal reflection and disclosure. The ideal is to achieve reactions like those in the example given below.

> "I've been thinking about what I did during that river crossing," says Jim. "I realize that pushing Susan into the water was just the sort of behavior I carry on with at work. You know, I often play the joker, and I've been told that I don't know when to be serious. But today, when I saw Susan's reaction to being pushed in, I guess it finally hit home."

You can see how a training miracle has occurred here. The experience has helped Jim see something about himself that is otherwise hidden behind the daily context of his relationships at work. Reflecting on that experience reveals a valuable learning outcome and the imprint of that event will last a long time for Jim.

How to Plan an Outdoor Program

When you are planning an outdoor program there are a number of issues to consider. All of them are important and some of them are crucial. One of the first issues to consider is the successful relationship between the outdoor experiences and the required learning outcomes. If the lasting imprints from outdoor learning are not linked to the learning outcomes, the experience may be of little or no value. The quality of the debriefing is the key ingredient to making this link.

Linking the Outdoor Model to Learning Outcomes

Outdoor learning takes many forms, including bushwalking, ball games, white water rafting, caving, orienteering, initiative challenges, abseiling, rope courses, and even scuba diving. No matter what the form, there are usually three broad categories of learning outcomes into which most corporate outdoor programs can be classified.

1. Team Challenges

These programs are designed to pose a variety of challenges to a group as a whole. They are usually intended to explore the interactions between team members and are most useful when addressing some kind of difficulty that a group may be having in terms of its level of trust or support or in interpersonal relationships.

The events may all be linked, such as in a distance challenge with obstacles along the way. Each event is debriefed as it is overcome and the group gradually approaches its end goal. Alternatively, the group may tackle a number of events that are independent of one another. The key is that each event is debriefed as it is overcome.

2. Leadership Challenges

These programs are similar in many respects to team challenges and even to the third category, individual challenges. The major difference is the goal of the program. Rather than trying to analyze the interrelationships among all of the group members, these programs try to explore leadership behavior and its influence on the group and the way the group tackles its challenges.

Another potential difference is that leadership challenges can be conducted with people who do not know one another. The individual challenges are often conducted in this way.

3. Individual Challenges

Common goals for individual challenges include increased self-esteem, adaptability, tolerance, confidence, and positive thinking. Also, of course, there are the goals of improved problem solving and decision making. As each person tackles his or her individual task, he or she must confront a whole range of personal challenges.

Interestingly, there are the "gun" people who simply leap off into the unknown and get a real rush from the attempt, and there are some people who find it physically or emotionally difficult to attempt a task, despite seeing others do it. Skilled facilitators help the cautious ones overcome their fear of the unknown by gradually taking them from easy challenges to the more difficult ones. Each step along the way, others in the group support the hesitant participants to confront the challenges with confidence.

Another way to link the outdoor model to learning outcomes is to consider an appropriate design for the program that maximizes learning potential. One such model is Kolb's experiential learning model (see Figure 10.2). Kolb, Rubin, and McIntyre (1984) argue for a cyclical explanation of the way people learn. They suggest that learning begins with a concrete experience. Learners then reflect on that experience, drawing from it ideas and perceptions about responses, interactions, and meaning for action. Next, learners use their reflections to develop new rules and abstract concepts for behavior, which are in turn used in a new concrete experience or in a pragmatic application of the concepts (or an imagined one) to test the validity of the abstract concepts developed.

An outdoor program that is designed around this model may well go like this: A group is given a physical challenge (concrete experience) and its behavior is observed and, perhaps, recorded. The facilitator debriefs the group about the experience, asking many questions to explore reasons and interrelationships between actions and reactions (reflection). The group members then develop new ways of interacting and working together to solve problems (abstract conceptualization) and finally puts their ideas into practice in a new physical challenge (pragmatic application).

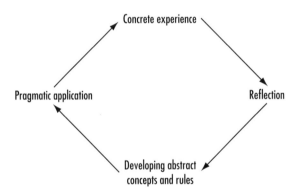

FIGURE 10.2. EXPERIENTIAL LEARNING MODEL

Source: Adapted from Kolb, D., Rubin, I., and McIntyre, J. 1984. *Organizational Psychology: Readings on Human Behavior in Organizations* (4th ed.), Prentice Hall, Englewood Cliffs, NJ. Reproduced with permission.

How Can the Risks of Outdoor Learning Be Minimized?

It is important to be aware of the possibility of risk in outdoor learning. There are both physical and psychological risks involved. The extraordinary level of personal exposure can easily create difficulties for some people. The process of self-disclosure is sometimes emotionally overpowering. Emotional safety is critical to people's ongoing peer support and respect once the program has ended. Therefore, there are a number of important factors to plan for in an outdoor program if it is to be both physically and emotionally safe.

Psychological Well-being

Many people are relieved to learn that the risks in outdoor learning are carefully managed. Although the level of perceived risk is high, the real risk is very low since a wide range of safety measures is put in place to protect people. Perceived physical and psychological "danger" build gradually in the program, and increased physical and emotional safety measures are built in to protect the participants from any real risk.

In a program that includes self-disclosure, participants are put through a number of exercises to promote trust and peer support. All participants get the chance to discuss their feelings and disclose previously hidden things about themselves. These activities are carefully monitored; the facilitator will draw out people who are obviously holding back while avoiding any outright demands on them to disclose their feelings.

People must always have a choice about their participation in experiential activities. This is even more important when it comes to activities that involve personal disclosure. However, it may be better to draw people out earlier, when there is low risk, rather than later, when the damage of speaking out is likely to be more keenly felt. For example, it may be that early in a program participants complete a trust walk. During the debriefing they are asked about their feelings of vulnerability. This is the time when it may be disclosed that a participant was intensely worried about his or her partner tripping him or her for a joke. It is only then that the facilitator can gauge the depth of feeling on this issue and perhaps conduct other activities to remove the barrier. By comparison, it is clearly not a good time to discover that one of the participants does not wholly trust his or her partner when they are all exposed on a cliff with a 90-foot drop below and (in his or her mind) only his or her partner to rely on for safety.

Physical Well-being

Safety precautions that fit the level of physical risk are, of course, a primary concern. Ropes, helmets, harnesses, belaying lines, and two-way radios are commonplace. The rule of thumb is to expect the unexpected and to be prepared.

Facilitators need to have first aid skills at the very least. The ability to immediately contact ambulance services is also a priority, and the group should never be far from a road. Of course, this is a good idea in any training, not just high-risk training. After all, a person can get a very nasty concussion simply from fainting on a tiled floor in an indoor training setting.

Remember, though, that physical danger is not a part of this method—physical challenge is. Learners should perceive the risk of outdoor activities in the appropriate place on a "continuum of risk."

Figure 10.3 illustrates how activities may be placed in order to determine their level of perceived risk for participants. The facilitator's role is often to manage the learners' perceptions of risk and to help them overcome their fears. Overcoming the perceived risks and powerful physical challenges is often where the real miracles lie.

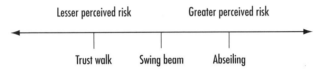

FIGURE 10.3. CONTINUUM OF RISK

Skilled Facilitation

One of the most significant things about outdoor learning is that the circumstances generate some very deep personal experiences and can result in profound emotional disclosure ranging from exhilaration, celebration, and joy to conflict and depression. When these things occur, it is absolutely crucial that the facilitator is skilled at using them for the purposes of the program or defusing them appropriately if they are of no benefit.

Open conflict may be a good thing if the purpose of the program is team building and developing better interpersonal relationships. It may also be useful for leadership training. However, when the purpose of the program is to develop self-confidence or positive thinking, this kind of disagreement is not necessarily productive for the group. Similarly, tears generated out of fear of falling from a height may well serve as a debriefing focus for personal challenge courses but are usually of less interest (as far as facilitation goes) in, say, a leadership program. (However, if someone is afraid it is interesting to see how the leader and teammates respond.) For these reasons, the facilitator has to be well-armed with the skills involved in debriefing.

EXAMPLE OF SKILLED FACILITATION

In a leadership/team-building program, group members have to help one another through a series of obstacles and challenges. An activity is used that requires the members to cross a muddy swamp without getting wet. After a frustrating day, their energy is low and feelings are raw. Jean, the team leader, just wants to get back to the cabin and yells to the group, "I don't want to hear five hundred ideas and arguments about how to get across! Bill, you're good at these things. You work it out and let us know!"

Bill tries, but the group gets stuck in the middle and Jean falls in the swamp. Jean screams about sabotage and storms back to the cabin without completing the event. As you can imagine, the commitment to the event wanes sharply at this point and the group decides, with the help of the facilitator, that they should follow Jean and try to resolve the problem.

Situations like this one wait for you in the outdoor learning arena. The challenge for the facilitator now is to go back to the cabin, call the group together, and try to resolve this conflict by asking questions such as the following:

- What happened?
- How did Jean fall?
- What made Jean give up? How did Jean feel?
- How did the others feel when Jean gave up?

The exact nature of the debriefing will vary depending on the responses that develop, but the broad intent should be to get the group members to discuss these kinds of difficulties rather than give up or sabotage one another. Another goal is to get the group to return to the event as soon as possible and complete it. The subsequent debriefing would compare the first attempt to the second and help the group identify positive and negative behaviors. Finally, to help create a miracle, some agreed guidelines for how to overcome this kind of situation should it recur at work are a must.

Realistic Goals

It is easy to develop outdoor learning programs with too many concurrent goals and objectives. It is important that a trainer keeps the desired goals to an achievable level—one or two broad aims at most. Many of the experiences take a lot of time to complete, and it is important to allow sufficient time for debriefing. For example, getting a group to develop positive communication strategies during conflict would be more than enough for a one-or two-day program. Tacking things on such as trust, supportive behavior, and asking for help are all noble pursuits but may simply serve to cloud the purpose and minimize the results. Keep it simple and the outcomes will be more effective.

Process Framework

There are some common denominators to the sort of processes that are appropriate to most outdoor learning programs. The following areas are a useful framework around which to structure your activities.

Orientation

Figure 10.1 shows a marked dip in the team index immediately prior to the outdoor learning event. This may be an indication of the apprehension that many people feel when they are about to embark on a program with high perceived risk. It is therefore important to conduct an orientation phase as soon as people arrive. It is imperative that their early exposure is comfortable and relaxing and that they become familiar with their surroundings.

The orientation phase is important for developing rapport, establishing expectations, building relationships, and minimizing inhibitions. In the orientation phase, you should explore the needs of each individual if it is an individual challenge program or crystallize the needs of the group for a group challenge program.

The orientation phase is the best time to begin icebreaker activities to help people to get to know one another (if that is relevant) or to generate enthusiasm toward the principles of outdoor learning.

Practice and Comfort

When people have been orientated, are familiar with their surroundings, and have discussed their expectations, fears, and excitement, the next step is to begin practicing some of the key skills to be used in the outdoor exercises. Again, the emphasis is on comfortable transition. Start easy and progress to the more difficult.

Naturally, outdoor learning programs expose people to activities that many of them have never attempted before and, as safety is a primary concern, it is therefore important to include practice elements so that when learners confront the more vigorous challenges there is lower risk. By practice, we mean, for example, simple stretching exercises, some balance practice, and also practice at "scouting."

Scouting is the process whereby people provide physical assistance, such as catching one another or preventing falls. A major principle of scouting is to avoid the need to catch someone already well into a fall. It is difficult and dangerous to actually catch a falling body. The primary goal is to keep the upper body and head from striking the ground, and the group should practice this skill before the need actually arises. Catching should occur as soon as the person loses his or her balance.

Scouts perform other functions, too. For example, if a group has to climb over a fifteen-foot wall of split logs, a scout may sit astride the top log to lend a hand. Also, if someone is walking a balance beam, a scout simply walks beside him or her to prevent falls. These simple scouting activities build the necessary trust and support required for emotional and physical well-being during the program. When someone is leaping from a platform twenty feet in the air to catch a trapeze, he or she needs to be supremely confident in his or her scout's ability to prevent a fall by using a belay line.

Another skill to be practiced in this phase is that of how to fall. The group should practice forward and backward rolls, first on gym mats and then on the ground, and then progress to falls from heights of up to six feet (three feet for backward rolls). Skilled trainers should instruct people how to fall. If you do not know how to do so, get an expert.

Practice in the actual activity may not be necessary, but practice in the discrete skills that make a program physically safe is important. The rule of thumb for the practice stage is that there needs to be a mood that is relaxed, calm, and easy, but in which skills are being practiced and people are not just having good fun. Clearly, expert scouting by the facilitator in this phase is important so that the participants truly develop the necessary skills for scouting for their colleagues. In this phase, the facilitator asks the participants to reflect on the simple yet challenging events already experienced. The intention is to clarify ideal behavior and establish ground rules such as focusing feedback on the behavior rather than the person. The trainer must also make absolutely certain that everyone understands the rules. The following dialogue illustrates the learners' understanding of the rules for a trust fall:

Faller (John): "Are you ready to catch me?"
Catchers: "We're ready, John."
Faller (John): "Okay. I'm falling."
John falls into a safe catch.

Go for It

Now it is time to progress along the path from simple to more complex events and from less to more physically demanding events. The perceived risk must grow gradually as should the support provided by scouts. Each event is a cycle from action to reflection to development of concepts to practical application of these concepts in yet more events. Each event encourages the learning and development of the group and the cycle repeats itself over and over.

Action Planning

The facilitator should allocate time for the group to identify action plans that specify on-the-job application of what has been learned. Key ingredients of action plans include specific objectives, milestones, accountabilities, and review dates.

Exit

Eventually, every program comes to an end. However, outdoor learning is a profound experience and the levels of disclosure and feedback serve to bind most groups into a close-knit team. Great and lasting friendships are known to have been formed on these programs. As a consequence of this, it is important that the facilitator provide a process or ritual for saying goodbye. Some facilitators choose hugging; others have a campfire where they give out mementos; others choose to have an awards ceremony and an informal closure over lunch or drinks. Whatever you do, it is a good idea to close the program with an appropriate farewell ritual.

What Issues Are Important for Planning an Outdoor Program?

There are many considerations when planning an outdoor learning program. The most important is the choice of facilitator. It cannot be too greatly stressed that a facilitator skilled in group dynamics and outdoor training is crucial.

Choosing a Facilitator

Consider your own skills before facilitating an outdoor program. Be sure you have the appropriate adventuring skills for the level of risk involved and also be clear on your debriefing capabilities. It is advisable to use the services of an expert and learn from him or her. As with any consulting contract, you should endeavor to learn from someone's expertise. As a new facilitator of outdoor learning, begin with building experience at debriefing more basic experiential learning activities that might be used in an indoor program. When you have mastered that, progress to low-risk outdoor activities and also embark on a course for learning outdoor adventure skills. A checklist covering important issues for organizing outdoor learning is provided in Appendix 4.

If you decide that you are not yet ready to facilitate an outdoor learning program, you will need to select an outside facilitator. The facilitator whom you choose must have, at the very least, experience with the type of outdoor activity being planned (experienced abseilers for abseiling programs, for example) and also skills as an educator so that he or she can competently debrief the activities. Otherwise, it may very well be little more than a "good weekend in the woods." Also, referrals are crucial. It is very important that you do not take an outdoor facilitator on face value. Obtain references and follow them up, particularly checking on the issue of educator ability.

Site and Travel

Choose a site that is remote enough to provide privacy but that has access to emergency services and nearby roads. Prepare for the unexpected when considering the level of risk involved. The site must have all of the necessary features required for your events and must be accessible before the program so that you can set up the activities that require preparation.

Participants will usually need to travel to the site in unusual ways due to the requirements for "real adventure." Consider their means of transport and whether group travel is appropriate.

Ascertain Whether Your Needs Are Suited

Outdoor learning is usually an enjoyable experience, there is little doubt. But it is useful only for a limited range of needs. Be certain that the needs you have are suited to the medium.

Cost and Cost Effectiveness

Outdoor learning programs can cost more than traditional workshops. These programs often require extra facilitators. Additional equipment must be purchased, maintained, and erected. Accommodations and meals must be arranged for, and the proper insurance must be acquired. However, while considering the costs, remember the cost effectiveness of the process. There is little argument that most well-run outdoor learning programs are unforgettable events and that therefore transfer of learning is more likely than with traditional workshops (all other things, such as facilitator skill, being equal).

Duration

Make sure that you have allotted enough time for the events you are planning and the debriefing. When planning the time required, calculate your best estimate, include time for debriefing, and then add 50 percent. An intensive half-day activity followed by a half day of debriefing is a reasonable yardstick to plan by. Remember, too, that the activities are not exclusive to the normal working time clock. Consider the full twenty-four hours in a day for the best impact of the activities. A midnight walk may achieve a better imprint than a daylight one.

Having too much time is preferable to having too little. It is better to have extra time for longer discussions than to have to hurry a discussion when there is insufficient time. Furthermore, you may uncover some serious personal issues that must be handled carefully and not hurried.

Events

Again, as with any program, carefully choose events that will have the best chance of achieving your objectives and that fit the skills of the facilitator. If you are personally attempting some of these experiences, select those that suit your skills. Some are covered briefly in Appendix 3 and the level of risk is indicated to help you choose from among them.

Insurance

Adequate insurance is also important since, even in the safest activities, someone can fall over or sprain an ankle. Make sure you are clear about the insurance coverage you or the provider has. Outdoor learning programs attract high insurance premiums, and some companies may refuse to cover you. The premiums are based on the level of risk involved: the higher the risk, the higher the premium. Simple waivers of responsibility from participants aren't worth the paper they are written on. Be sure you have adequate insurance coverage before you take a step outside.

Summary

Outdoor learning is becoming a very popular training technique. The primary advantage is that it produces long-lasting behavioral change by using the natural capacity of individuals and teams to confront challenges. These challenges are carefully selected to be metaphors of workplace scenarios. As with all training techniques, success depends largely on effective planning and debriefing.

The fact that people are outdoors means that added precautions need to be taken. Physical safety must be a priority at all times.

Outdoor learning is a powerful, enjoyable, and energetic learning experience that leads to longer lasting change when compared with regular classroom training and creates imprints on the memory that are hard to forget.

Bibliography

Clements, C., Wagner, R.J., & Roland, C.C. (1995, February). The ins and outs of experiential training. *Training and Development, 49*(2).

Corporate Adventure Training Institute (CATI). (1993). *Research Update No. 9.* Brock University, St. Catharines, Ontario, Canada.

Kolb, D., Rubin, I., & McIntyre, J. (1984). *Organizational psychology: Readings on human behavior in organizations* (4th ed.). Englewood Cliffs, NJ: Prentice Hall.

Michalak, B., Fischer, S., & Meeker, L. (1994). *Experiential activities for high performance teamwork.* Amherst, MA: HRD Press.

Rohnke, K. (1984). *Silver bullets.* Dubuque, IA: Kendall Hunt.

Rohnke, K. (1989). *Cowstails and cobras.* Dubuque, IA: Kendall Hunt.

Rohnke, K. (1994). *The bottomless bag again* (2nd ed.). Dubuque, IA: Kendall Hunt.

11

A PILOT'S GUIDE TO FACILITATION

This chapter follows a simple model that explains the role of a facilitator. It shows a trainer how to navigate a path that leads toward a learning destination and how to pilot the program over hazards along the way.

"Risks must be taken because to risk nothing is the greatest hazard in life."
ANONYMOUS

Gems Mined from These Pages

- Facilitators must begin by clarifying their role.

- They must develop broad strategies to achieve their aims.

- They must be equipped with an array of intervention skills.

- Most assignments have two equal goals: facilitating learning and facilitating group dynamics.

- Facilitators need to help groups through stages of development.

Declan Controls the Steering

The time had come for both Cheryl and John to make the transition from trainers to facilitators. Cheryl Eccleston and John Metcalf were consultants with a medium-sized training and consulting firm. They had each worked for the company for about two years and both had challenging assignments coming up in the next week.

Until now, their assignments had been merely to deliver training in areas associated with personal and management development. However, over the past year they had been coached by their manager, Declan Power, in facilitation skills, and it was time to use the skills they had been practicing.

Cheryl is to facilitate a team process for an advertising firm. The various division managers of the firm meet weekly, and the CEO, Michael Kennedy, normally does most of the talking. Occasionally, the others would have something to say, but rarely, if ever, would they directly challenge Michael's opinions.

It was Michael's idea to run this program with Cheryl because he felt that the managers agreed with everything he said too easily and he wanted them to be more forthcoming with ideas and feedback. What Cheryl didn't know was that the division managers had tried to give feedback to Michael in the past and he was, in their perception, opposed to everything they suggested. Their view was that Michael was the root of their difficulties, but they were not inclined to tell him this since it would probably be met with strong resistance.

John's assignment was different but equally challenging. His client was a transport company that had initiated a staff training program for its drivers for the very first time. John's job was to put the drivers through a customer-service program. The challenge, however, was that these people had had very little training since leaving school and for many of them that was years ago. They generally resisted formal training and they had been educationally disadvantaged in the past.

Cheryl and John each had a different assignment, but both of them were presented with a challenging facilitation opportunity.

In both cases, they were to begin with a half-day session during which some agenda setting would occur and the participants would have an opportunity to state their expectations. From that point onward, though, their processes diverged markedly.

Cheryl had no content to deliver up front but had to facilitate openness and two-way communication. She first had to provide the group with some communication experiences and then observe group behavior and identify what was consistent with the goal and what was inconsistent with it. Then she had to help the group members learn more effective behavior if that was what they needed. In a sense, her role was to begin with diagnosis and then to help the group to implement the solution. John, on the other hand, already had a solution (customer service); his task was to get the group to accept this.

John had to train the group members in service skills but also had to facilitate the group dynamics so that the participants would accept training even though they were unaccustomed to it and perhaps held negative preconceived ideas about it.

Before Cheryl and John began their assignments they had a briefing meeting with Declan. He reminded them of the need for professionalism. Then he said, "It's probably worth going over the issue of what facilitation is before we go any further."

What Is Facilitation?

Facilitation is about helping. The term has become almost synonymous with training since many trainers regard themselves as facilitators of learning. However, there is a little more to it than that. A facilitator is a catalyst who takes a person from being a passive learner and transforms him or her into a person possessed of the power to take control of change. There are a number of models, frameworks, and skills that can create the chemistry for real and lasting change. In this chapter we will explore facilitation from the perspective of three variables:

1. The role of the facilitator;
2. Strategies used by the facilitator; and
3. The outcomes being pursued.

"I think it would serve a useful purpose if we just review what we know about facilitation," said Declan. "I think each of you has a different role here even though you both have clear learning outcomes as your goal."

Declan stood up and drew a series of circles in the center of some flip-chart paper attached to an easel in the conference room where they were talking. Ever the comedian, John quipped, "Don't tell me you're going to start talking in circles again." Cheryl stifled a laugh. Declan proceeded to draw (see Figure 11.1). When he had finished he said, "We just need to look at the center issue for now."

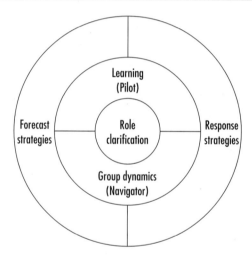

FIGURE 11.1. FACILITATION MODEL

Role Clarification

Facilitation skills encompass a wide spectrum of roles from helper, adviser, coach, and mentor to director, counselor, and expert. Some people believe that facilitators should remain neutral at all times, having no role in the content of a group's decisions. This definition, however, denies the reality that facilitators also have a teaching role. They often need to facilitate group dynamics while still delivering content. Therefore, although there are certainly occasions in which facilitators need a neutral standpoint in relation to various opinions in a group, it is often more complex than this simple model suggests. The key variable is the context within which facilitators operate.

Clarifying the appropriate role for the trainer given the context is a critical beginning to the process of facilitation. Facilitation is therefore contextual, meaning that the skills you employ will depend on the situations in which you find yourself. In some cases, to help means to leave alone. In other cases, of course, the help you provide can take a much more significant and active part in the relationship. It may mean that you have to be quite directive and spell out exactly what a learner needs to do.

Facilitator Role and Power

The central perspective from which we will examine the issue of the facilitator's role is the way power is shared among the participants and the facilitator. The distribution of power is a key issue that influences other dynamics in a training program, such as motivation to learn, rapport among the people involved (trainer and learners), and respect for the process.

Declan finished his diagram and said, "As I stated earlier, it is important for a facilitator to begin by clarifying his or her role. For example, is your role to help someone learn in a directive way by acting as the expert or is it to be a coach and take a much more cooperative stance or is it to be more of a supporter, letting the learner run his or her own learning and take almost total control for the decisions he or she makes over learning?"

"These role decisions are based on how you want power to be distributed," Declan said. "In some cases, the power will be almost totally invested in the facilitator, while at the other end of the spectrum the power may belong to the participants. This power sharing belongs on a continuum with the trainer at one end and the participants at the other." As he said this he jumped up and added the continuum to the easel (see Figure 11.2).

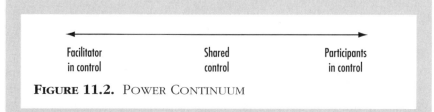

FIGURE 11.2. POWER CONTINUUM

"If you take an expert role and are directive and very structured in your design, then you are taking a position at the left end of the continuum," continued Declan. "On the other hand, if you take a purely neutral position and merely share your observations and allow the group to discover things for itself using its own processes, then your facilitation position is at the other end of the continuum."

"In between there are varying degrees of shared power and responsibility; most facilitation belongs somewhere in the middle. In situations like this, the group, including the facilitator, is a team, and the facilitator, although an outsider, exists as part of the team since he or she is integral to the experiences of the group. As a result, the activities, rules, discoveries, and actions undertaken by the group are jointly decided on with varying degrees of direction, prodding, and probing from the facilitator to help the group achieve the aims it set out to achieve. Whichever power structure you adopt, it is important to remember that it is central to the process of learning," Declan continued. "That's why I put the issue of the facilitator's role in the center of the model."

"Finally," Declan said as he sat down again, "the power structure will also influence the strategies you intend to adopt as you design the program—but that's another story. First we need to look at your facilitator style."

Facilitator Style and Program Outcomes

The second perspective to examine is the style of facilitation required. This relates to the outcomes that are intended for the program. Program outcomes can be broadly categorized as facilitating learning (piloting) and facilitating group dynamics (navigating). The style the facilitator uses will depend on which category the outcomes fall into.

Pilot Facilitation

The first style is best suited to a situation in which the primary outcome is to facilitate learning. It is equivalent to a teaching role. The facilitator chooses the process and activities that will show the group a solution. We call this style "pilot facilitation." The facilitator is really flying the plane and directing the group along the route he or she has chosen. The learning goal (destination) has been decided and the facilitator takes the group there.

Navigator Facilitation

The second style is for situations in which the major outcome is to improve group dynamics by helping a group to analyze its own processes. In this case, the facilitator is in more of a guiding role. The group is working on finding a solution itself rather than having the facilitator provide one. The facilitator merely keeps an eye on things. We call this style "navigator facilitation." The group is flying the plane and the facilitator advises when the steering needs adjustment.

John and Cheryl each considered the outcomes of the programs they were about to begin. Cheryl decided that since her goal was to help the group find its own solutions through joint diagnosis, a navigator style was more appropriate for her. She wanted to help the group permanently improve its process and reduce its dependence on a facilitator so that the members could help themselves in the future. To this end she saw herself advising the group when to adjust the steering.

When she considered the power continuum, she felt that her role would be a transitional one. She felt that initially she would need control. She would need to be more directive than John since she was going to have to confront some potentially sensitive issues. She would need to be an expert observer and evaluator of the members' behavior toward one another. She also considered the need to adopt a flexible approach and adjust the level of power as the program progressed. As the members became more aware of their behavior and the effect they had on one another, she would move to a cooperative control process whereby they would begin to learn improved behaviors through guided discussion and participative exercises. Finally, if she was going to achieve her aim of eliminating their dependence on her, she needed to end with an autonomous process in which they took control of their own learning and change.

From the information he received at the briefing meeting with his client, John believed that his program needed pilot facilitation since he was intending to help the group improve its level of service. He also considered the power sharing issue in relation to his pilot style and decided that, since motivation might be a difficulty, a cooperative control process would be a good idea. He believed that this would help to build ownership for the program and also help the participants see what they had at stake.

When they had finished discussing the issue of roles, Declan reminded John and Cheryl that it was important not to be too structured before the program began. "You may find things to be different than what you expected, and it will be necessary to adapt to the real dynamics in the program as they unfold," he advised. He also reminded them that it was important to consider their facilitation strategy. He stood up again and motioned to his model. "There are two kinds of strategy," he said. "Keep the pilot and navigator facilitation styles in mind as I explain this."

Facilitation Strategies

Earlier, we said that the role of a trainer in facilitation is to facilitate learning. As you know, there are many ways to design this facilitation. In doing so, you are designing a *structure* that provides information or skills in a sequence that will maximize the possibility that the learners will make sense and order of it. It is equally important to design a *process* that will achieve the same end. Facilitation strategies are a way of exploring how to design these processes. They are divided into two broad categories: forecast strategies and response strategies.

When a pilot and a navigator plan a flight, they attempt to forecast the weather patterns they will encounter. Then they choose a flight path that will avoid the worst storms and take them through the least turbulent areas and yet be the most direct route to their destination. However, as they make their way the weather can take a turn for the worse, and they need to be equipped to respond to whatever arises. The safety of their passengers is paramount.

Facilitators (whether pilot facilitators or navigator facilitators) also need to *forecast* the way the program will go and choose processes that will move them through the storms to their destination. Likewise, they need to be ready with skills and strategies to *respond* to what arises and protect the (emotional) safety of the learners they are facilitating.

Facilitation is therefore a combination of forecast and response strategies. Whether your style is as a pilot or a navigator, your journey will still need forecast and response strategies. The model in Figure 11.1 is drawn in a way that represents this overlap and shows how each style needs both kinds of strategy.

Forecasting strategies are those things a facilitator does that enhance the overall learning environment and may include issues such as environment and climate setting, sequence and methods used in training, level of risk and open communication required, and even specification of course objectives.

The facilitator uses response strategies for the moment-by-moment management of the program. There are responses to both the discrete events that occur and also to the individuals in the learning setting. These strategies might include questioning technique, conflict management, changes to room layout, level of inclusion or exclusion of the group as a whole or of individuals within the group, and the trainer's own disclosures, such as not knowing the answer to a question.

Forecast Strategies

John considered his program and discussed the forecast strategies he had in mind with Declan. As a component of his forecast strategy, he decided to adopt a fun element for the program as a means of building motivation. He decided to begin with some enjoyable activities and gradually move on to the more serious and confrontational issues surrounding behavior change. His intention was to develop a solid rapport with the learners first;

then he would be more capable of fostering personal reflection and change.

Because he was going to maintain a relatively high degree of control over the process, John decided that more effort would need to be put into developing a rapport with the participants in order to have the group accept him as credible. Furthermore, he decided to design increasing levels of group discussion and activities that would keep the interest up and commitment high. As John considered these ideas, Declan reminded him of a simple model that would be quite useful in his situation.

"Since you really are in a learning facilitation role," said Declan, "you might use the GRIPS model. Make sure the group is clear on each of the elements in that model and you should be okay."

John thanked him and left. Back in his office, he searched through his journals for the GRIPS model.

The GRIPS Model of Group Needs

The GRIPS model is a mnemonic that represents the needs of a group. The model implies that a group that has these needs met will be more effective. The mnemonic represents these elements:

- **G**oals that are mutually agreed on, achievable, and challenging
- **R**oles within the group that are clearly described
- **I**nterpersonal relationships that are healthy and open
- **P**rocedures that are clearly understood and agreed on
- **S**ystems influence, which is the ability to influence the external environment and systems in which the group functions

For training purposes, these issues can be further clarified to show what individuals will require in order to function well as a part of the group and therefore to learn in the environment that they are in during the length of the course:

- A clear goal or purpose for every session;
- A clear structure—what happens first, second, etc.;
- Appropriate recognition for contribution;
- Approval of the leader and the leader's authority;

- A feeling of belonging;
- A participative process;
- Low threat;
- Knowing that the group respects each of its members;
- Empowerment to act on the system in which they learn; and
- A clear idea of the "big picture" (i.e., the business and political issues affecting the content of what they are discussing).

If these things are not provided, there may be subsequent tension, anxiety, frustration, confusion, and aggression. It is therefore the facilitator's responsibility to provide for these needs.

John immediately began to plan how he might satisfy these needs. "After all," he reasoned, "the program is less than a week away."

Meanwhile Cheryl and Declan were still locked in intense discussion. Cheryl decided that her forecast strategy would be based on developing the group since her goal was just that. She would need to work out a way to help her group of advertising executives become more effective and find their way through various stages of group maturity until they could effectively work together. How to do this was the focal point of the discussion with Declan.

A Model of Group Development

Five sequential stages of group development are commonly experienced in groups that are organized for a specific learning activity or, indeed, for any kind of activity. These stages have been described by Tuckman (Pfeiffer, 1991) using the terms "Forming," "Storming," "Norming," "Performing," and "Adjourning." From our experience with group development, the stages that a group moves through can be described using two criteria. As time goes on and the group becomes more mature, so too will its effectiveness improve. However, the intervention of a facilitator is vital to the development of this maturity and effectiveness. Otherwise, the group may stall and not reach its true potential.

The facilitator of group dynamics needs to navigate the group through the first three stages and into the optimal fourth stage as

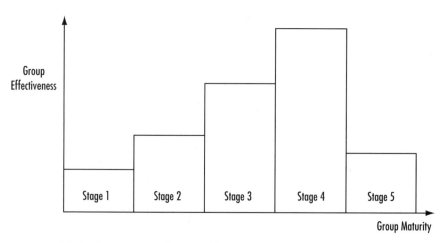

FIGURE 11.3 STAGES OF GROUP DEVELOPMENT

quickly as possible. The growth of a group can be arrested at any one of these stages. For example, if a group has not established trust and cooperation among its members, it would have a difficult time progressing to a fully satisfying and successful completion of a project. In this situation, it may never reach the fourth stage. The participants may be entrenched in bickering and one-upmanship and until they move past this they will never be truly effective as a group.

Stage 1

The first stage is the early life of a group—when the group is just getting together and the members are getting a feel for the climate of the group, whether this be warm or cold. In this stage each member may have concerns about membership in the group, what role he or she will play, what it will be like to belong to this group, and to what extent he or she will be included or excluded from the activities of the group. Members may be anxious about rejection or acceptance, their own adequacy and self-esteem, and where they fit in the group. They are also concerned about the task and are trying to orient themselves to it.

Stage 2

This stage is typified by open conflict and clashes over procedure and structure. It is in this stage that the facilitator is usually put to the test as the group begins to assess its goals and procedures with debate about the best way of operating. Effective facilitators will be sensitive to the stress levels within the group during this phase particularly. As conflict grows, some people display negative reactions, such as withdrawal, frustration, or bitterness. Scan the group frequently for signs of these reactions and treat them with some of the intervention strategies outlined later.

To move beyond this stage, the group needs to be able to progress from conflict that is framed aggressively (e.g., "That's the stupidest idea I've ever heard") to a manner that is less threatening and more conducive to solution seeking (e.g., "Can you explain how that idea will influence my area's output?").

Stage 3

This stage is characterized by cohesive behavior as the group reaches a level at which the contribution of each member is acknowledged. It is at this stage that the group begins to establish what acceptable behavior is and what the acceptable norms of the group are. The practicalities of this stage mean that people must take a few risks while checking out what is acceptable and what is not.

Stage 4

It is in this stage that the group really begins to function effectively. Not all groups get this far since, as we have said, some groups stagnate and get stuck at earlier stages. This stage is recognized for its constructiveness and creativity. Earlier stages can have a destructive effect on a group, but if the group perseveres, rewards await it on the other side.

The focus of the group in this stage is on quality and enhancements to systems and procedures. The group is also focused on support, affection, team spirit, competency, independence, and interdependence.

Stage 5

This stage occurs in the closing period of the life of the group. In a learning group that is together for a finite time, for example, there are distinct characteristics in the final hours. Typically, the group members return to being introverted and keep to themselves. Ritual closing behaviors take place, such as exchanging addresses and phone numbers. Conversation returns to polite discussion about personal issues. Discussion about the task diminishes markedly. Energy for further work is lowered to the point of lethargy, and people also cut themselves off from the facilitator to some extent. As Figure 11.3 shows, the effectiveness of the group takes a sharp turn for the worse in the final stage.

Moving Through the Stages of Development

In order to use the information about the stages of group development to help facilitate group dynamics, it is helpful to understand some of the techniques for advancing the group from one stage to another so that it reaches the fourth stage as efficiently as possible. These techniques are the basis of the forecasting strategy used to foster group development.

From Stage 1 to Stage 2

Each individual needs to relinquish the comfort of nonthreatening topics and risk the possibility of raising unacceptable ideas. This can be achieved by creating risky discussions. Many trainers create icebreakers that require varying levels of self-disclosure as a means of progressing through the first stage. In this way, the facilitator provides structured experiences and discussion that encourage interaction. This allows members to size one another up and even establish cliques so that progress can occur. It is also important that the facilitator helps to establish ground rules for dealing with conflict. This can be done either by the explicit expression of operating guidelines or by modeling. Modeling means that the trainer needs to be able to say things like, "You can do what you see me do."

From Stage 2 to Stage 3

It is important in this stage that the facilitator mixes up the membership of subgroups and often creates new teams and project committees. This should eliminate the possibility of entrenched cliques. Also, the facilitator should take an active role in the management of conflict. The facilitator should encourage the group to question and challenge him or her as well as others in the group.

From Stage 3 to Stage 4

The facilitator should praise and reward assertive challenges to inappropriate behavior or statements. He or she should introduce high levels of autonomy to the group processes and ask for direct and constructive feedback about his or her own role with questions like, "What do you want more of from me, and what do you want less of?"

From Stage 4 to Stage 5

It is advisable to keep the closing phase brief since the energy and commitment for further learning is dramatically reduced. It is important to maintain the rituals of closing but also to keep the energy high during the last few hours by including more active experiential learning activities.

Once Declan had finished explaining to Cheryl how to move the group through the stages of development, Cheryl was more confident that she had the framework for a workable forecast strategy. She would design some activities that led the group along the power continuum she had envisaged. It was then that she noticed how these activities also fit nicely into the stages of the development model that Declan had shown her. There seemed to be a good fit between the power continuum and Declan's model. She left the room beaming.

Declan sighed and felt a warm glow as he realized that he had, himself, facilitated the exchange with John and Cheryl pretty well. He stood and gazed out the window and admired the sailboats as they glided effortlessly across the bay. Suddenly, John disturbed the serenity by rushing into the room. He apologized for his dramatic entrance but explained to Declan that he was having a little trouble making the connection with one of the elements of the GRIPS model. He wasn't quite sure how to apply the "roles" element.

Declan sat down again. The sailboats would have to wait. "The point of that element," he began, "is to help clarify what the group wants from you and what you want from the group. How will you cooperate and collaborate? In a sense, it is the same as the role issues we discussed earlier. In any case, I have an exercise you can use to satisfy the need of the group in that element."

EXERCISE 11.1. ROLE CLARIFICATION

"Give copies of the items listed to the group members," Declan said. "Then ask them to identify the roles or behaviors they believe are appropriate for you and the roles they believe are appropriate for themselves. They can add to the lists as well if they believe there are items missing. Be sure to get explicit permission from each person to comply with these roles."

Participant Roles
- Listen
- Participate fully
- If you disagree, do so openly
- Make decisions by consensus
- Be hard on issues but soft on people
- Confront taboos and challenge their validity
- Invite people to disagree and offer alternatives
- Be open about needs and interests, not just positions
- Reflect on your own behavior through self-analysis
- Discuss specific, observable behavior—use examples when criticizing
- Keep the discussion focused
- Disclose all relevant information
- Confront assumptions and distortions

Facilitator Roles
- Listen
- Be patient
- Try to see things from the learner's side
- Identify assumptions and distortions
- Trust the group to be responsible
- Model effective behavior (practice what you preach)
- Use clear expression, free of ambiguity
- Don't jump to conclusions about what the group says or does—suspend judgment until you have the facts
- Give feedback on significant behavior and statements
- Give constructive feedback without being negative and critical

At last it seemed that Declan had been able to satisfy the needs of both John and Cheryl. They went to work planning their overall strategies.

The next day, he called them into his office to discuss their progress. Both were happy and satisfied and were comfortable with the progress they were making. Neither seemed to have any concerns about their respective projects, and Declan reminded them that they were highly competent consultants who had many years' experience. "I know you will be able to handle this," he proudly confided.

A week later, however, Declan found himself in familiar territory. The three of them were back in the training room discussing the half-day programs that Cheryl and John had facilitated. Both of them had struck obstacles and had come to Declan for advice.

Response Strategies

"All right then, one at a time," Declan pleaded as both Cheryl and John tried to explain their plights. Rain was slamming against the windows with a terrible force—there would be no yachts today.

Slowly, John began to outline his difficulty. The people in his group had not reacted well to his forecast strategy of beginning with some enjoyable activities. John's plan was to get them motivated and establish a rapport but the reverse had occurred. It seemed that in the short space of half a day he had managed to get every person up in arms against him; there was a significant level of anger and frustration. His belief was that, essentially, they were taking out their anger about recent company changes on him.

Cheryl had a different dilemma. There was no aggression and anger for her to deal with. Her main concern seemed to be about how to begin to intervene in the group's process.

Declan stood and turned some paper over on the easel. He soon found the model he had drawn a week earlier. "I think we need to clarify the final part of this model," he said. "We looked at forecast strategies that could help you to plan your broad approach. Now we should consider how to respond to these situations. That is what response strategies are all about. Let's start with you, John."

"Remember how you wanted to create some cooperative power. Maybe you could resolve the difficulties you are now having by applying what I call the 'tell. . . sell . . .well?' model."

Response Strategies Using the Tell . . . Sell . . .Well? Model

As a program unfolds, it is not uncommon for difficulties with process to occur. Sometimes, for example, people in the program find it is not meeting their expectations or they have concerns about content. The facilitator will need to negotiate these difficulties and resolve them in order to maintain effective rapport and group process. This can be called "process negotiation."

Process negotiation occurs whenever the trainer feels that the process in use is an ineffective one. This can be because the facilitator's own chosen process strikes trouble or because the group's solution-finding or communication processes are inappropriate. One model for negotiating the program process with participants is known as "tell . . . sell . . .well?" The purpose of this model is to put the responsibility for change in the hands of the learners. Each of the elements of the model can be included or excluded to allow flexibility in the way you respond to various circumstances.

To use this model, in its simplest form, the trainer tells the learners about facts relevant to the query or dispute and asks them to give an alternative. The alternatives are then discussed, and the learners decide on a procedure. In effect, the trainer reiterates what is going on and then asks, "Well, what shall we do about it?"

The level of control given to learners may be varied by adapting the model. The facilitator can, for example, be responsible for all parts of the model. This variation can be used when it is unlikely that the learners will be able to provide a suitable alternative themselves. In this situation, the trainer recites the relevant facts surrounding the program, then sells several alternatives of his or her own to the group, and next asks the learners to choose by using the "well?" question.

EXAMPLES OF THE TELL . . . SELL . . .WELL? MODEL

1. A trainer notices that the energy level in the group wanes sharply after lunch and decides to follow the tell. . .well? model.

    Trainer: I notice that the energy in the group is getting very low and I still have about another thirty minutes worth of material to cover *(tell)*. What do you want to do about it? *(well?)*

2. A trainer becomes involved in a disagreement over a point of little relevance. The disagreement is amiable enough but has become more time consuming than the issue warrants. The trainer decides to use the tell . . . sell . . . well? model.

    Trainer: The way we are going we'll be here forever with each trying to convince the other. I don't think it's important enough to take up everyone else's time at this stage *(tell)* so I suggest we continue the discussion during the next break *(sell)*. How do you feel about that? *(well?)*

"Remember," Declan cautioned, "when you are confronting this conflict, approach it assertively. Conflict-resolution skills are a very important part of a trainer's tool kit."

Response Strategies for Resolving Conflict

It is generally agreed that confronting conflict assertively is the best approach to resolving it, and, depending on the circumstances involved, this is also the recommended approach for trainers. One exception to the rule may be in situations, for example, in which the participants do not know one another and are unlikely to meet again and the conflict arises near the end of the program. The time it takes to resolve the conflict may not be well spent nor advantageous to the group, and it may be preferable to speak to the protagonists separately and negotiate an "armistice" for the remainder of the program.

Broadly speaking, the following basic skills can be helpful for a trainer taking an assertive approach to conflict management. While it is not the goal of this book to develop assertiveness skills, there is some merit in understanding these concepts.

1. *"I" Statements.* So called because they commonly begin with the letter "I," "I" statements are intended to remove the indication of value judgment or blame that we often place on another person in conflict situations. However, to limit the concept to a notion that statements must begin with the letter "I" and avoid the use of "you" is to deny the real intent behind "I" statements and oversimplifies their true structure.

For example, when confronted with a person who is late to a learning event, many trainers might say, "This is the third time you have been late and you are the only one who ever is." The implied value judgment here is that the person is not as "good" as the other people and that somehow he or she isn't trying. Clearly, both of these implications could be incorrect but by implying them the trainer may be likely to anger the learner because he or she feels under attack. The result of the attack on a learner's values is often a counterattack leading to arguments, aggression, and diminished learning.

Imagine, instead, that the trainer has said, "I've noticed that you've been late a few times now. Is there something wrong that I can help you with?" This "I" statement is much less likely to anger the trainee and will lead to a more rational discussion about the issue.

Now imagine the learner responds with, "No, there is nothing wrong. I just don't feel like breaking my neck to get here any earlier."

An appropriate "I" statement that doesn't use the word "I" might be, "You have every right to feel that way if the program is not helping you. However, my responsibility to the organization requires me to ensure that people attend for the duration of the program. There might be some merit in us talking about how you are finding the program and whether there is anything that can be done to help you get the best from it."

While it may not be a perfect resolution to the conflict, this statement is nevertheless an "I" statement in that it does not carry any value judgments about the behavior of the learner and is therefore much less likely to fuel a dispute. Imagine the difference if the trainer had said, "Well, that's your choice, but if you don't come on time I'll have to arrange for your pay to be reduced."

Other examples of "I" statements include the following:

- I feel that there is more to this.
- I understand that you mean . . .
- I am concerned about . . .

- I recognize that . . .
- I appreciate that . . .

"I" statements minimize the use of judgmental language.

2. *Empathy.* Another response strategy to conflict is for the trainer to empathize with the learner's view. Essentially, the trainer needs to acknowledge the person's view and try to see it from his or her perspective, that is, "meet the person in his or her world." Furthermore, a trainer needs to let learners know that he or she is aware of their feelings and how he or she is aware. Paying lip service to the cliche "I hear where you're coming from" is not true empathy and will only be seen for the false friendship that it is. For more detail on empathy, see Chapter 6.

3. *Paraphrasing.* In order to display empathy, it is also a good idea for a trainer to first demonstrate understanding of the message by paraphrasing what the person has said to him or her. A trainer should check assumptions and reactions by clarifying to the person how he or she perceived the message. For example, if someone says, "I'm not happy with the time we've spent on this issue," a trainer could paraphrase by asking, "Are you saying you'd like more time or less time spent on it?" or "If we spend more time on it, will you be happy to spend less time doing something else?"

> Declan turned his attention to Cheryl. "Your concern is quite different and seems to begin with your own uncertainty about how to intervene. Take a few minutes and write down the concerns you have and then let's have a look at them."

Facilitator Intervention

Many facilitators become anxious and uncertain about their intervention role. They begin to question their ability and doubt the timing of their interventions. They fear they will make things worse and be unable to adequately resolve the issues that their interventions might identify. Their concerns might be summarized with the following questions:

- Am I skilled enough to intervene?
- Is there time to resolve the issues we might identify?

- Has the group agreed how and when I can intervene?
- If I do intervene, will I create information overload?
- If I do not intervene now, will I be able to successfully intervene later?
- Is the issue important enough to warrant intervention?
- Have I got enough information from my observation to make a reliable diagnosis?
- Will the group be able to use the information productively?

"I think your concerns would be resolved if you were clearer about how to intervene," Declan said. "I know you have the ability—perhaps you just need a clearer framework in which to apply that ability. First of all, you need to remember the models we spoke about with John because they, too, might be helpful to you. Then you should keep in mind the following intervention model to help you structure your own intervention with your group. It's based on the intervention of a doctor with a patient. Just remember the steps a doctor might go through if you were to have a consultation and you should be able to recall the model any time you need it."

The six-phase intervention model involves the following parts: examining, diagnosing, challenging, exploring and prescribing, administering a cure, and preventing.

1. *Examining.* When you first visit the doctor, he or she will examine you in an effort to discover the issues that are the keys to your ailment. This phase of intervention is, similarly, an effort to examine the facts surrounding an observation or the circumstances that led up to it. Typically, the facilitator will intervene in the group's process at that moment in order to examine the issues with questions like the following:

- What caused that to happen?
- What happened next?
- Can you tell me more?
- What is it that she does that bugs you?
- What is it about her attitude that you don't like?
- Let's go through it one step at a time.

- What, exactly, did he say?
- When he said that, what was your response?

2. *Diagnosing.* This phase moves the facilitator beyond exploring group actions and into actually diagnosing what caused them (just like a doctor would move beyond actual observations of your symptoms and try to diagnose the cause). The facilitator needs to call on skills such as understanding different origins of behavior and recognizing similarities and differences in statements made by others. The facilitator needs to examine the behaviors first, as in the first phase of the model, and then prepare questioning strategies that help the group to make the same diagnosis. Such interventions will require questions like the following:

- Can you see a consistent pattern of behavior here?
- What does that pattern indicate?
- What contribution does that make to the group?
- What might be an alternative behavior?

3. *Challenging.* In this phase, the facilitator needs to confront inconsistencies between actual behavior and desirable behavior. This requires the facilitator to employ his or her ability to remember statements and actions as well as the ability to comprehend different perspectives of behavior, give constructive feedback without creating defensive behavior, and diagnose and describe effective and ineffective behavior. The facilitator takes on a more directive role here and must be ready to speak up about inconsistencies. For example, the intervention might go this way: "Yesterday you said that you wanted to start calling those customers. Today you say you haven't called any of them. Do you agree that you are the only one who can make this happen?"

4. *Exploring and prescribing.* When you visit a doctor and he or she feels that some form of treatment is required, the doctor may consult you about the form of that treatment if he or she feels a number of alternatives may be equally appropriate or if he or she feels that the symptoms are not sufficiently serious to warrant more direct intervention. Likewise, this phase of facilitation requires the adoption of the tell . . . sell . . . well? model explained earlier. There will be times when the intervention can solicit alternatives from the group and times when the facilitator must be more directive about the prescription for the

best way ahead. Essentially, though, the facilitator states what he or she has observed and asks the group what it wants to do about it or suggests what to do about it. For example the facilitator might say, "I notice that whenever this issue arises, only two or three people seem willing to express their opinions. What should we do about that?" (tell . . . well) or "I notice that whenever this issue arises, only two or three people seem willing to express their opinions. Since we agreed on full participation as one of our ground rules, I would like to use a process that encourages everyone to have a say but without putting them on the spot. Would everyone be willing to give it a try?" (tell . . . sell . . . well).

5. *Administering a cure.* This phase is fairly self-evident. Just as a doctor will administer a cure for an illness, a facilitator will administer a cure for a failing group process. It requires the facilitator to teach the group some skills so that it can more successfully deal with its own difficulties. For example, if the facilitator observes aggressive statements, he or she might teach the group some assertiveness skills and then foster the use of these skills during the rest of the process.

6. *Preventing.* This phase is about helping group members to develop ideas to prevent the "illness" from recurring. This can be done by establishing self-generating group processes such as a regular review and diagnosis process in which the group appraises its methods. Another prevention strategy is to help people develop alternative meanings to their preconceived ideas. For example, people are often unwilling to say what they think for fear of upsetting other members of the group. The facilitator can show people how to alter their messages so that others are not upset, thus preventing people from repeating the original habit of holding back their true thoughts.

Cheryl thought over Declan's medical model for intervention and agreed that it might help the situation, although her face seemed to suggest that she still had some concerns. "You still seem unsure," Declan said.

"It's not that your model won't help me," Cheryl said. "It's just that the project was to get people to challenge their boss, Michael Kennedy, more than they do now and they really do seem to behave like sheep. They don't question anything he says. It's like they just want to follow the leader and have no original thoughts of their own."

"Do you mean that they are suffering from group-think?" Declan asked.

"That's it precisely," Cheryl replied.

"Then it seems to me that you need an activity that will put them in a simulated group-think situation. Then you can use the medical intervention model to cure the illness."

Group-think

Learning does not occur in a vacuum. The phenomenon of group-think influences the way individuals in a group behave, react, attend, and contribute. Facilitators need to build a rapport with a whole group and with the individuals within that group. A successful rapport can have the effect of helping to create a team environment in which learners feel comfortable about challenging the facilitator and one another.

Furthermore, as we discussed earlier, it is sometimes the facilitator's role (as a navigator) to improve group processes. Many trainers will see this as threatening—and indeed it can be. When the group starts to challenge the facilitator and take over the process, the trainer can feel powerless, and concerns about real progress toward the goal begin to surface. However, if it is your goal to develop critical thinkers and autonomous people who can become independent of you, then see it as a challenge and go out to meet it. Take the risk.

EXERCISE 11.2. GROUP-THINK

To see the power of group-think, announce to a group that you have something very important to discuss, you need to get a group decision, and that you'd like to get a vote on it. Ask everyone to close their eyes and to vote by "secret ballot." Then put a challenging question to the group such as, "Who can stay an extra forty-five minutes today to go over some very important information?" As the participants sit with their eyes closed, begin to count at a random, changing rate: 1 . . 2 . . . . 3 . . 4 . . . . . . 5 . . 6 . 7, etc.—even if no hands go up. You will soon see people putting up their hands as they begin to feel the unseen pressure of voting along with their colleagues despite their true feelings.

Facilitating group dynamics is about creating the right environment to generate healthy debate, challenge, and confrontation about risky issues. It is also about developing independent thinkers who are not swayed by popular opinions.

A month later, after the rain had long since stopped and the yachts were back out on the bay, Declan was enjoying a tacking duel between two catamarans when John and Cheryl came in.

"I'm so glad your facilitation projects worked out well," he said without turning around from the window. John and Cheryl had sat down on the other side of the desk when Declan finally turned and sat in his own chair. "What can I do for you?" he asked.

"Well, we just wanted a bit of a chat," said Cheryl. "We have been talking a lot about the models you showed us."

"Particularly the pilot and navigator metaphor in the circles model," John chimed in.

"We realized, after quite a bit of discussion, that you had been facilitating us in a way," Cheryl continued. At this Declan smiled. "We thought that you had been piloting us. We kept coming to you for advice and expecting you to hand us solutions. We left all the responsibility to you and effectively gave you the power to find our solutions rather than taking responsibility for them ourselves. Your response strategy to our concerns consisted of interventions that prescribed solutions for the difficulties we were having."

"We appreciate the help you gave us but know deep down that you must have also had a forecast strategy in mind that would help us to move into the fourth stage of our development. So, we decided to do some thinking on our own and have come up with a little metaphor that we think you can use. Hopefully, you will see this as adding value to your circles model of facilitation."

At that moment, John reached down and from under the desk he took what looked to be some kind of trophy mounted on a wooden stand. Declan immediately recognized it as a steering wheel from a small airplane.

"This is for you," John said. "This steering wheel represents your model: the pilot and navigator steering the plane on its course. Now you need a name for your model. We were thinking of something like 'Controlling the steering—a pilot's guide to navigating groups.'"

"I love it," Declan said. "Now we're ready to fly."

Summary

In this chapter we have outlined a model that helps to place facilitation in a framework. The framework acknowledges the importance of clarifying the role a trainer wishes to play in relation to the sharing of power and control. It also illustrates the style of facilitation that suits the outcome a trainer intends and the need to plan forecast strategies that are congruent with this style and to be ready with response strategies if the forecast proves wrong.

The intervention used as a response strategy can be likened to the actions of a doctor treating a patient. Beginning with examination and diagnosis, the facilitator moves through various stages and on to cure and prevention.

Facilitation is a complex and exciting skill and requires continuous development. People are themselves complex and there may never be a definitive answer about how to help them learn. Facilitation is a nonlinear discipline that requires constant flexibility and versatility to be successful.

Bibliography

Bradford, D. (1984). *Group dynamics*. Chicago: Science Research Associates.

Burns, S. (1996). *Artistry in training: Thinking differently about the way you help people to learn*. Warriewood, NSW, Australia: Woodslane Press.

Dick, B. (1984). *Helping groups to be effective*. Brisbane: Interchange.

Dyer, W. (1987). *Team building—Issues and alternatives*. Reading, MA: Addison-Wesley.

Hart, L.B. (1992). *Faultless facilitation—Resource guide*. Amherst, MA: HRD Press.

Heron, J. (1989). *The facilitator's handbook.* London: Kogan Page.

Hyman, R. (1979). *Strategic questioning.* Englewood Cliffs, NJ: Prentice Hall.

Kinlaw, D. (1996). *The ASTD trainer's sourcebook: Facilitation skills.* New York: McGraw-Hill.

Pfeiffer, J.W. (Ed.). (1991). *Theories and models in applied behavioral science, volume 2: Group.* San Francisco, CA: Pfeifffer.

Schein, E. (1987). *Process consultation—Lessons for managers and consultants.* Reading, MA: Addison-Wesley.

Schwarz, R. (1994). *The skilled facilitator.* San Francisco, CA: Jossey-Bass.

12

REACHING FOR THE STARS

This chapter reviews the learning highlights of the book to discover the five ingredients for creating training miracles. Also, a list of practical tips for enhancing training skills is supplied.

Gems Mined from These Pages

- Creating training miracles requires the right spirit, techniques, awareness, resilience, and structures.

- Invest in a self-nurturing plan.

- The trainer holds the key to his or her fulfillment.

- Avoid trying to be perfect in everything.

- Maintain an honest assessment of your strengths and areas for improvement.

Just for You

Creating Training Miracles has focused on helping others to learn and to reach their full potential through effective training. This final chapter will enable you to reflect on your key discoveries and develop actions for further professional development and personal growth. To begin this challenge, we will start by asking you to review the learning highlights.

EXERCISE 12.1. LEARNING HIGHLIGHTS

Step 1. Grab a large piece of white paper and a collection of colored pens.

Step 2. Using colored pens of your choice, write out the words, or draw icons or symbols, for each chapter you have read. Make sure you space these evenly over the page as displayed in Figure 12.1.

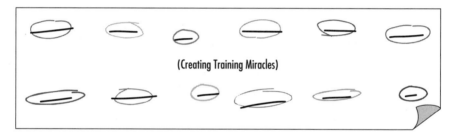

(Creating Training Miracles)

FIGURE 12.1. WHITE PAPER WITH CHAPTER HEADINGS OR DRAWINGS SPREAD EVENLY OVER PAGE

Step 3. Using each chapter title as the central focus, note any ideas, feelings, and thoughts that you may have had. Do this by branching out into outcomes, observations, and unresolved issues from each chapter. For example, a reader could draw a mind map like the one shown in Figure 12.2 for the four issues that he or she gained from Chapter 1.

Translated, the mind map shown in Figure 12.2 summarizes the following learning highlights:

● Training provides an exciting range of offshore market opportunities within the global marketplace;
● Interactive multimedia needs to be studied further;

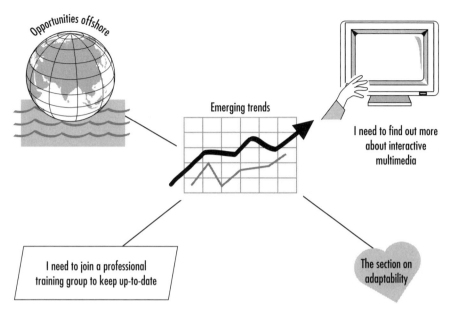

Opportunities offshore

Emerging trends

I need to find out more about interactive multimedia

I need to join a professional training group to keep up-to-date

The section on adaptability

FIGURE 12.2. A READER'S MIND MAP OF CHAPTER 1

- The reader feels that he or she should join a professional group; and
- The discussion on adaptability was loved and was seen as very important to the future of training.

Step 4. When you feel that you have recalled all that you can, place your mind map in a notable and visible spot. This may be somewhere like in your action file at work, in this copy of *Creating Training Miracles,* on your desk blotter, or even on the fridge in your kitchen.

Step 5. Over the course of the next week, add to your mind map as new memories or insights surface. If you decide to revisit and re-read *Creating Training Miracles,* you can also add to your mind map.

Step 6. If your paper becomes too cluttered, contemplate expanding and redrawing your mind map onto a larger piece of paper.

Step 7. When the week is ended, grab a colored pen and draw a five-pointed star (see Figure 12.3) next to the six most important issues that came out of *Creating Training Miracles.*

Step 8. List these six major issues in your diary for further action.

FIGURE 12.3. DRAW A FIVE-POINTED STAR NEXT TO IMPORTANT ISSUES

Step 9. Next to each idea, write down what you will do in the next month to enhance your understanding and application.

Step 10. Set a review date and note a reminder of this day in your diary. For example, if during the next month you wish to review the current literature on interactive multimedia, make sure you remind yourself well in advance of your deadline.

The Wonder of the STARS

EXERCISE 12.2. REMEMBER THE STARS

Take a minute to remember the last time you looked at the stars in a clear, moonless, night sky. Where were you and who was with you? What sort of night was it? Was it cold and windy or was it calm, serene, and quiet? As you looked at the stars sparkle and glow, what were you thinking and feeling? How did you react to this tapestry of lights in the sky?

The stars in the night sky provide us with a powerful metaphor for creating and accepting training miracles. At times it is easy to be mesmerized by their beauty, complexity, and enormity. On other occasions, stars can feel somewhat distant, remote, and unavailable. To embrace the wonder of the night sky we need to be open, connected, and receptive to the beauty and wonder that are unfolding above us. It is only then that the true miracle of the universe can be explored. Questions that are brought to mind include the following:

- Is the night sky one big miracle or is it trillions upon trillions of separate miracles?
- How is it that one moment a single star appears to struggle for recognition while an instant later it shines and pulsates?
- How is it possible for the stars to shed twilight on the Earth's surface at nightfall?
- Will the stars and the force that created them affect our future destiny?

Stars provide us with a powerful way to remember how to create training miracles. As displayed in Figure 12.4, we feel part of the answer to creating training miracles lies in understanding the five qualities of stars. These qualities are developing the right *Spirit,* choosing excellent *Techniques,* being *Aware* of oneself and others, displaying *Resilience,* and seeking good *Structure.*

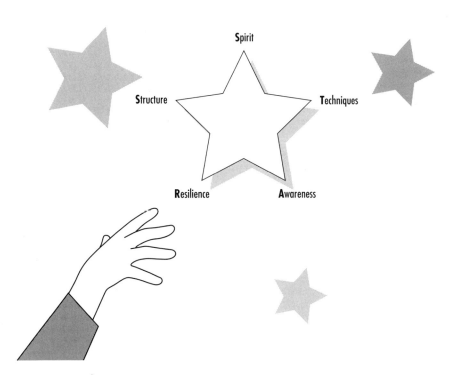

FIGURE 12.4. REACHING FOR THE STARS

Developing the Right Spirit

Spirit is one of the enduring themes that has run through *Creating Training Miracles* from start to finish. Spirit is about making a commitment to those mindsets discussed in the preface and then trusting that they will allow the process of discovery to unfold. Without that trust and reassurance, the potential for people to learn together in partnership becomes limited.

Spirit is also about adopting some philosophical principles that govern your actions in learning experiences. To generate or be part of training miracles, people must be connected, confident, and receptive to the possibility of learning. When people live and breathe the spirit of training miracles, the capacity for change and learning in all aspects of their lives will increase dramatically. Start with small steps first, like taking greater time to listen and gain the support of others, and then move on to longer-term changes like repositioning one's career to an area of training that one finds more interesting and exciting.

Choosing Excellent Techniques

In *Creating Training Miracles,* we have profiled an exciting array of new, innovative, and well established *techniques* that provide high-leverage learning to people in a variety of settings. Some of the areas discussed, in order of appearance, include the following:

- Taking the time to predict future trends;
- Clarifying outcomes with decision makers before a training process begins;
- Recognizing prior learning in training design, delivery, and assessment;
- Empowering learners to draft learning contracts;
- Using energizers and icebreakers to adjust the mood and the commitment to a training process;
- Adapting to the visual, auditory, and kinesthetic modality preferences of learners;
- Conducting whole-brain learning;
- Using music to soothe and stimulate the subconscious and conscious mind;
- Adding spontaneity to role playing by using role training;

- Adjusting the delivery methods of case studies to achieve different learning outcomes;
- Supporting and encouraging people during outdoor learning with quality coaching and debriefing; and, finally,
- Navigating and piloting facilitation.

In addition to these techniques, there are many others that could quite easily be grouped under the umbrella of creating training miracles. Examples of these include how to design tools for performance-enhancement, the intricacies of undertaking skill audits, advanced public speaking skills, adapting and using high technology, and benchmarking best practices.

Given that there is such a wide array of techniques involved in creating training miracles, it is important to recognize that it is impossible to be brilliant in every area—particularly as the field is growing and expanding so quickly. It is, therefore, necessary to be mindful of learning and training trends and to develop techniques that you most enjoy, while also recognizing that there will be times when you will need to stretch outside your comfort zone to get results and to grow.

Being Aware of Oneself and Others

Paramount to the success of being a trainer is to first have a good *awareness* of the nature and direction of change and second to know how to get things done. Finally, a trainer must be prepared to develop himself or herself in areas that need improvement.

Understanding Change

Trainers have a unique responsibility for identifying how learning can best meet the challenges that come with change. To do this, trainers need to be aware of, anticipate, and meet the opportunities associated with living in today's rapidly evolving world.

As a minimum requirement, trainers need to help people to keep informed, up-to-date, and resourced for the challenges of change. As highlighted in both Chapters 1 and 2, one of the best ways of maintaining a clearer picture of the nature and direction of change is to form strategic alliances with a wide range of parties and organizations. Ideally, trainers should use learning as an agent of change.

Getting Things Done

To survive in today's world of competing resources, trainers need to be aware of the political, economic, and social issues that support or hinder getting things done.

Trainers need to project a professional image, deliver high-quality services, and supply products that meet the evolving needs of key decision makers. Particularly important is promoting the cause of successful learning for internal and external customers by rigorous marketing and influencing strategies.

Self-development Needs

Trainers need to be aware of their strengths and areas for personal and professional growth. Without doubt, one of the most contagious factors of creating a training miracle is when a trainer is seen to be investing in his or her own development.

Being Resilient

To regularly reach for the STARS requires physical, emotional, and intellectual *resilience*. Trainers must therefore be prepared to develop their resilience by constantly investing in self-nurturing behavior. Creating training miracles requires an excellent balance between giving and receiving. In many ways, as we reach for the STARS, we must keep our feet firmly on the ground and care for ourselves before we can be expected to care for others.

As displayed in Figure 12.5, trainers must be prepared to maintain and recharge their batteries if they wish to create training miracles and avoid becoming flat or burned out.

From our experience, trainers are very susceptible to burnout, chronic fatigue, stress, and ill health. The primary reason is that the nature of their responsibilities involves giving to others for extended periods of time. Doing this day after day can take its toll, unless a conscious effort is made to recharge the batteries. A sure sign that a trainer's energy is waning is when he or she begins to view requests from learners and clients as chores rather than as wonderful opportunities to explore and discover.

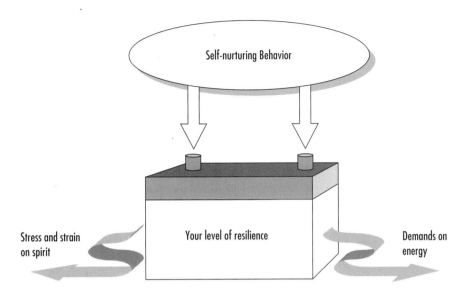

FIGURE 12.5. MAINTAINING RESILIENCE

Developing a Personal Self-nurturing Plan

As shown in Figure 12.6, there are many areas in which activities can be initiated to increase resilience. What is most important, however, is that you develop a self-nurturing plan that works for you. The biggest mistake is to impose on yourself self-nurturing activities that do nothing for you. For example, if you hate gardening, do not take it up as a self-nurturing activity just because someone else you know loves it. Self-nurturing is a very personal business.

To help you to develop your personally tailored self-nurturing plan, complete Exercise 12.3.

EXERCISE 12.3. CHARGING YOUR BATTERY

Using the following headings, list as many preferred self-nurturing activities as you can. The best self-nurturing activities are short, specific, and creative. A sample is provided, followed by a blank form for you to fill in with your own ideas.

At Work

- Renegotiate the current two-month training plan and work schedule with the manager of Human Resources.

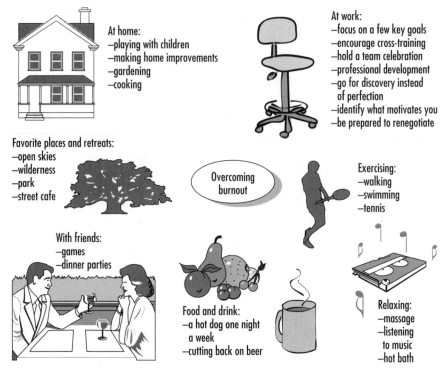

At home:
—playing with children
—making home improvements
—gardening
—cooking

At work:
—focus on a few key goals
—encourage cross-training
—hold a team celebration
—professional development
—go for discovery instead
 of perfection
—identify what motivates you
—be prepared to renegotiate

Favorite places and retreats:
—open skies
—wilderness
—park
—street cafe

Overcoming
burnout

Exercising:
—walking
—swimming
—tennis

With friends:
—games
—dinner parties

Food and drink:
—a hot dog one night
 a week
—cutting back on beer

Relaxing:
—massage
—listening
 to music
—hot bath

FIGURE 12.6. OVERCOMING BURNOUT

- Publicly praise volunteers' efforts at the next meeting at the local volunteer center.

At Home

- Twice a week, spend half-an-hour reading poetry in the sun room overlooking the garden.

Relaxing

- Once a week, give and receive a massage with a loved one.

Favorite Places and Retreats

- Attend one football game per month.
- Have breakfast at my favorite cafe once every two weeks.

Food and Drink

- Eat more fresh fruit and vegetables and less sugar, fat, and butter.

- Allow myself the luxury of having my favorite dessert, chocolate mousse, once a week.

With Friends

- Rent a video recorder and invite some friends over.
- Organize a monthly card game.

Exercising

- Take a half-hour walk outside my place of work each day.
- Establish a ten-minute ritual of stretching each morning before I have breakfast.

Self-nurturing Ideas for Yourself

At Work

-
-
-
-

At Home

-
-
-
-

Relaxing

-
-
-
-

Favorite Places and Retreats

-
-
-
-

Food and Drink

-
-
-
-

With Friends

-
-
-
-

Exercising

-
-
-
-

Having completed your list, create a mind map like the one displayed in Figure 12.6 and place it in a visible spot for easy referral. Alternatively, you can photocopy your answers and place them in a regularly seen place.

Seeking Good Structure

The final ingredient in reaching for the STARS is *structure*. The importance of structure should not be underestimated. Creating training miracles is not a matter of luck; it is the result of careful planning and good strategy. High-leverage learning doesn't just happen; it requires quality preparation, good process, and exemplary instructional design, delivery, and assessment.

Good structure provides the medium to inspire confidence, build self-esteem, and obtain results. When used correctly, structure gives the freedom for both trainers and learners to discover and learn. Whether studiously following competency-based training from design to assessment or logically presenting a video case study for discussion, trainers need to ensure that the process is clear and meaningful to the learners involved. Poor structure can destroy any well-intentioned training session.

Practical Tips on Developing Your Advanced Training Skills

As a final postscript to *Creating Training Miracles,* twenty-five practical tips are provided to help you develop your skills in advanced training. Use the list as a discussion starter for your development and that of others.

1. Visualize where you want to be in five years' time and develop a plan of action to get there. Write down a measurable twelve-month plan for training and development and self-nurturing behavior. Update your progress on a monthly basis.
2. Find a wide range of mentors and advisers who have a track record in enhancing the skills you need.
3. Regularly attend training conferences or seminars that enhance your competency.
4. Seek out and role model international best practices in training.
5. Define and meet industry, national, and international competency standards in training provision and skills enhancement.
6. Join and actively participate in training professional groups, associations, and networks. Leave groups, associations, and networks that are not enhancing your skills. Be prepared to explore interstate or international options for dialogue.
7. Accept that stretching your comfort zone of training is a natural part of learning. Practice, rehearse, and perfect new frontiers and existing skills. Ensure that you celebrate personal growth and success. Start with low risk and, as your confidence grows, move to higher risk activities.
8. Studiously collect and review feedback on your strengths and areas for improvement.
9. Undertake team participation, project work, and special courses that enable you to connect and learn from other fields, disciplines, and endeavors. For example, a person may learn about one-on-one coaching skills by talking to counselors.
10. Research and enhance your understanding of how to learn. Become a person who is committed to being well-versed on

learning how to learn. Be prepared to do activities that encourage you to learn in different ways. When enhancing your skills, build on success by developing your expertise.

11. Become part of the high-technology and information revolution; get access to a high-quality personal computer with a CD-ROM drive and a modem. Join networks on the Internet and electronic mail and explore distance-learning options. Use these communication channels to access the latest information and advice.

12. Visit other training centers. Build strategic alliances and share resources and expertise.

13. Gauge your skills on the job market to determine your market value and to gain feedback on your development needs.

14. Write an article or a book or produce a video on training ideas.

15. Maintain a learning journal of your discoveries. Keep a summary of your achievements and the skills that you have developed.

16. Undertake formal accredited and competency-based training programs at a university or equivalent institution. Select the mode and topic of study that suits your lifestyle and professional development needs.

17. Start a newsletter or network for exchange of views on an area of interest.

18. Conduct community-based training programs. Do this to build your skills and to test your more innovative programs.

19. Visit exhibitions at trade shows on training and related fields.

20. Every six months, spend a half-day in the library to get yourself up-to-date on the latest trends that you may have missed in the hustle and bustle of modern life. Read the popular media as well as recent journals and articles.

21. Videotape and audiotape yourself in action. Note your strengths and areas for improvement.

22. See yourself as a learning consultant and resource person rather than just a pure training provider or presenter.

23. Employ people with the expertise that you wish to develop and learn from them. Request a coaching relationship from the training provider.

24. Develop your skills in speed reading and other techniques of memory-enhancement such as mind-mapping and mnemonics.

25. Give yourself full permission to explore and build on new ideas.

EXERCISE 12.4. LET'S MAKE IT THIRTY

Set yourself a learning goal of extending this current list of twenty-five practical tips to at least thirty.

26. _____

27. _____

28. _____

29. _____

30. _____

After building your own ideas, share and exchange them with another person or team. See how many more you can come up with.
   Extras:

31. _____

32. _____

33. _____

34. _____

35. _____

Having completed the above exercise, place a five-pointed star next to each of the six best ideas for your development in creating training miracles.

Summary

Reaching for the STARS and creating training miracles requires a genuine belief that successful and high-quality learning can be achieved through the use of the right strategies and methods. It is also important to recognize that creating training miracles requires energized and enthusiastic trainers who are committed to learning and discovery in all aspects of their lives.

Creating Training Miracles has explored many avenues to increase the capacity of people to face their individual and collective futures with greater hope and increased confidence. It is our dream that this book will in some small way help and promote this cause.

APPENDIX 1

Chapter 5: Examples of Icebreakers and Energizers

Ten Important Questions

Process

Ask the participants to form subgroups and to write ten questions they want to be able to answer by the end of the course. The ground rules are simple: participants should write questions, not topics, and the questions should be as specific as possible, giving details of specific situations if appropriate. Post the questions on the wall and refer to them throughout the program. As the program closes, have the subgroups return to their lists and attempt to answer the questions. If the course is only a day long and there are several subgroups, limit the questions to fewer than ten (perhaps five).

Uses

- Is suitable for any course
- Establishes ownership of the course by the participants
- Builds motivation to learn (everyone now sees "something in it for me").

Climbing the Steps

Process

Give participants a list of issues that relate to the program. For example, for a career-development program, you might list job security, income, challenge, variety, interest, and autonomy. Distribute a diagram of a flight of steps to the participants and ask individuals to rank the items on the list from the most important (placed at the top of the steps) to the least important (placed at the bottom). Next form small subgroups and ask members to share their views with the other members of the subgroup.

Uses

- Is suitable for a program in which there can be multiple views about the order of the items. These differences of opinion will generate discussion.
- Is suitable for a program in which there is a single, correct answer to the order of the items. This method can be used as a way of exploring the prior knowledge and values of the participants.

Three Statements

Process

Give the participants three statements that are related to the issues in the program. One of the statements should be false and the other two true. Ask the participants to form subgroups and to discuss the statements and identify the false one. Repeat this procedure with new lists of three as often as you like.

Uses

- Is suitable for any program, but especially technical training
- Can be used when a trainer is confident of the correct answer (answers should be clearly true or false—no grey areas).

Chalk Lines

Process

Draw a chalk line on the floor. (It will easily wash or vacuum off.) Tell the group that the line represents a continuum of experience related to the course material—one end representing very experienced and the other representing ignorant. Ask people to stand at the place on the line where they think their experience places them. Take the people at either end and pair them up. Then take the next two from either end and pair them up and so on. Give the pairs some questions to discuss that relate to the content of the program. The intended effect is that the more experienced partner will become a coach for the less experienced one, and team teaching will begin to evolve.

Uses

- Is suitable for any program, especially those in which there is likely to be a wide range of experience
- Is suitable for technical training

Toy Metaphors

Process

Ask participants to select a toy that would be an effective metaphor for their workplace (or for the content of the course). Be sure to have a large array of toys to choose from. Ask participants to describe the metaphor—why they chose it and what characteristics it shares with the workplace—first to the person next to them and then to a small group. Then have each small group choose its favorite metaphor to share with the whole group.

Uses

- Identifies the creative people and the risk-takers in the group
- Helps to promote self-disclosure and remove inhibitions
- Creates a fun beginning

Brain Pleasers

Process

Ask participants to form subgroups and to discuss their favorite brain teasers (brain pleasers) and choose one that they like. Each subgroup then poses its teaser to the rest of the group and the facilitator. Give a reward to any subgroup that stumps the group (or the facilitator). Have a lot of rewards handy, such as small chocolate bars, fresh fruit, or stick-on stars.

Uses

- Provides a good introduction for a problem-solving course
- Stimulates thinking
- Provides a good energizer any time, but especially as a transition from reflection to action or vice versa

Jigsaw

Process

Create jigsaw puzzles using pictures related to the content of the program. For example, select a photograph of a clean work environment for an occupational health and safety program or a product specification sheet for a course on technical skills. Instead of using a picture, you can write a series of questions on the jigsaw puzzle such as those described in the story that began Chapter 5. Make as many puzzles as subgroups you desire and have as many pieces in each jigsaw as the number of people you want in each subgroup. Make each jigsaw a different color to minimize chaos. Give each person a piece of his or her subgroup's puzzle and ask him or her to find the people with the other pieces. The participants then assemble their jigsaw puzzles and sit together. Next, distribute a question sheet related to each jigsaw puzzle and ask the participants to complete the questions.

Uses

- Is suitable for technical training
- Is suitable for small groups (it's very difficult for 100 people to find their partners)
- Is a good transition energizer to introduce a new topic at any time in a program

Chaos

Process

Decide on some categories that relate to the content of the training program. Write ten items that relate to each category and number them 1 to 10. Divide the participants into subgroups and assign a category to each subgroup. For example, on the topic of time management your list of ten items might be as follows:

1. Planning
2. Objectives
3. Goals
4. Stress
5. Diary

6. Interruptions
7. Structure
8. Meetings
9. Priorities
10. Urgency

Without revealing the ten items on the list, give a team one minute to call out as many items, terms, or definitions related to the topic as it can think of. For each one the team guesses from the list it scores a point. The effect is a free-for-all yelling match that is great for getting the group hyped up. Give each subgroup a turn with a different topic. The activity is useful for highlighting the importance of establishing rules and norms in group behavior. It's also a novel way of reviewing the material at intervals during the program.

Uses

- Is suitable for any program
- Can be used as an energizer to raise the level of excitement
- Can be used for course review

Picture Perfect

Process

Divide the participants into two teams and ask each team to appoint a drawer who then stands at a whiteboard or flip chart that has been assigned to each team. Next, give the drawer for each team a word or phrase from the training program. Give each team the same word or phrase. The challenge for the drawers is to represent this word or phrase pictorially. One limitation is that the drawing may not include letters of the alphabet, numbers, or any other recognizable symbols such as dollar signs. The teams now compete against each other as each team's members attempt to guess the word or phrase that is being drawn. The first team to guess the word or phrase is the winner of that round and is awarded points. For each round, assign a new drawer for each team. Repeat the process as many times as you like, or until one of the teams reaches a predetermined point total.

Uses

- Is suitable for a communications course
- To open a discussion about individual strengths and weaknesses (e.g., some people can't draw and get frustrated)
- To open a discussion about feedback (often in this game, people become critical of colleagues who can't draw)
- As an energizer to raise the level of excitement
- As a course review (groups draw things related to the course)

"Don't Worry, Be Happy"— Group Stretch and Breathing Exercise

Process

Ask the participants to form subgroups of five to seven people each. Subgroup members form a circle and stand facing one another. Each subgroup selects a leader who will then lead a group stretch to the music of "Don't Worry, Be Happy" by Bobby McFerrin (EMI). The role of the leader is to demonstrate some simple stretching exercises and breathing patterns to complement the stretch. Change the leadership every sixty seconds or so. Caution each subgroup to be aware of the physical ability of its members and to encourage participation rather than force it. The value of breathing exercises cannot be underestimated as a means of refreshing people, and it is this feature of the activity that should be focused on.

Note: Ensure that your client or workplace has obtained permission to use the music in accordance with copyright laws.

Uses

- After lunch or an early morning start
- To relax participants
- For team building and support

Humming Energizer

Process

Lead the group through a process of saying the vowel sounds out loud. Everyone stands and begins to say the vowel sounds: a, e, i, o, u. Start in a low pitch and ask people to follow your vocal lead. Repeat the sounds, gradually increasing the pitch and volume. (The use of vowel sounds energizes the brain and connects both left and right hemispheres.)

Uses

- To relax the participants
- To stimulate mental activity
- To build fun and enjoyment

Learner Stories

Process

Ask people to form subgroups of three. Instruct each subgroup member to take a turn sharing a positive story about a time when he or she learned something important about himself or herself. The other two members of each subgroup are to actively listen but not pass judgment. When all three members have shared their stories, the members choose the best story to recount to the entire group.

Uses

- Sets the tone for a positive learning environment
- Is suitable for self-disclosure programs
- Is suitable for career-development programs
- As an introduction to the value of learning

APPENDIX 2

Chapter 6: Suggested Answers to Exercises

Exercise 6.1: The surgeon is the boy's *mother.*

Exercise 6.2: The second "the" is usually deleted.

Exercise 6.3: Divide the shape as shown below:

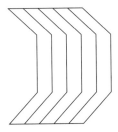

Exercise 6.4: Suggestions for establishing rapport:

1. Are you saying that you want to be sure your time is well spent today?
2. Who says that?
3. What, specifically, can't you do?
4. Are you saying you want practical suggestions?

Exercise 6.7: Possible positive intent:

1. Wanting to have expertise acknowledged.
2. Having other important priorities.
3. Needing to vocalize thoughts in order to internalize them.

Exercise 6.12: Possible alternative positive language:

1. We have a challenge.
2. This is going to be good for development.
3. I'm really going to have to stretch to solve that.

APPENDIX 3

Chapter 10: Some Outdoor Activities

The activities we have described in this Appendix are intended as a sample that can be part of an outdoor program. They represent varying levels of risk. The earlier examples require less equipment and lower adventure skills and contain less potential for injury while the later activities are at the higher end of the risk continuum (see Figure A3.1) and will require an experienced trainer.

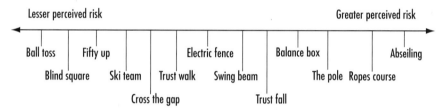

FIGURE A3.1. THE RISK CONTINUUM

Ball Toss

Ask the group members to stand in a circle and to toss a ball randomly from one person to another. Each person should toss the ball to someone who has not yet received it. As the ball is tossed, members count off to establish an order. Time the exercise to determine how long it takes to toss the ball to everyone. Next, instruct the team members to throw the ball to one another in the same sequence as before, but this time in under five seconds. Typically, they will see this as impossible. However, if they can break from the assumption of having to remain in the circle, they may have success.

Blind Square

Blindfold all of the group members. Then give them a length of rope (the length depends on the number in the group, but, for example, ten people need sixty feet of rope) and instruct them to form a perfect square with it, with group members to be spread at equidistant intervals around that square.

The behavior that emerges can serve well for debriefing a range of issues including leader behavior, interpersonal communications, inclusion and exclusion of group members, and problem solving.

Fifty Up

Ask the group members to stand in a circle and to hit a beach ball or any large soft ball in the air fifty times without allowing it to touch the ground. However, the same person must not hit the ball twice in a row. This activity is particularly entertaining when there is a slight breeze blowing. The activity appears to be quite easy on the surface but it does require leadership and teamwork. One of the issues to be explored as the activity unfolds is the way group members support or ridicule one another when someone allows the ball to drop.

Ski Team

This activity is designed to help team coordination and also to provide insight into team relationships and behavior. Four or more people (eight maximum) stand on two long planks. Along each plank is a series of foot stirrups into which each person places his or her feet so that one foot is on one plank and the other foot is in a corresponding stirrup on the other plank. The effect is that of one long pair of skis to which all team members are connected. To move the skis in a coordinated way so that the group can make forward progress requires high levels of communication and cooperation (the more people in the shoes, the harder it becomes). The group is then tasked with crossing an open space (for example, a field) in a set amount of time. Extra challenge can be provided by having some people face the other direction.

You might also wish to consider varying the activity by instructing that the planks be used in ways other than by walking on them. The problem solving takes on a new dimension under these circumstances as the group must look for creative ways of using the tools it has. For example, the group might simply stand on top of one of the skis, leaving the other vacant. The group then lifts the unoccupied ski and places it down farther along the path to be traveled. The team then walks along this ski until all members are standing on it. Without touching their feet to the ground, the team members then pick up the ski left behind and place it in front of them. They then walk along this ski until the ski they were standing on is unoccupied. They repeat this procedure until they reach their destination.

Cross the Gap

Create an open space and draw two parallel lines approximately twelve feet apart. The gap between the lines has to be crossed by the group. Instruct the group that it is to cross the gap in the best way it can but is only allowed to touch the ground three times (not three per person, but three for the entire group). Tell the group that the gap is an electronic minefield and if touched in more than three places the alarms will be triggered. It doesn't matter how the group crosses or what part of the participants' bodies touch the ground, so long as the participants only touch the ground between the lines three times in total. The only successful way we have seen this achieved is as follows. Person A places his or her right foot three feet into the minefield, then steps another three feet with the left foot. Person B steps on Person A's feet, using them as "stepping stones." Person B pivots on Person A's left foot and steps out from there, ending up with one foot in the minefield and one in safety on the other side. In this way, the gap has been bridged with the ground only having been touched three times. The remainder of the group crosses by stepping on the feet of A and B while they provide support to those treading on them. Finally, Person A steps onto Person B's feet and crosses out of harm's way. (See Figure A3.2.)

The event is good for building support, for problem solving, and for physical contact. It is also a fun event to videotape and replay after dinner that night, like so many of the events of outdoor learning. Take some precautions about stepping on feet. You might need to have people remove their shoes and allow a small space around the feet, say 6 inches, so that nobody has feet crushed.

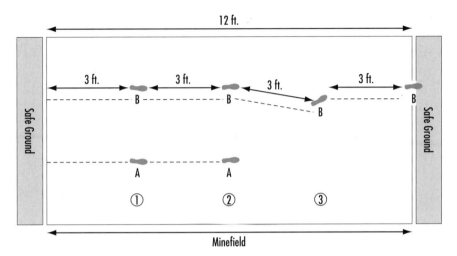

FIGURE A3.2. THREE EASY STEPS TO CROSSING A MINEFIELD

Trust Walk

This is perhaps one of the better known events because it does not necessarily have to occur in an outdoor context. One of its strengths is that it helps build trust among team members and also skills in listening and coaching.

Participants are paired up and one person in each pair is blindfolded. The sighted partner leads the blindfolded partner through an obstacle course. The obstacles vary and the person is forced to walk, crawl, run, squeeze, and wriggle at different points along the way. The sighted partner begins by physically leading the blindfolded partner, but the level of trust grows so that, for example, after a few minutes of comfortable leading the sighted partner tells the blindfolded partner to run for five steps. This takes an incredible level of trust, and the blindfolded partner's confidence can be observed by just how vigorously he or she runs.

The sighted partners may be instructed to use only their voices or physical touch as a guide, or a combination of both. We prefer the combination because it helps build trust rather than put it at risk. When people need to run (with just a hand on the partner's arm), there is sufficient risk to really challenge the trust in the partner without the need for additional, unnecessary physical risk.

Normally in the trust walk, the sighted partner holds the hand or arm of the blindfolded partner. Variations include (1) holding hands but not talking and (2) no holding or contact at all (unless to prevent a fall) but with speaking allowed.

An interesting observation to make is to compare how many of the blindfolded partners feel the need to have their hands out in front of them. Those who do not may have greater trust in their partners' ability to guide them safely.

Electric Fence

Erect a triangular fence about three-and-a-half feet tall. Each side should be just long enough to closely confine the group. There should only be a small amount of room to move inside the fence. The participants are advised that the fence is "charged" with one thousand volts that creates an electric field from the top of the fence to the ground. Touching the fence is obviously not allowed. The challenge is for everyone to get over the fence (not under it). It is too high to simply step over and so the group members must physically help one another to succeed. If any members touch the fence while they are outside the fence, they must return to the inside.

Swing Beam

The swing beam is a pole or thick tree branch that is suspended by ropes or chains so that it swings free from the ground as a person attempts to cross it. The swing beam is a good event to use for practicing balance when more difficult balance events are to follow (such as a ropes course) and is also good development for scouts and a good activity for building trust between group members. Extra interest can be added by having the swing beam suspended over a muddy pool.

Trust Fall

Each member of the group, one at a time, stands on top of a five-foot ledge and falls backward into the waiting arms of scouts, who act as catchers. The fallers place their arms across their chests and close their eyes. The scouts stand in two lines with arms extended and alternately interlocked. The interlocking procedure involves the catchers working in pairs. Each catcher grasps the wrists of the catcher standing opposite him or her. When the faller falls, the catchers should ensure that no part of the body touches the ground while paying particular attention to supporting the faller's head, neck, and lower back.

It is important that the facilitator is not the first to fall. The facilitator should be in the line of catchers at about where the person's shoulders and chest will fall; if all else fails, at least he or she can help break the fall. It is also wise to practice with a dummy of similar build and weight as an average person. Also, swinging arms and elbows of fallers may become a problem, so it is useful to have the fallers hold something in their hands. This is a good exercise for scouting practice.

Balance Box

The balance box demands high levels of physical contact and is an excellent way to introduce touch as an important aspect of outdoor learning. A box about one-and-a-half feet square is placed in an open space (or in the middle of a muddy pool with a plank leading up to it). One member of the team stands on the box and one by one the others join him or her. Eventually, as more people get on the box, people need to sit on one another's shoulders, hold on tightly in a huge bear hug, and balance at all sorts of awkward angles. (Be careful of the risk of falls here.) The real benefit is simply the physical contact required to complete the event. It helps to break the ice about physically helping one another since this is sometimes a very sensitive issue.

The Pole

A pole about nine feet tall is embedded in the ground. A number of car tires are then placed over the pole so that the tires are stacked one on top of the other around the pole (see Figure A3.3). The team is tasked with removing the tires from the pole and then replacing them in the opposite order. (The tires can be numbered to help identification.)

This exercise challenges the team on issues such as cooperation, communication, and problem solving. Furthermore, the need

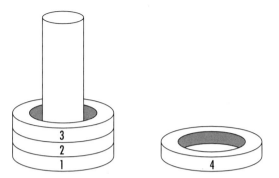

FIGURE A3.3. THE POLE

for physical contact as they lift the tires over the pole can be a useful icebreaker for further activities that require close physical support among team members.

Ropes Course

Ropes courses are very popular events in outdoor learning programs, especially those at the higher risk end of the spectrum. They are many and varied and often involve a number of different elements. The common feature is that they involve heights with little evidence of safety except a belaying line. An example is a rope stretched between trees thirty feet above the ground, across which people are asked to walk. There is another rope above participants' heads that they can hold on to for balance, but this is still a very demanding activity. It is important to ensure that there is yet another rope above participants that is connected to a belaying line from the harnesses they are wearing. If someone falls, the belaying line will stop his or her descent.

Many ropes courses are similar to this one. The key is the challenge of the height and the trust a person must place in his or her scout. For a work team, this can also be a valuable experience as the team explores its levels of peer support.

Abseiling

This is another popular event, particularly for individual challenges. It has benefits in team challenges as well. As each person attempts the descent, the level of support and encouragement from team members is a useful issue to reflect on. The major challenge is for the individual to be confident enough to let himself or herself step backward into a 30-to 150-foot void.

Clearly, safety issues are critical and each person needs to be well trained in the check points before he or she steps off. Remember, most accidents occur simply due to carelessness.

APPENDIX 4

Chapter 10: Outdoor Learning Checklist

Logistics and Learning

1. What outcomes do you want?
2. What other training or events will this experience coincide with?
3. How much time is available for the event?
4. What dates are intended? Do you have an alternative?
5. What is the budget?
6. Will weather conditions alter the program significantly?
7. Where will the training occur? Is the location critical?
8. What transportation arrangements do you need to make?
9. Will you have easy access to emergency services and roads?
10. What insurance coverage do you have?

People

1. How many people will take part?
2. Do they need to be trained at the same time?
3. Is the group already organized into predetermined teams? Will the participants benefit from being trained in these teams?
4. Will you have mixed gender groups?
5. Are your exercises gender-balanced?
6. What is the age range of the participants?
7. What is the physical condition of the participants?
8. Have the participants been examined for suitability to the activities you are planning?
9. What clothing and other equipment will they require?

Provider

When choosing an expert trainer to provide the adventure learning experiences and debriefing, consider the following questions:

1. What experience does he or she have with outdoor training?
2. What references does he or she provide?
3. Can he or she competently provide the adventure element as well as the education element?
4. Do you need him or her to help with follow-up training?
5. How does he or she gauge the level of success of his or her programs?
6. What is the safety record of the facilitator personally and/or the firm he or she represents?

ABOUT THE AUTHORS

Alastair Rylatt, B.Bus., Grad Dip. Employment Relations, is acknowledged as an expert international trainer, strategist, and award-winning author in workplace learning, advanced training skills, and change management.

Alastair is the director of Excel Human Resource Development based in Sydney, Australia. He is also a fellow of the Australian Institute of Training and Development, a charter member of the Australian Human Resource Institute, a member of the International Alliance for Learning, and a member of the American Society for Training and Development.

Since 1986, Alastair has completed more than 200 projects involving over 1,500 public, private, and tertiary-sector organizations. Some of Alastair's well-known clients include Ampolex; AVIS; Australian Broadcasting Corporation; Australian Institute of Management; BOC Gases; Coca-Cola; the Australian Department of Education, Employment, Training and Youth Affairs; Energy Australia; Harlequin Mills & Boon; Total Quality Management Institute (New Zealand); Sydney University; Vodafone; and Zurich Insurance.

More recently, Alastair has built a reputation as an excellent author in human-resource related issues. He contributed to the Jossey-Bass publication, *Organizational Career Development: Benchmarks for Building a World Class Workforce,* released in 1993, and then followed that up in late 1994 with his very popular book, *Learning Unlimited: Practical Strategies and Techniques for Transforming Learning in the Workplace* (Business and Professional Publishing, an imprint of Woodslane in Sydney). *Creating Training Miracles* was then released, initially with Prentice Hall Australia in 1995, followed by this custom-designed version for the U.S. and Canadian marketplace. Alastair is currently writing his next book on the theme of helping individuals cope with turbulent change.

In the years ahead, Alastair hopes to increase his international consulting and publishing still further as he pursues his mission of stimulating greater learning, meaning, and enjoyment for people in the world of work.

Alastair can be contacted by e-mail at arylatt@ozemail.com.au.

Kevin Lohan is a director of Endeavour Training and Development on the New South Wales Central Coast and is one of Australia's leading practitioners of self-directed learning and trainer development. To further his passion for learning and trainer development, Kevin established the National Institute for Trainers and Assessors (NITA) in Australia with business partner Betty Sheppard in 1995. NITA is dedicated to developing trainers and assessors in Australia and promotes a range of development opportunities as well as publishing a periodic newsletter that is received by 2,000 people around Australia.

He has a Bachelor of Education (adults) and an Associate Diploma of Adult Education from the University of Technology, Sydney, and has also been a lecturer and adviser for the same diploma program. He has also been a regular presenter for the Australian Institute of Management (AIM).

Kevin's training experience spans appointments to positions in the Australian Department of Defence, the Family Court of Australia, and the Special Broadcasting Service (a multicultural broadcaster). Since he formed his own consultancy, Kevin's clients have included BHP, Coca-Cola, Coopers and Lybrand, Philips Australia, Sydney Electricity, the University of Technology (Sydney), and the Human Rights and Equal Opportunity Commission.

Kevin has previously been published in the AIM journal *Management* and in the *Australian and New Zealand Training and Development Management Manual* (CCH Australia Ltd, Sydney, 1992). Kevin is a member of the Australian Institute of Training and Development (AITD), AIM, the American Society for Training and Development (ASTD), and the Australian Consortium of Experiential Education (ACEE), and is a past vice-president of the Accelerative Learning Society of Australia—New South Wales Division (ALSA). Kevin believes that his writing and his membership in these organizations act as his vehicle for returning some of the excitement he has received from his profession back to his colleagues.

Kevin can be contacted by e-mail at endeavr@manuka.terrigal. net.au.

INDEX